पुरातत्त्व
PURĀTATTVA

Bulletin of the Indian Archaeological Society

No. 27 1996-97

Editors

K. N. Dikshit & K.S. Ramachandran

D.K. Printworld (P) Ltd.
New Delhi

Cataloging in Publication Data — DK
[Courtesy : D.K. Agencies (P) Ltd. <docinfo@dkagencies.com>]

Purātattva : bulletin of the Indian Archaeological Society, no. 27, 1996-97 / editor, K.N. Dikshit & K.S. Ramachandran.
p. cm.
Includes bibliographical references.
ISBN 8124603022

1. Archaeology — India — Periodicals. 2. India — Antiquities — Periodicals. 3. India — Civilization — Periodicals. I. Dikshit, K.N. II. Ramachandran, K.S. (Kattalai Sivasubramanium), 1939- III. Indian Archaeological Society.

First Published in 1997
First Reprinted in 2005
ISBN 81-246-0302-2
Price for volume 27 (1996-97): Rs. 800 US $ 40

Reprint authorised by
Indian Archaeological Society
New Delhi - 110 016

Purātattva is published annually.

Manuscripts (whether in the form of articles or notes or book reviews) offered for publication should be sent to the Editor, Purātattva, Indian Archaeological Society, B-17, Qutab Institutional Area, New Delhi - 110 016.

Published and printed by:
D.K. Printworld (P) Ltd.
'*Srikunj*,' F-52, Bali Nagar
New Delhi – 110015
Phone : (011) 2545 3975, 2546 6019 Fax : (011) 2546 5926
E-mail : dkprintworld@vsnl.net
www. dkprintworld.com

PURĀTATTVA

CONTENTS

Obituaries

Professor R.N. Mehta
(1922-1997)

Professor Ramanlal Nagarji Mehta, born on 15th December 1922 at Mardi in Valsad Distt., Gujarat, died on 22nd January, 1997 after a very brief illness at his residence in Vadodara. The country has lost a veteran Field Archaeologist, an eminent historian and a well known epigraphist; he was indeed a leading Indologist.

Commonly known as Dr. Mehta in the world of archaeology, he was very popularly known as 'Bhikubhai' by his family and close associates. His parents were a very worried lot as none of their issues lived long prior to the birth of Ramanlal. Therefore, when he was born his mother immediately put him near the dung-heap debris and begged for his long life. Since then he was called Bhikhubhai. But see the strangeness of fortune that this Bhikhubhai lived his entire life just with debris and debris alone, examining them, ransacking them, interpreting them and making them public.

Prof. Mehta received his training in art and archaeology from Prof. Binaytosh Bhattacharya, Sir Mortimer Wheeler, Dr. Hermann Goetz and Prof. H.D. Sankalia. He joined the Department of Archaeology and Ancient History of the M.S. University of Baroda and retired as the Professor and Head of that Department. He had a deep insight into the history, culture, art, architecture as well as archaeology, epigraphy and numismatics of Gujarat. He was well versed in Sanskrit, Prakrit, Arabic, Persian, Marathi, Bengali and French languages besides Gujarati, Hindi and English. It was his great asset. He had always something new to offer regarding the interpretation of Vedic, Pauranic and Epic texts as also Islamic literature.

He started his career from Ahmedabad as a curator of Calico Mills Tapestry Museum. After dedicating his services to the M.S. University of Baroda for nearly three decades, he joined the Gujarat Vidyapith, an institution of higher learning founded by Mahatma Gandhi in 1920 in the wake of non-cooperation movement, as a Visiting Professor of Historical Archaeology and remained there for over a decade. During his stay at the Gujarat Vidyapith his contribution to the Salvage Archaeology, Jaina Archaeology, Place-name study will be remembered for a long time. His publications on the following four topics are constantly referred to by students and researchers alike: Discovery and Excavation of Buddha-Mahastupa and Buddha-Mahavihara at Devnimori in the vicinity of the Hindu Tirtha Shamalaji in Sabarkantha distirict of Gujarat; Horizontal excavations of the lost city of Champaner near Vadodara; The study of place-names of Towns and Cities of Gujarat; and Study of living towns and cities with the help of Salvage Archaeology. He, by such efforts, had brought to light the past of Ahmedabad, Vadodara, Surat, Kambhat, etc.

A loving teacher and above all a noble soul, he was, no doubt, a fountain of love, inspiration and encouragement. Always deressed in simple clothes of *kurta* and *pajama* of coarse *khaddar* he was an embodiment of sincerity and hardwork. He was selfless in helping one and all, a source of strength for all his students and friends. His touching simplicity, caring nature, thoughts and services for pupils and researchers come to my mind. A person like him never dies since their academic experiences and attainments ever remain with us. His gentle nature, compassion, strong principles, integrity and dedication to research will always be alive in the hearts of his friends, colleagues and students.

Rasesh Jamindar

Dr. Shashi Prabha Asthana
(1947-1997)

Born at Hardoi (U.P.) on 16th April 1947, Dr. Shashi Prabha Asthana obtained M.A. degree in 1965 from the Lucknow University, passing in first division. She obtained Ph.D. in 1976 from Magadh University. She joined the National Museum, New Delhi in 1972 as Technical Assistant and was elevated to the position of Deputy Keeper (Pre-Columbian and Western Art) in 1979 and Keeper (Archaeology) in 1982. In 1992 she took charge of the post of Assistant Director, National Museum.

Within a brief period of her academic career, spanning hardly two decades, she had made immense and lasting contribution in the field of Indology and emerged as an outstanding archaeologist and art historian of international repute. Latterly she was engrossed in Buddhist art, particularly Vajrayana Buddhism. She authored the following major monographs and catalogues:

1. *History and Archaeology of India's contacts with other countries from earliest times to 300 B.C.* (1976).
2. *Pre-Harappan Cultures of India and its Borderlands* (1985).
3. *Indian Art through the Ages* (Catalogue for an exhibition held in USSR-1987).
4. *Indian Bronzes* (Catalogue for the exhibition put up in Hungry and Italy-1993).
5. Mathura Art: Hindu, Buddhist and Jain (in Press).
6. Catalogue of Gandhara Sculpture in the National Museum (in Press).

Dr. Asthana also contributed a large number of research papers in Indian art and archaeology, each one of which speaks about her great insight and grasp of the subject. Her meticulous planning and active involvement resulted in the National Museum organising most successfully fourteen international and eight national exhibitions besides several academic meets. She was also an excellent teacher and made an unforgettable impression on the students of the National Museum Institute where for sometime she taught Egyptian and West Asian Art.

Recipient of Bursary Merit Scholarship, Commonwealth Scholarship, British Institute Fellowship, J.D.R. 3rd Fund Fellowship, British Institute of Persian Studies Fellowship and similar other fellowships, Dr. Asthana, was widely travelled and a well sought after scholar. She visited and worked in U.K., USA, erstwhile USSR, Japan, Iran, Iraq, France, Germany etc. Under the short-term fellowship of British School of Archaeology she participated in exploring in Iran and Iraq. She also had the privilege to study important collections in various International Museums, viz. Stein collection and Mesopotamian antiquities in British Museum, London; West Asian material in Iraq Museum, Baghdad; Bostan Museum, Tehran, and National Museum of Art, Rome and Indian Art collections in the museums of New York, Brooklyn, Cleveland, Los Angeles, etc.

She had also a passion for editing. She jointly edited *Frontiers of the Indus Civilisation* (Sir Motimer Wheeler Commemoration Volume) along with B.B. Lal and S.P. Gupta, and also the *Journal of the Museum Association of India,* New Delhi.

She was actively interested in the day-to-day working of the Indian Archaeological Society. She was elected its Hon. Treasurer. She also became member of the Board of Management of the Indian Archaeological Society in 1994. Her donation in kind and otherwise to the Society will be always remembered.

Her sincerity, deveotion, compassionate love and affection to one and all, including scholars from every part of the world was immeasurable.

Whom God loves die young. Dr. (Miss) Shashi Prabha Asthana, after a successful life, left for her heavenly abode in her fiftieth year on the 26th September, 1997 in the Golden Jubilee year of India's Independence. We the members of the Indian Archaeological Society express our deep sympathy and condolences on the sad and untimely death of Dr. Asthana to the bereaved family.

PURĀTATTVA

Number 27 **1996-97**

Editorial

We are happy to convey to our members that the construction of the first phase of our Society's building at B-17, Qutab Institutional Area, New Delhi has commenced. At the time of writing this we would have reached plinth level of the basement, which will have an area of about 290 sq. metre with 2.15 metre high large opening on the south-east for proper light and ventilation. Over the basement, there will be three floors for archaeological studies, conservation laboratories, class-rooms, seminar rooms, etc. The construction work was started on the 14th August, 1997 and as per our contract we should get possession of the complete building by the 15th August, 1998. When complete in all respects, it will cost us around Rupees one crore. We hope to make it the biggest centre of archaeological studies in South Asia.

* * *

The Society has recently launched a new venture, called **Heritage Helpmates,** meant primarily to cater to individuals, groups and governmental agencies in their efforts to explore and excavate as well as to conserve and preserve standing monuments, movable antiquities and buried sites.

* * *

The Govt. of Delhi has established the **Delhi Institute of Heritage Research and Management** to conduct a Post-Graduate Diploma course from early next year. In due course of time this may be given 'Deemed to be University' status so that even degree classes could get started. It has been a long-felt need since archaeology is taught at several places and there is no institution of higher learning, teaching and training in Heritage Management in India. We expect that there would be close coordination between the Indian Archaeological Society and the new Institute as both have common programmes of activities.

* * *

We have also decided to launch a quarterly **Newsletter,** the first issue of which is expected to come out in January, 1998. The main objectives of this are to further the cause of archaeology, including lobbying and campaigning.

* * *

We are glad to inform our members that Shrimati Usha Narain, wife of Prof. A.K. Narain formerly of the Banaras Hindu University has kindly endowed a sum of Rs. 50,000/- to create a permanent fund for assisting "Indian scholars, not older than forty five years in age, for the best work/contribution in the form of published book, contribution of major articles (at least 3 in number) or unpublished doctoral thesis or a significant fieldwork with a report in one of the disciplines which come under the purview of the three Societies and which is related to the study of cultures and civilisations of countries and people other than India'. The award amount will be met from the interest of the amount donated by Shrimati Narain and shall be rotated among the three Societies viz., the Indian Archaeological Society, The Indian Society for Prehistoric and Quaternary Studies and the Indian History and Culture Society. The Award is named as **"AK Narain Award for the Study of Cultures and Civilisations of countries other than India."** The award will be an annual feature and the first awardee will be in the year 1998.

* * *

The current issue of *Puratattva* has many articles ranging from Prehistory to Historical Archaeology but one –the article by Shri Bhagwan Singh is very thought-provoking which seeks to prove, on the basis of his Vedic studies, ethnological history and archaeological evidence that in the history of South Asia, agriculture and language originated in north-western India and then moved on towards West Asia and beyond.

* * *

This number of Puratattva has come out with financial support from the Archaeological Survey of India, New Delhi and Indian Council of Historical Research, New Delhi. We are thankful to these organisations for their kind gesture.

* * *

We are thankful to Dr. S.P. Gupta, Chairman of the Society for his guidance.

* * *

Once again we would like to emphasise our contributors to follow the British system of referencing in which references are numbered and arranged serially and printed at the end of the article.

* * *

We deeply regret the untimely, sad and sudden demise of Dr. Shashi Prabha Asthana, a beloved collegue and a member of the Board of Management of the Society on the 26th of September 1997 at New Delhi. May her soul rest in peace.

Editors

Cunningham : Explorer and Excavator

S. Silas*

Alexander Cunningham initiated archaeological explorations in India, a subject which had not received any attention from scholars engaged in the study of Indian antiquities before him. He pioneered the archaeological movement in India, with excavations getting systematised to some extent under official patronage. His ideas and principles on archaeology formed the framework of the Archaeological Survey of India in 1861. However, his concept of archaeology was devoid of the scientific inputs it received in the West from the pioneering labours of Mariette and Petrie in Egypt, Layard and Schliemann in Greece, and Pitt-Rivers in England.

The life and works of Cunningham gained some importance with the concise study attempted by Abu Imam in his work titled, *Sir Alexander Cunningham and the Beginnings of Indian Archaeology.* Mortimer Wheeler, in his foreword to Abu Imam's work calls Cunningham as 'the "father" of archaeology in India.' Earlier, A.L. Basham, in his account of the initial antiquarian researches and archaeological explorations in India expressed a similar opinion about Cunningham.

Alexander Cunningham, second son of Allan Cunningham, a Scottish poet of note, was born at Westminister on January 23, 1814. Cunningham's father was till then domicile in Dalswinton near Dumfries and had come to Westminister 'in the hope of bettering his circumstances' some three years before Alexander was born (JRAS 1894:167). Along with his next younger brother, Peter, Alexander had his preliminary education at Christ's Hospital, London. He later joined the Military College at Addiscombe, receiving his final training at the Royal Engineer's Estate at Chatham. Following this, he obtained his first commission as Second Lieutenant in the Bengal Engineers in June 1831. He arrived in India for military service on June 9, 1833.

Cunningham was nineteen years of age when he started his career with the Bengal Engineers, and put in twenty-eight years of distinguished service in the army till his retirement in 1861, as Major General, in June 1862 after being already appointed as the first Archaeological Surveyor to the Government on December 1, 1861.

Cunningham had given a memorandum to Lord Canning regarding a proposed investigation of the archaeological remains of upper India in November 1861. Canning's Minute, which led to his appointment as Archaeological Surveyor, is dated January 22, 1862. The first two volumes of his Survey Reports carry the results of the archaeological tours he undertook from 1862 to 1865. (ASR: I i-viii). Though at another place he speaks of having begun his operations as Archaeological Surveyor to the Government of India in November 1861. (ASR I: xli)

Alexander Cunningham was well immersed in his quest for Indian antiquities from the beginning of his career. He made the most of the opportunities, well pro-

*Department of History, St. John's College, Agra.

vided through his postings in significant areas while still in military service. He was as much favoured by luck, as his interest and acumen for research oriented activities. But his rise to fame was not predestined. It was an uphill task, involving years of hard labour.

Because of his stay in Calcutta in the initial years of military service, Cunningham had the oppurtunity of joining a band of followers of the august antiquary, James Prinsep. At that time, Prinsep was involved in his study of 'the newly discovered Baktrian and Saurashtran or Kshatrapa coins, and on the Asoka and Sanchi inscriptions' (JRAS 1894: 168). Gradually Cunningham came closer to Prinsep and as he himself reminisced: 'With our mutual tastes and pursuits this soon ripened into the most intimate friendship.' This, (the years 1836 and 1837) recalled Cunningham was 'the most active period of his (Prinsep's) career ......' (ASR I: vii). As early as 1836, Prinsep, writing in the *Journal of the Bengal Asiatic Society,* observed: 'Henceforward my readers should understand, and they will soon perceive the fact, that my coin essays are joint productions, and that I have an auxiliary at my elbow, far better acquainted with the contents of, I may say, all the collections of coins in India, than I have leisure to become' (*Arch. in India,* 1-2). This association with Prinsep, inbred in him an antiquarian taste and archaeological insight which he exhibited sufficiently during the early stages of his career in India. Cunningham was proud of his association with Prinsep of which he acknowledged;' ... when I recollect that I was then only a young lad of twenty three years of age, I feel as much wonder as pride that James Prinsep should have thought me worthy of being made the confidant of all his great discoveries' (JRAS 1894: 168). But of his very first excavations, undertaken at Sarnath, Banaras, at the Dhamek tower (Dec. 1834-Jan. 1836) and in the vicinity of Dhamek (1835-36), Cunningham partly refuted the charge that these excavations were suggested to him by James Prinsep.

Cunningham wrote his first paper titled, 'Correction of a mistake regarding one of the Roman coins found in the Tope at Manikyala, opened by M. Court.' He wished to emulate General Court's technique of opening the Topes. From 1840 onwards Cunningham frequently wrote in the Society's Journal but several of his essays on Indo-Greek and Indo-Scythian coins published in the *Numismatic Chronicle* later on. Among his other papers contributed to the *Journal,* the one, 'An Essay on the Arian order of Architecture as exhibited in the Temples of Kashmir' is referred to as 'a more ambitious attempt in a new direction and was perhaps, the least successful of his works.' The value, whatever remains of this work, is owing to its plans and drawings which 'were most valuable and instructive' (JRAS 1894: 171).

On the two missions to Ladakh, Cunningham had ample oppurtunity to observe and document the various historical, topographical, statistical and physical features of the whole region. This enabled him in publishing his seperate work, *'Ladak : Physical, Statistical and Historical with Notices of the Surrounding Countries'* in 1853. The result of the excavations undertaken by him at Bhilsa (Vidisha) in January and February 1851 along with his friend and associate F.C. Maissey were published by him in his work, *The Bhilsa Topes,* in 1854 from London. This work embodies a sketch of the rise, progress and decline of Buddhism in half of the text, with about a fourth devoted to the donative inscriptions found chiefly on the rails and pillars, of which Cunningham copied about 200 from the Great (Sanchi) Stupa and 43 from the smaller ones. This work has been termed as 'the first serious attempt to trace Buddhist history through its architectural remains' (Enc. Brit. Msc. III:295). It is also significant owing to the complete translations of the inscriptions 'which considering the state of Prakrit scholarship forty years ago - were very creditable to his (Cunningham's) scholarship' (JRAS 1894,:171).

The proceedings of the year 1848, were significant, as they had direct bearing upon Cunningham's long association with archaeological explorations in India. In the beginning of the year, he initiated a 'new subject, to which he constantly recurred in succeeding years' (JRAS 1894:170). M.M. Remusat, Klaproth and Landresse had translated the *Foe-Koue-ki,* or Travels of Fa Hian, into French, appending to their version the itinerary of Hiuen Thsang with its English translation with additional notes by J.F. Laidlay, minus the itinerary. Major Wm. Anderson questioned the authenticity of Hiuen Thsang's work, and suggested that it was a modern compilation, to which Captain Cunningham replied in his paper: 'Verification of the Itinerary of Hiuen Thsang through Ariana and India, with reference to Major Anderson's hypothesis of its modern compilation.'

It was in June 1848 that Cunningham sent to the Calcutta Society a note drafted upon a "Proposed Archaeological Investigation" to be carried out with the services of 'at least two persons' ; with the one to whom the responsibility of 'the selection of objects for preservation' is entrusted. '..... should be conversant with the sculptured forms and religious practices of the present day and with the discoveries made by Prinsep and others in Indian Paleography and Numismatology' (JASB 1848:I, 535-536). This was the first seed sown of what he was afterwards personally to nurture and reap.

Gradually, time drew nearer for the recognition of Alexander Cunningham's pioneering efforts. His scheme, for a proposed investigation of the archaeological remains of Upper India, submitted in his Memorandum to the Viceroy, Lord Canning in November 1861 was accepted. Lord Canning agreed to create an Archaeological Survey 'at least' of Upper India, through his Minute in Council on the Antiquities of Upper India, dated January 22, 1862. (Canning's Minute, ASR: I, i-iii). General Cunningham was appointed to superintend this Survey and he began operations in December 1861. During the four years succeeding his appointment, Cunningham undertook the Survey of the historical remains in the North, North-West, Central India, Rajasthan, Bundelkhand and Bihar. He reported upon numerous sites along with his attempts at identifying the chief cities of ancient India, the results of these two tours were initially published as supplementary numbers to the society's Journal of 1863 and 1865. These were later reprinted in two octavo volumes (with maps, plans and sketches of the remains) in 1871 on his reappointment as Director General of the newly constituted Archaeological Survey of India. To the first volume he added an introduction of 43 pages with a brief sketch of the history of antiquarian studies in India, his own achievements and contributions and his close relationship with Prinsep.

Cunningham was in England when he was reappointed to his new post and returned to resume, 'those interesting labours which had already occupied so many years of his life, in December 1870' (JRAS 1894:174). He was in the fifty-eighth year of his life then and continued in his renewed service to the cause of Indian archaeology upto 1885. Added to these fifteen years was the initial term of four years as Archaeological Surveyor. These twenty years of service to the cause and development of Indian archaeology was sustained well owing to his prolonged experience in the field of excavations, epigraphy and numismatics, which formed his chief interests while still in military service.

For his exemplary services in this field the British government bestowed upon him several commendations, – Companion of the Star of India (May, 1871), Commander of Indian Empire (January, 1878), Knight Commander of the Indian Empire (February 1887). While in office, as Director General of the Archaeological Survey of India, General Cunningham was a honorary member of the Bengal Asiatic Society, member of the Royal Asiatic Society and the Anthropological Institute as also the Numismatic Society of London. He was also the corresponding member of the Oriental Society of Germany, the Imperial Academy of Sciences of Berlin and the Ethnological Society of Berlin.

After his retirement from the Survey on Oct. 1, 1885, Cunningham returned to England completing a long and fruitful career in India. During the remaining seven years of his life, till he died in 1893, he continued in his relentless pursuit of antiquarian studies. These last efforts resulted in the publication of a few more papers and works of unmitigated value. Notable among them are his two seperate works in his favourite field of study i.e., numismatics. His *'Coins of Ancient India'* was reproduction of a number of his papers on numismatics where he detailed his opinions regarding the origin of money, the various measures and units in use in different parts of the world, with an attempt at deducing the relative as well as comparative values in some cases. He also refuted the popular belief that the Indians were ignorant of the art of coinage at the time of Alexander's invasion. The notable aspect is his publication of numerous obscure coins of Ancient India, which he assigned to their respective periods and dynasties. His other work and the last one of his career, the *Coins of Medieval India,* in continuation of his account of the ancient Indian coins was still in the press, when he died on November 28, 1893. It could be published owing to the kindness of E.J. Rapson of the British Museum, who read and corrected the entire proofs.

During his initial explorations as Archaeological Surveyor to the Government, Cunningham set out to discover and identify some of the chief cities and historical sites of ancient India. The result of his identification of sites are found in volumes I and II of his Survey Reports and later discussed more widely in his *Ancient Geography of India*. Though most of his identifications do not hold ground now in the light of recent researches, yet the work done by him in this respect, still remains indispensable.

Cunningham claimed to have identified the sites of some of the famous cities of ancient India with certainity. Few prominent ones, as noted by him were - Aornos, Taxila, Sangala, Srughna Ahichchhatra, Bairat, Sankisa, Sravasti, Kosambi, Vaisali, and Nalanda. Some of his identifications like those of Shahdheri with Taxila; Manikapura, in the Rawalpindi district of Punjab, with Manikyala; Kapitha or Sankasya with Sankisa, forty miles south-east of Atranji, and fifty miles north-west of Kanauj; ancient Kosambi with Kosam village on the Jamuna, 48 km south-west of Allahabad; Sravasti with Saheth-Maheth lying on the borders of Gonda and Bahraich districts of Oudh (Lucknow) in U.P.; Kusinagara with Kasia, a village 56 km in the east of Gorakhpur district; Vaisali with Basarh or Basar (Muzaffarpur district, Bihar), have been accepted by modern researches.

It has been pointed out that most of these identifications had been made earlier by scholars like 'Wilson, St. Martin and even Kittoe' (Abu Imam: 235-239). This fact was acknowledged by Cunningham, regarding the identification of Kasia with Kusinagara, first proposed by Wilson. Cunningham also acknowledged his first becoming acquainted with Sangala-wala-Tiba in 1839, from a copy of Mogal Beg's manuscript map, compiled by Wilford, who described its position three times in the *Asiatic Researches*. In order to accommodate the factual authenticity of this criticism, the term 'located' seems to be a better option in place of 'identified' (Lar. Enc. Arch.. 386).

In the sphere of excavations, Cunningham could not comprehend stratigraphic archaeological excavation, already evolving at that stage in India. It was Captain Meadows Taylor, who, as early as 1851, in the excavations of numerous megalithic monuments of Southern and Central India, drew stratigraphic sections of the discovered remains. In almost fifty years of his familiarisation with archaeology, Cunningham explored innumerable number of mounds, most of them representing remains of ancient Indian cities. But there are no illustrations of sections showing stratigraphy in his accounts, so as to establish the approximate age of the mound. However, his section of the remains in the Manikyala Tope (previously opened by Ventura in 1830), chiefly consisting of coins of the Kushan Kings, Kanishka and Huvishka (exclusively in the lowest deposit C of the plan), and mixed with other coins of a later period i.e. sixth and seventh century A.D. (in deposits A and B) made him conclude that the tope was originally built in sandstone in the reign of Huvishka and was later repaired with 'Kankar facing and mouldings' around A.D. 720, probably by Yasovarmma of Kanauj whose gold coin was found in deposit A. (ASR: V, 77-79).

This is due to the ignorance of the principle of stratigraphy and the near total dependence upon evidence from written, numismatic and epigraphic records. In the 'archaeological well' dug by him in the fort of Multan, Cunningham assigned the time period of one century to depth of 1 1/2 feet, beginning with A.D. 1700 and gradually progressing downwards till the total depth of the "well" which was 40 feet, made him fix 800 B.C. for the lowermost layer. Utilising the same principle he calculated the age of a 45 feet high mound at Sahri Bahlol as a whopping 3000 years, beginning at A.D., 800 with 1 1/2 feet intervals for every century.

The initiation of systematic and controlled excavation by Mariette in Egypt or Fiorelli's concept of 'total excavation' applied at Pompeii or even Schliemann's application of the principle of stratigraphy for the determination of the age of ancient mounds, seems to have no impact upon Cunningham's concept or perception of archaeological details. Did he know of these or ever cared to learn? His total silence upon the subject speaks otherwise. His scope of study chiefly extended to the study and description of hundreds of historical sites with ascertainment of their antiquarian importance. For these he would consider the traditional accounts and legends, native histories, traveller's testimonies, architectural styles in vogue, sculptured reliefs, and the coins, inscriptions and seals discovered therein. The real purpose of archaeology for assimilating the sum total of man's past achievements concealed in the history of civilisations, thereby evolving in a study of behavioural patterns and cultures, hardly occurred to him. Cunningham and his assistants did not display any tendency of undertaking a methodical study of man's material vestiges in their entirety. It creates an impression sometimes that 'ordinary dwellings, the habitations of the common people were clearly outside the scope of their programmes,' though stated otherwise in his memorandum of instructions (Roy: 47). The tools and implements associated with the finds seem to be treated likewise. On the contrary, in the ethnographic findings, attention should have been focussed upon these objects, so as to form a comprehensive account of the behavioural patterns evolving in different races in the course of time. It would have helped in understanding and tracing the very evolution of race from hominoid (man like) to hominid (family of man). The archaeological pursuits of Cunningham in India would then have become considerably elevated in the context of modern archaeology. Unfortunately what was primeval in archaeology became perennial with him.

Hence Cunningham could not apply his ideas in totality to his numerous excavations conducted in Northern and Central India. Digging never became dissection for him. The excavations effected by him never proceeded beyond what might be called 'prospecting' (JRAS 1895 : 655). His indifference to prehistory made him ignore the findings resulting from the conjoined labours of Babington and Harkness, Congreve and Keanes, Newbold and Meadows Toylor in the megalithic monuments, where he noticed only an earlier form of the *Stupa* (Roy: 59). Likewise the ignorance cast upon paleoliths deprived him from gaining an idea of the scientific parameters of the findings of geologists in this connection. These discoveries were no doubt significant and it is regrettable to note that they could not be assimilated in the mainstream of the activities of the archaeological department. As it was only with the establishment of the Survey that 'systematic records' of fresh discoveries could be compiled, which 'were impossible' before 1870 (Lar. Enc. Arch. : 386).

Similarly, protohistory, recognition of which has been significant for archaeology as well as the history of civilisation in India, did not merit attention by Cunningham. He visited Harappa thrice, lastly during the tour of 1872-73 (the first two visits were accomplished in 1853 and 1856 respectively), and was much disillusioned by the devastation carried out by the railway contractors with 'very little worth preserving'. He found the ruins of Harappa as 'the most extensive of all the old sites along the bank of the Ravi,' 'with a complete gap of 800 feet' on the east side, the reason for which was beyond his comprehension. From his account the remains consisting of a 'continuous line of mounds' on each side appear square in form. He spoke of these mounds, with the highest of them to the north-west, 60 feet above the fields. He has cited Burnes, who mentioned "a ruined citadel on the river-side" as the eastern side. Here (i.e. the north-west mound) he discloses of having traced 'the remains of flights of steps on both the eastern and western faces of the high mound to the north-west, as well as the basement of a large square building'. He reported of having seen at, 'the south face of the southern mound ...... traces of a large square building with rooms on four sides surrounding a courtyard' which he took as similar to Buddhist Monastery. 'The walls' he notes, 'were very massive; but the whole have now been removed to form ballast for the Railway.' He suggested a wide extant to the ruins at Harappa owing to the fact of it having 'sufficed to furnish brick ballast for about 100 miles of the Lahore and Multan Railway' (ASR: V, 105-108).

Concluding his notice of the site, Cunningham estimated the importance of Harappa from the account of Hiuen Thsang, who mentioned the city of Po-fa-to, or Po-fa-to-lo, measuring 20 *li*, which Cunningham believed to correspond with Harappa. From the account of the Chinese pilgrim, he learned about the site as having possessed 'four stupas and twelve monasteries counting about 1,000 monks, besides twenty Brahmanical temples' (ASR: V, 107-108).

His 'chief discovery there consisted of number of stone implements for scraping wood or leather.' Other objects discovered were 'numerous specimens of ancient pottery,' and the 'most curious object .... a seal, belonging to Major Clark ....' He described this seal as 'a smooth black stone without polish' having a humpless bull with an inscription in characters 'unknown' to him. In his opinion the seal was 'foreign to India' owing to the humpless bull and the non-Indian character of the letters of the inscription (ASR : V, 108).

For him the antiquity of Harappa extended to the seventh century A.D., i.e. the period of Hiuen Thsang's visit. In another reference which he makes relying upon a local tradition is the destruction of the city by Mohd. ibn-Kasim in A.D. 713. For this purpose he tends to identify the local Raja Har Pal or Hara Pala, with Raja Dahir of Alor, as both of them were related as having committed incest with a near relative.

Sometimes he would tend to get logical in his explorations. As early as 1835-36, in his excavations in the precincts of the Dhamek tower at Sarnath, he could notice 'a piece of terraced floor.' He attempted to trace the 'flooring' but it, 'terminated on what appeared to be the edge of a small tank .....' (ASR: I, 120). In another instance, Cunningham informs of 'something like a piece of terraced flooring' at the western edge of the mound K at Khukundo. He was successful in uncovering a portion of the terraced floor which was broken up by the widespread roots of the Tamarind tree (ASR: I, 89-90). Again, at Bodh Gaya, but towards the close of his career, he excavated several floors, one beneath the other in the Buddhist temple. His efforts at correlating the ground level outside the temple with the floors uncovered inside, followed by an attempt at the reconstruction of the site in different epochs is indeed a sign of a systematised approach.

Regarding the Iron pillar of Delhi, Cunningham initially spoke of it as constituted of 'mixed metal' on the authority of Fred Cooper, Deputy Commissioner of Delhi. Other European writers (Bishop Heber, Emma Roberts and Sleeman) had described it variously as of 'cast metal', 'mixed metal', and 'of bronze'. But upon realising the fact that 'a bronze pillar would never have escaped the rapacity of the Muhammadan conquerors', Cunningham submitted 'a small bit from the rough lower part of the pillar' to Dr. Murray Thomson for an analysis of its nature. He was informed by the latter that the metal was 'pure malleable iron of 7.66 specific gravity.' This fact was accepted by Cunningham. (ASR: I, 170 & f.n.).

His suggestions for the future excavations of the mound K at Khukundo, seem to emphasise the concept of 'total excavation'. But instead of the success in uncovering of the layers, the success of the whole exercise for him depended upon the discoveries made therein. At Nirandpur, in spite of the discovery of several discontinuous walls in his 'numerous excavations' of mound F, he thought it fit to give up the excavations as nothing was discovered there. (ASR: XI, 161).

Recalling the developments which took place in world archaeology in the nineteenth century, we are aware that cross-dating and sequence-dating evolved with Flinders Petrie (from 1880 to 1904, with the principles of his systematic method of excavation summarised in his *Methods and Aims of Archaeology,* 1904), with his success in dating Palestinian and early Greek (Aegean) sites by reference to the Egyptian ones. He extended the 'absolute chronology' of Egyptian sites to Greece and Asia Minor during 1889-91. The principle of relative dating was based upon the fundamentals of stratigraphic analysis. Dendochronology, the dating of trees by counting their growth rings was developed and applied for archaeological purposes by A.E. Douglas in the United States. Though unaware of the scientific relevance of this principle for dating the historical remains, Cunningham attempted to ascertain the age of the Pipal tree at the mounds of Hatila or Asokpur, on the basis of its annual rings. The tree was cut down by the Tahsildar of the neighbouring village of Vazirganj in A.D. 1862, as the lingam of Asoknath Mahadeo Temple, was 'almost covered' by its matted roots. Upon seeing the section of the stem Cunningham deduced thus: 'As the cut stem of the Pipal shows 849 annual rings, the tree must have been planted in A.D. 1013, during the reign of Mahmud of Ghazni.' This, he notes, corresponded with the date of the temple itself which was said to have been built by Suhridal, Raja of Asokpur, the antagonist of Sayid Salar. (ASR: I, 329).

In this background of developments in world archaeology, how far is it correct to accept the charge by Abu Imam that Cunningham did not know about sequence-dating or its handmaid typology (Abu Imam: 1966) His chronology of the coins of Mathura, is related as done on a 'typological basis' (Sunil C. Ray: 140). By alleging that: 'Also the importance of pottery and corpus of finds completely escaped him' (Abu Imam: 199). If the indication is towards their relevance for the purpose of dating the objects, then this charge looses much of its authenticity in the light of the above facts. Cunningham did mention the pottery pieces he noticed during the course of excavations at some sites and also drew sketches of the same. His reflections on Bhita are symptomatic of a comparative approach which he often exhibited in suggesting similarities or differences in the architectural styles and sculptured reliefs noticed at different sites. The glazed pottery which he found at Bhita was discovered by him in 'all the more ancient sites' with a specimen 'exhumed in one of the Bhilsa Topes' (ASR: II, 51).

Cunningham did not possess any workable knowledge of stratigraphy and strata-wise analysis of objects; so one cannot expect him to have known relative dating either. Neither did he have any idea of the Four Age classification of objects. However, as early as the 1860's Bruce Foote of the Geological Survey divided the Indian paleoliths into 'ten types' (Cumming: 93).

But on the whole, apart from acknowledging the damage caused to significant sites by the initial excavations of the Archaeological Department, Sir John Marshall calls for exonerating Cunningham and Burgess in the context of the developments taking place in world archaeology elsewhere. In his words; 'In those days modern methods of scientific excavation were unknown, ... We must not, however, blame General Cunningham or his colleague, Dr. Burgess, for what explorers were at that time doing everywhere, in Europe as much as in Asia and in Egypt, in the name of archaeology' (cumming: 2).

Cunningham's tours of exploration have been described as 'hurried visits from site to site .... visiting as many as thirty sites in one single season, doing scarce justice to them during these brief visits.' (Abu Imam: 181). It ought to be considered rather a credit to Cunningham that he could survey around thirty sites in a single season in those days of difficult travel. Moreover, the survey tour undertaken encompassed a whole region or even two at a time with a responsibility to delineate all which remained of the past. His main objective, as also emphasised in Canning's Minute, was to effect a complete search in order to record all noticeable remains along with the records of them as far as traceable. In his official capacity, firstly as Archaeological Surveyor, and then as Director General of Indian archaeology, Cunningham altogether surveyed and reported upon almost 492 sites and districts (including those revisited by him), most of them being prominent . His assistants on the other hand, who joined him in 1870, surveyed and reported almost 428 sites and districts along with sketches and photographs of the site maps, plans, objects of sculpture and architecture etc., respectively as done by Cunningham. That his Survey tours were well chalked out and planned before is clear from this observation, which he made about Kakupur. He wrote thus: 'I have not yet visited this place, which lay out of my line of route, but I hope to have an oppurtunity of examining it hereafter' (ASR: I, 296).

Abu Imam has also characterised Cunningham's excavations as degenerating 'into mere object - hunting expeditions', at times (Abu Imam: 181). It has however, to be borne in mind that Cunningham was not professional archaeologist possessing adequate technical skills for the job at his command. His methods of excavation were entirely traditional, taking into scope the entire survey of the north, east, and central parts of India, of which many areas he could not visit at the end of his tenure. Even then he exhibited a deep understanding of the architectural styles practised in India since ancient times, often pointing at the 'stylistic relationships, and highlighting many prominent sites with historical remains, ruined or intact. (Lar. Enc. Arch.:3). To some extent it was through his initial explorations that the cultural importance of Taxila could be estimated (Lar. Enc. Arch. :382).

At many places in his Reports Cunningham has acknowledged his inability to effect a complete survey of some sites owing to paucity of time (more particularly during his first term in office). He would be satisfied with accomplishing surface or superficial excavations therein as he himself has admitted. At times he would return twice or even thrice to an important site to satisfy his quest of making significant finds. In his tour of 1875-76 we find him extending his operations at Sravasti to period of eleven days in the course of which he asserted to have 'made a very careful examination of the site' (A SR: XI, 78). During the same tour Cunningham spent five days at Tandwa, where he is reported to have made 'a complete survey of the ruins' (ASR: XI, 72).

Cunningham took special care in publishing the results of his extensive survey tours on an annual basis, in the form of 'systematic records' (Lar. Enc. Arch., : 386). Though at times delay occurred in carrying out this important task, it did not hamper the publication of the reports of any archaeological tour. However, Abu Imam has criticised Cunningham for this delay in the publication of the survey reports, which as he says, led to an 'unnecessary duplication of work' (Abu Imam: 203 fn.). In the light of this criticism we should consider this fact; 'An excavation is not complete until the printed report is available to the world. Often the publication of the report takes as long as, or much longer than, the actual work in the field' (Enc. Brit. Mac.: I, 1081).

Whatever was discovered was reported upon, comprising the discovery of minor objects, insignificant sites, along with the important ones. At the end, each survey report was supplied with several plates carrying neat hand-drawn sketches and diagrams of the site plan, maps, monuments, discovered objects, architectural styles, sculptures, eye-copies of inscriptions discovered etc. These hand-drawn sketches were later supplemented with photographs, with the services of his assistants J.D. Beglar and H.B.W. Garrick. Photography was first utilised for the illustration of excavation reports by Alexander Conze who worked at Samothrace in 1873 and 1875. Cunningham was convinced of the importance of photography as emphasised in his memorandum to Lord Canning. Though, Abu Imam has alleged that Cunningham 'did not properly exploit photography for the purpose of illustration ....' and, '.............. it was not until Report IX that Photographs appeared in any number when Beglar began to help him with photography' (Abu Imam: 201-202). Further, he testifies that some photographs 'appeared' of 'the illustration of the Appendix on Indian architecture' in Report V (201). Before giving any weightage to this criticism we should remember that Report V gave the results of the survey tours undertaken during 1872-73, and Report IX of the tours of 1873-75.

The Survey reports broadly deal with Cunningham's interpretations of Indian history and culture upon the basis of his excavations, discoveries and observations of people. However, the places described by him are seldom dealt as vibrant portions of a whole civilisation. The idea of the whole as a sum of its parts never possibly dawned upon him in this connection. Through him, it could not be the archaeological history of a civilisation or a culture, but of sites, preferentially Buddhists which were desired to be recorded in the archaeological annals.

REFERENCES

Ancient India No. 9, Bulletin of the Arch. Sur. of India, 1953. Special Jubilee Number New Delhi: 11 & f.n.

Archaeology in India. 1950: Bureau of Education, India, 1-2.

Basham, A.L. 1996. *The Wonder that was India,* London, twenty-eighth edition, New Delhi: 4-8.

Buhler, G. 1895. Some Notices on Past and Future Archaeological Exploration in India, *Journal of the Royal Asiatic Society,* London: 1905, 653, 655.

Childe, V.G. 1958. *A Short Introduction to* ***Indian*** *Archaeology,* (Reprint) London : 20, 35.

Charles Gilbert–Picard. 1977. *Larousse of Encyclopedia Archaeology,* (Lar. Enc. Arch.), New Jersey: 207-237, 245-146, 315-316, 328, 382, 386.

Cumming John (ed.), 1939. *Revealing India's Past,*London: 2, 9-10, 93-96.

Cunningham, A. *Archaeological Survey Reports,* Calcutta.

___________, 1834. Correction of a mistake regarding one of the Roman Coins found in the Tope at Manikyala, opened by M. Court': *J.A.S.B.* 1834 : iii, Calcutta: 635-637.

___________1848 a. An Essay on the Arian Order of Architecture as exhibited in the Temples of Kashmir, *Journal of Asiatic Society of Bengal* (*J.A.S.B.*), 1848, XVII, Pt. II, Calcutta: 241-242.

___________1848 b. 'Verification of the Itinerary of Hiuen Thsang through Ariana and India, with reference to Major Anderson's hypothesis of its modern compilation, *J.A.S.B.* 1848, XVII, Pt. I, Calcutta: 476-477.

___________1848 c, Proposed Archaeological Investigation, *J.A.S.B.* : XVII, 535-536.

___________1853. *Ladak : Physical, Statistical and Historical with notices of surrounding countries.* Simla. (Reprint), New Delhi, 1970.

___________1892. *The Mahabodhi or the Great Buddhist Temple under the Bodhi Tree at Buddha Gaya,* London: 17-23.

___________1891 *Coins of Ancient India from the earliest times down to the Seventh Century A.D.,* London, 8vo, Reprint, 1965·Varanasi: Preface v, 19-22.

___________1854 *The Bhilsa Topes or the Buddhist Monuments of Ancient India,* London, (Reprint,) 1966 Varanasi.

____________1893 *Coins of Medieval India from the Seventh Century down to the Muhammadan Conquest,* London, (Reprint,) 1967 Delhi: Preface vi, f.n.

Dey, N.L. 1927. *The Geographical Dictionary of Ancient and Medieval India,* London: 92, 96, 111-112, 125, 189, 201-202.

Daniels, Glyn E. 1952. *A Hundred Years of Archaeology,* London, (Reprint): 25, 28, 54, 69, 140, 165, 177, 260.

Imam, Abu, 1966. *Sir Alexander Cunningham and the Beginnings of Indian Archaeology,* Asiatic Society, Dacca: Preface, vi-vii, 181, 198-199, 201-202, 203 f.n., 208, 235-239.

JRAS, Obituary Notice, Major General Sir Alexander Cunningham, 1894. London : 167, 168, 170, 171, 174.

Khanna, A. 1992. *Archaeology in India,* New Delhi: 14.

Kosambi, D.D. 1965. *The Culture and Civilisation of Ancient India in Historical Outline.* London : 15 f.n.

Law, B.C. 1967. *Historical Geography of India* France : 117, 121, 147, 153-154.

Majumdar-Sastri S.N. (ed.) 1924. *Cunningham's Ancient Geography of India,* Calcutta : Preface, lxxii, Preface to the New edition, v, pp. 67 ff., 120-125, 206-207, 387-393, 395-399, 412-417, 423, 448, 469, 507, 536, 537.

Rapson, E.J. 1922. *Cambridge History of India.* vol. I, Cambridge: 315, 317.

Ray, Sunil C. 1989. 'Stratigraphic Evidence of Coins from Excavations at Mathura in Dorris Meth Sreenivasan, (ed.), *Mathura: The Cultural Heritage.* New Delhi: 140.

Roy, Sourindranath 1961. *The Story of Indian Archaeology,* 1784-1947. Delhi: 47, 49-50, 59.

Sheratt, Andrew, (ed.), 1980. *The Cambridge Encyclopaedia of Archaeology.* Cambridge: 20, 23.

Smith, Vincent A. 1927. *Early History of India.* Oxford : 27.

The New Encyclopaedia Britannica, Macropaedia, (En. Brit. Mac.) 1973-1974. I & III, Chicago: 1078-1082, 295-296.

Wheeler, Mortimer. 1954. *Archaeology from the Earth.* Oxford,: 8-9.

Recent Archaeological Investigations in Trans-Ghaghra Plains and identification of some city sites of Kosala

B.R. Mani*

Archaeological Survey of India (ASI) is presently ɜxploring the Trans-Ghaghra Plains, Sarayupar area in the 3asti and Siddarthnagar districts of Uttar Pradesh. 3esides excavations at Siswania in Basti district and trial liggings at Deoraon and Orai near Siswania and Dharamsinghwa, Pipari and Mundiar in the bordering ırea of Siddharthnagar and Basti are also being undertak-ːn. Although some of the sites were visited in July, 1995 Tewari and Mani 1996: 149-68) but regular explorations vere conducted firstly from February to June, 1996 and ubsequently from February to May, 1997 by the ∃xcavation Branch-II, New Delhi of the ASI under my lirection. In the process 126 sites have been explored, of vhich 91 sites are new discoveries.

The area of Trans-Ghaghra plains, in general, covers ıorth-eastern Uttar Pradesh comprising modern districts ıf Bahraich, Gonda, Siddharthnagar, Basti, Gorakhpur, Aahrajganj, Padrauna and Deoria, besides the adjoining order areas of Nepalese Terai and some parts of north-vestern Bihar. This area forms the major part of the ncient Kosala mahājanapada which was ruled by the *kshvākus* of the solar race besides the states ruled by *'ākyas,* Koliyas and Mallas.

The entire region is a monotonous flat land with a igher elevation of 102 m in the north-west dropping in a lope of 70 m in the south-east. It forms a distinct geo-raphical and cultural entity. The plain is bound on the south and the west by the Ghaghra and east by the Gandak and extends upto the foothills of the Himalaya. The northern part is studded with streams, lakes, swamps and forests. Rapti and Ghaghra, emanating from Himalaya, have a number of important tributaries– Manwar, Kuwano and Ami– which run through the twin districts of the region.

Dynastic lists in the *Purāṇas* and the legend of Videgha Māthava in the *Satapatha Brāhmaṇa* testify to the region being inhabited in the pre-Buddha times. Archaeological evidence also confirms this. The area attracted the attention of British archaeologists in the middle of last century. Lassen, Alexander Cunningham, A.C.L. Carllyle, A. Führer, V.A. Smith, W.C. Peppe and P.C. Mukharji carried out archaeological investigations here. Cunningham identified and located the ancient Sravasti in 1863. The focal point of these investigations was Kapilavastu which was identified by these archaeologists variously– Nagar Khas, Bhuiladih, Tilaura Kot and Piprahwa. Carllyle and Führer tried to identify various Buddhist sites mentioned in the Pāli texts and by the Chinese pilgrims on the basis of distances and directions mentioned therein by orienting themselves from Bhuiladih which they thought to be Kapilavastu. But after the discovery of Aśokan Pillar edict at Lumbini in 1896 by Führer and an inscribed relic casket at Piprahwa in 1898 by Peppe, a number of identifications of sites made earlier were proved to be incorrect. In the post-indepen-

uperintending Archaeologist,Archaeological Survey of India, Excavation Branch II, New Delhi.

dence era ASI, the Gorakhpur University, the Banaras Hindu University and the U.P. State archaeological organisation carried out excavations and explorations in the region. Sravasti, Piprahwa-Ganwaria, Tilaura Kot, Kodan and Ayodhya were excavated by the ASI while Sohgaura, Narhan, Imlidih and a few other sites were dug by the universities. A large number of inscribed sealings bearing the legend *Om Devaputra Vihāre Kapilavastu Bhikhu Sanghasa* with a little variation were discovered at Piprahwa which strengthened its claims to be the site of ancient Kapilavastu.

Excavations at Sohgaura, Narhan, Imlidih and Dhuriapar in Gorakhpur district provided new evidence of cultural movements in the middle and second half of the second millenium B.C. The dates were confirmed through radiocarbon method. The occupational deposits revealed a sequence of neolithic and chalcolithic ceramic traditions, which coincides with the chronological framework and suggests the extension of the eastern neolithic-chalocolthic traditions of Bihar.

Earlier, Northern Black Polished Ware (NBPW) was identified as the principal ceramic industry of the region which had its beginning somewhere around 600 B.C. But with the discovery of Pre-NBPW levels at the above mentioned sites in Gorakhpur district yielding earlier ceramics of at least two distinct cultural periods; the earliest represented by cord-impressed red ware (pre-1300 B.C.) and later by the black-and-red ware and black slipped ware with white paintings (*c.* 1300 B.C. to *c.* 800 B.C.), it was considered necessary to examine earliest cultural movements in other parts of the region. Secondly, more than three dozen *grāma, nigama* and *nagara* sites have been mentioned in the earliest Pāli Buddhist texts which fall in this region– the Kosala, Sākyas and Koliyas– during Buddha's time. It was felt that they need their proper identification which is a difficult task but which could be possible through explorations, study of the already explored material, revisit to the important sites, study of philological similaritis of ancient names with modern names of sites as also a study of routes and traditions. Similarly, a need is also felt for the exact identification of ancient Devadaha, Rāmagrāma, Pāwā and Pippalivana in the territories ruled by Sākyas, Koliyas, Mallas and Moriyas extending towards east and north-east of the region under study which may be located in the Nepalese Terai and present districts of Gorakhpur, Mahrajganj, Padrauna and Deoria.

So far, nearly 150 ancient and medieval sites have been reported from the districts of Basti and Siddharthnagar by various explorers. During our two seasons' explorations we visited 126 sites, out of which 91 were new discoveries in the two districts. Since the objective of this paper is mainly related to the earliest cultural movements and assemblages and the identification of ancient sites, it would be not out of place to mention here that out of 126 explored sites 33 belong to the medieval period but the rest of 93 provide materials for further study on the above lines.

The cultural assemblage noticed during excavations and explorations in the two districts points to the emergence of townships towards the end of the second millennium B.C. which also suggests the ushering of the Iron Age, the ceramics of which can be classified in the pre-NBPW group. Main caramics were cord-impressed red ware, black-and-red ware, black slipped ware and grey ware; all are devoid of painting. Important shapes are dishes, variety of bowls including channelled or lipped bowls, dish-on-stand, vases, water vessels, storage jars etc. The associated material include bone points, terracotta animal figurines, discs, gamesmen, beads and hopscotches. Lumps of burnt clay with reed marks suggest that the inhabitants lived in huts made of wattle and daub. Lahuradeva and Gulrihwaghat (Singh 1990), district Basti have earlier yielded white painted black-and-red ware and black slipped ware. The problems related to emergence of neolithic-chalcolithic cultures and early Iron Age settlements in this region require further investigation at a few promising sites.

The next phase is represented by the introduction of NBPW along with the earlier ceramics, although a few earlier shapes like dish-on-stand fell into disuse. Silver Punch-marked and uninscribed copper cast coins are found associated with NBPW period. Other associated antiquities include terracotta human and animal figurines, beads, bangles, ear-studs, toy carts, wheels, gold foil bull-shaped pendant, iron nails, arrow-heads and other minor objects besides those similar to the pre-NBPW phase. The above two phases along with later cultures are represented by Piprahwa-Ganwaria complex (already well known), Siswania, Deoraon, Lahuradeva, Chandidiha, Benipur, Pipari, Ama, Mahjidia II, Bhatolva, Sevaidih, Itawa,

Buddhikhas, Paun, Behil I, Behil II, Siyara Jhunri, Baksari-banni, Gedar, Deokali, Karahna, Itauwa and Gharighat.

The post-NBPW phase is represented by sites having Sunga-Kushan assemblage including the earlier mentioned sites. They are Kopia, Bhuiladih, Ghoswa, Mahdeva, Dharamsinghwa, Orai, Nagar I, Jata, Kopa, Ukada, Buddhi Khas, Chharaunchha and the Kushana complexes of Sarpoka-Pipari group of seven sites in one locality besides Kushan sites at Pedar, Hansudi, Dhaurahra, Barhari Gaura, Ramnagar, Mundiar, Dakharwa, Meerganj, Udsara, Devdand, Gana, Jogiya I, Birdpur, Naugarh, Bhelwal, Pipra Gautam, Gaura Rohari, Shankarpur, Belava, Thokawa, Selhara, Mundiari, Kusauna Khurd, Yashoval (Jaswal), Kanwar-Kanwari, Khajura Khurd, Arail, Katesar, Bhangura, Madain, Uchahra Kalan, Uchahra II, Amilahwa, Dhuriadih, Lohrauli-Sonaura, Bhaukhari, Dasia, Imlidiha, Chetia, Bhadana, Bharat Bhari I, Bharat Bhari II, Ganauna and Thalapar. Representative antiquities including Ayodhya and Kushan coins, terracotta figurines, seals and sealings, terrocotta pestles and red slipped ware and associated red ware with sprinklers, incurved bowls with string cut base and other shapes have been found. A late phase of this is represented at Chando, across river Kuwano and about 1km from Siswania and at Rampur Reoti and Hatawa. Rest of the sites such as Tamesarnath, Painra, Nagar II, Nagar Fort, Amorha Fort, Chhavni, Mahjidia III, Shahpur, Jignadham, Kotia, Ganawar, Bahkechor Bargadwa, Chando Tal, Gaighat, Charadahi, Kalvari, Rampur, Jogiya II, Othganpur, Bahera Mafi, Pala, Kotia II, Chhitahi-Majharia, Ghosiari, Aosara, Baksari II, Chhitahi, Ajanv, Gahba, Siktaur I and II, Majhauwa, Tedhawa, Baudhara and Siswa have yielded evidence of early and late medieval remains. Forts of Nagar, Bankechor, Bargadwa and Amorha were sacked during the revolt of 1857 and are important for the study of India's struggle for freedom.

During the last quarter of the second millennium B.C. two main painting traditions of ceramics were prevalent in the Ganga-Yamuna plains. Linear, hooks and floral patterns in black or white pigment on the surface of pottery is seen. In the west it is represented by Ochre-coloured pottery and Painted Grey Ware and in the east by white painted black-and-red ware and black slipped ware or black polished ware. Representative sites in west fall under the *mahājanapadas* of Kuru, Pañchāla, Sūrasena and Matsya. Similarly representative sites in the east are in the old territories of Kāśī, Magadha, Vajji and Malla. Kosala which was perhaps strongest *mahājanapada* in pre-Buddha times was full of streams, swamps, forests, lakes and was bounded by Himalaya in north, river Ghaghra in west and south and parallel running rivers to Gandak like Rapti, Ami and other tributaries in the east besides the forests like Naimishāraṇya in the west. Thus, the geo-political barrier seems to be one of the reasons for preventing painting traditions of ceramics from penetrating the area. The universal feature in the pottery of the age is the continuance of ceramics like black-and-red ware, black slipped ware, red ware, including corded pottery and grey ware in the entire north India or Āryāvartta but the painting traditions seem to be confined and restricted to certain areas. With the weakening of Kosala as a political power and with the rise and development of Buddhism new centres came into existence. This was the period of the beginning of the so called second urbanisation in which period the upper route of Uttarāpatha connecting Vaiśālī and Pāṭaliputra with cities of Pañchāla like Ahichchhatrā, Kāmpilya and Sānkāśya crossing the territories of the Mallas, Sākyas and Kosala was more frequent by the traders and pilgrims than before. This gave rise to the growth of urban centres which reached its climax during Sunga-Kushan rule.

The identifications proposed here for certain city sites such as Setavyā, Ukkaṭṭhā, Nagaraka, Medatalumpa, Sālavatika and Vebhaliṅga are based on the references in Pāli Buddhist texts about the status of the sites and distance or route followed for their approach, philological similarities between ancient and present names, size of present mounds and their cultural assemblage.

Setavyā

The famous ***Pāyāsisutta*** of the ***Dīghanikāya*** (Rhys Davids 1911: 349-79) mentions about the discourse by Kumāra Kassapa to Pāyāsi Rājanya on the rebirth and *karma* in the Simsapāvana to the north of Setavyā nagara in Kosala kingdom; the name of Simsapāvana or the grove of *Simsapa* (Sisam) tree *(Dalbergia Sisu)* is still preserved in the name of the place Siswania, 9 km towards south-east of Basti city on the left bank of Kuwano. Three mounds in a series are found along the river in north-south orientaton in an area of approximately 1000×300 m. Towards north and north-west are situated villages of Bankata and Deoraon with habitational remains of ancient times. Names of villages also suggest that towards the north of the main habitational centre the forest was cut in the past and probably there was some monastic establishment called Devārāma.

Excavations were carried out at Siswania and Deoraon in two seasons, in 1996 and 1997 in a layout of 44 quadrants of 29 squares measuring 10×10 m indicated a cultural assemblage (Pl I. 1 and Fig. 1) beginning from Pre-NBPW period (*c.* 9th to 6th centuary B.C.) to the

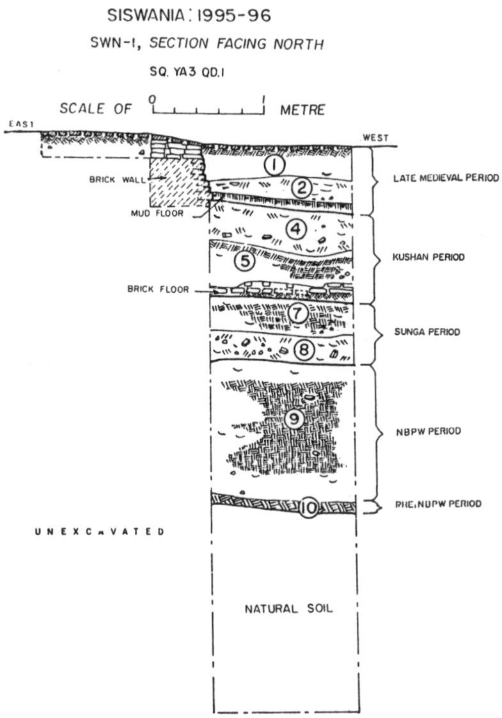

Fig. 1

Kushana period (first three centuries of the Christian era). More than 1500 antiquities both from excavations and surface were found. In the past the site yielded thousands of coins, seals and sealings, terracotta figurines, beads and other antiquities (Mani 1991: 43-50,. Excavations brought to light circular rammed floors with post-holes and hearths in the NBPW levels and a terrocotta ring-well and hearths and floors in Sunga levels. The Kushan levels were found rich in structures with brick walls, mostly showing evidence of brick robbing, brick floors, rammed floors, two terracotta ring-wells and a brick well. The site extended along the river Kuwano in north-south direction for nearly 1000 m and about 300 to 350 m in east-west direction. Punch-marked silver and copper coins, uninscribed copper cast coins, Ayodhya and Kushan coins, terracotta plaques of Maurya-Sunga period representing Gajalakshmi, *Yakshis,* figures and Kushan human figurines including Naigamesa-Naigamesi, Hariti and others, terracotta animal figurines bone points and arrowheads, copper antimony rods and other objects, iron, bone and ivory objects, a gold– foil pendant of bull shape, beads of semi-precious stones, terracotta and glass, terracotta *ghata*-shaped and arecanut beads, bangles of copper, terracotta and glass, terracotta gamesmen, and toy carts, stone weights, crucibles, terracotta pestles and skin rubbers, footed stone, querns and mullers, terracotta sling balls, hopscotches and discs and clay seals and sealings with legends in Bhāhmī script of second-first century B.C. reading *Idadevasa, Akatha* etc. were found. Ceramics include typical shapes of black slipped ware, plain black-and-red ware, grey ware, red ware including hand-made, cord impressed and fine red ware sherds, Northern Black Polished Ware and Kushan red are, both plain and with red slip (Fig. 2).

Setavyā is also mentioned in the *Vatthugāthā* of the *Pārāyanavagga* of *Sutta Nipāta* (Chalmers 1932: 106-44) in the context of Bavari's story who despatched a group of scholars, to get answers to some metaphysical questions from Buddha, who travelled † Sāvatthi (Śrāvastī) and then to Setavyā, Kapilavatthu (Kapilavastu), Kusinārā (Kuśīnagara), Pāvā and Vesāli (Vaiśālī).

Ukkaṭṭhā

Ukkaṭṭhā was a *nagara* in Kosala and was connected to Setavyā and Vaiśālī by high roads (*addhānamagga*). Pāli texts (Sarao 1990: 118) of *Dīghanikāya, Majjhimanikāya, Jātaka,* and *Papañcha Sūdanī* mention it in different contexts. It was located near forests of Ichchhānaṇgala Vanasaṇḍa and Subhagavana. This site can be identified with modern Ukada located at a distance of about 27 km north of Basti and about 1 km west from Bhanpur which was discovered during present explorations. The area of the extensively destroyed mound is approximately 150x150 m. A 4 m high brick mound roughly circular on plan is located there which is locally called Kotia, but which may probably represent the remains of a *stupa.* The local residents informed that there

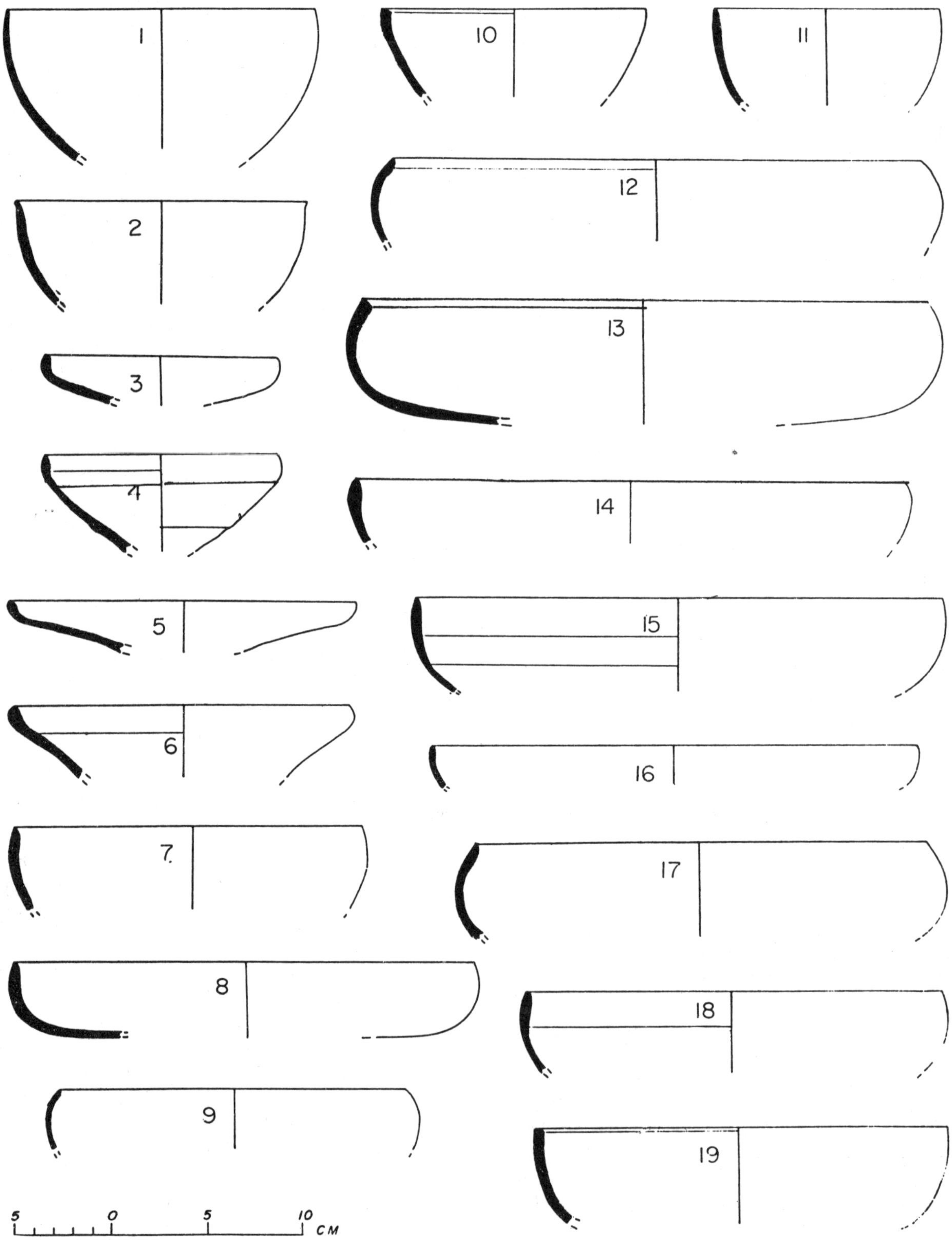

Fig. 2 Siswania: Red ware 1–8, 10, 15; Black slipped ware 9, 11–13, 18, 19; Black and –Red ware 14; NBPW 16; Grey ware 17.

were two forests full of *Sal* and *Mahua* trees in the past on its southern and western sides which were cut in due course of time to make the land cultivable. They might represent the old forests mentioned in Pāli texts. Another village called Ukadaha at a distance of about 9 km. towards west of this site was also examined since the name was philologically nearer to Ukkaṭṭhā; however, no archaeological remains were found. Besides the *stupa* mound, only red ware was found from Ukada. Yet it is most probable that the site may represent the ancient Ukkaṭṭhā.

Ātumā

The Pāli *Vinaya* and other texts (Sarao 1990: 108) refer to a *nigama* called Ātumā that lay between Kusinārā and Sāvatthi. The Buddha stayed there many times at the Bhūsāgāra. We propose the identification of modern village having large mound called Ama with Ātumā. Its location is also almost in between Kusinagar and Sravasti.

The site of Ama was discovered during present explorations on the right bank of Bainra nala, 27 km north of Basti and 1km east of Sonaha on Basti-Doomariaganj road (State Highway No. 26). It is about 3 km south of Bhanpur. The extensive mound is partly under cultivation and spreads in an area of about 300 m in north-south and 200 m in east-west direction with an average height of about 3 m. The cultural assemblage at the site includes NBPW of both delux and degenerated varieties, black slipped ware including convex sided bowls, red ware comprising storage jars, incurved Kushan bowls, red slipped dish, lids. channelled bowl and vases of medium size. Terracotta pestle, glass bangle pieces, iron slag, glass pieces and brick-bats were found. There are three ancient wells located on the mound. A burnt-brick measuring 32 (?)x 25x7 cm was also found.

Nagaraka

The *Dhammachetiya Sutta* of the *Majjhimanikāya* of *Suttapiṭaka* (Dhammagiri 1993: 56, 328-29) mentions about Kosalan king Pasenadi (Prasenajit) visiting from Nagaraka, a Kosalan *nigama* along with Dīgha-kārāyaṇa to Medatalumpa where Buddha was staying in the Śākyan *nigama*. The distance of 3 *yojanas* which might have been 40 to 50 km was coverd by them in a chariot.

The site of Nagaraka can be identified with present Nagar or Nagar Khas, a township about 10 km south-west of Basti on the eastern bank of Chandotal. The area of the site is about 600x800 m and pottery and brick-bats are scattered everywhere on the low mounds. Potsherds collected from the site are either of early historical period in small quantity or of medieval period. Black slipped ware and red ware of different shapes and types were found.

Medatalumpa

The *Dhammachetiya Sutta* (Dhammagiri 1990) calls Medatalumpa as a Śākyan *nigama*. The present Mehdawal market and township can be identified with the ancient *nigama*. This is located on the north of Bakhira tal at a distance of about 40 km from Basti. On the basis of philological similarity of the ancient and modern names, the site's proximity with Śākyan territory and its being famous traditionally even today as a market, the identification has been proposed. The area is fully occupied by modern township although ancient remains have been occasionally found in the vicinity. Local popular legends claim that there used to be an old town which had submerged in the Bakhira lake about which stories in poetic form are familiar.

It was observed that within the township of Mehdawal there are some evidences of ancient remains at Pashchim tola, Belbanava in western and northern part of the township and in east at Pakka Pokhra and in the north around Kubernath and the medieval tomb. These ancient mounds have been covered under continued habitation and modern structures. Two Kushana sites in the close vicinity of Mehdawal were discovered at Amilahwa, 2 km south of it and at Lohrauli-Sonaura, 1.5 km north of it. The former site covers an area of about 100x100m with an average height of 1.5 m. The latter site extends in an area of about 500 m in north-south and 300 m in east-west direction with the average height of its mounds between 1.5 to 2 m from the surrounding ground level. Red ware of Kushan period having the typical shapes of incurved bowls, lids, knobbed lids, sprinklers, carinated *handis*, basins and vases and decorated pottery with incised designs along with terracotta figurines and terracotta pestles and other minor objects were found. The surrounding area of Mehdawal around a radius of 15 to 20 km is rich in archaeological remains, which was noticed in about 20 such sites; the remains ranging from NBPW period to Kushan period.

Sālāorsālavatikā

In *Sāleyyaka-Sutta* (PGM : 12.73, 358) and *Apaṇṇaka-Sutta* (PGM : 13.28, 71) of the *Majjhimanikāya* of *Suttapiṭka*, Sālā has been mentioned in connection with Buddha's visit to the place in the country of the Kosala. In the same area of Kosala *Dīghanikāya* mentions a place called Sālavatikā or Sālavatī where *Lohichcha Sutta* was preached by Buddha and it is also mentioned that the village was given by Pasenadi (Prasenajit) to Lohichcha, a brāhmaṇa (Digha: I. 224; Malala sekera 1995: 1121). We propose its identification with a huge mound towards east of Saltauwa bazaar which is also known as Sevaidih, located on Basti-Doormariaganj road at a distance of about 19 km from Basti. The area of the mound is about 300x200 m with an average height of 2 to 3 m. Among two modern Siva temples, one is constructed on top of a *stupa* which still retains its height upto about 4.5 m. The other temple has an Ekamukhī Siva lingam of post-Gupta period. Sherds of black-and-red ware, black slipped ware, NBPW, grey ware and red ware with a variety of shapes and terracotta figurines, hopscotch and pestles were found.

Vehalinga

According to the *Ghaṭikāra-sutta* of *Majjhimanikāya* (Majjima: II, 44 ff; Sam. I. 34.60; Malalasekara 1995: 951) Buddha had preached the *Ghaṭikāra-Sutta* to Ghaṭikāra, a friend of Jotipāla at Vehaliṅga or Vebhaliṅga, a *gāma-nigama* of Kosala. The *grama-nigama* of Vehaliṅga or Vebhalṅga can be identified on philological grounds and archaeological evidence with the two mounds at Behil, located at a distance of 17 km from Basti on Basti-Mahuli road to its northern side, almost in between Basti and Mahuli.

A Siva temple, octagonal on plan, called Behilnath is located on the top of the circular mound having brick structures of Kushan period. The circular mound with a height of about 3 m seems to be a *stupa,* probably erected in the memory of the place having been blessed with Buddha's preaching at the site. The bricks of the circular structure measure 33 to 34x22x5 to 6 cm. Worship of Siva linga at Behilnath is singificant as it coincides with the proposed ancient name of the place Vebhaliṅga.

Remains of brick structures were also noticed on the western side of the mound with more than two courses of bricks. Towards further west of the above mound is an area of about 250 m in north-south and 200 m in east-west direction with a height of about 1 m from where black slipped ware, degenerated NBPW, grey ware, fine red ware sherds of mostly bowls and dishes were found along with Kushan red ware bowls, carinated *handis,* basins and vases which take back the antiquity of the site to *c.* sixth century B.C. to the Kushan period. A piece of ring of a terracotta ring-well was also found. About 300 m north of this site is another mound with the height of about 3 m. It spreads over an area of approximately 250x250 m. Black slipped ware, grey ware, coarse black-and-red ware and red ware sherds were found which represents Sunga-Kushan period.

There are two mounds at a distance of about 500 to 700 m south of Behil at Hatawa abutting the Basti-Mahuli road from where red ware sherds of post-Gupta period were found. The name Hatawa suggests it to be market place *(hat),* most probably connected with the *gāma-nigama* (village corporate guild) of Vehaliṅga.

Attempts have been made earlier to identify the present Mahso near Siswania with Mahāśrama of Sundarika Bhāradwāja, mentioned in the *Sutta* of his name under *Mahāvagga* of *Suttanipāta* (SBE: X.II. 73). A circular brick mound was located during present explorations on the bank of Kuwano which is identified with Sundarikā river mentioned in the *Sutta.* The brick mound is definitely a *stupa* of which the bricks measure 24 (?) x 20.5x6 cm. A few red ware sherds were found near it. Village Mahjidia is located in the vicinity.

An 86 cm high headless sandstone *yakshī* dating back to about first century B.C. (Pl. I-2) was discovered in the village Buddhi Khas in Siddharthnagar district. From the same village site sculptures of Vishṇu, Narasimha, Buddha, Umā-Maheśvara and Kushan ceramics were also found. A complete sculpture of Vishṇu holding *śankha, chakra* and *gadā* in his three hands and the fourth in *abhaya mudrā* was noticed in a medieval temple at Jignadham. A large number of antiquities including terracotta human and animal figurines, stamps, beads, dabbers, wheels, net-sinkers and pestles were found alongwith Kushan ceramics at Sarpoka-Pipari group of mounds extending over seven villages on the dry bed of an old river formed in the shape of a crescent.

Exploratory soundings at Pipari, Orai, Deoraon, Dharamsinghwa and Mundiar revealed cultural sequences of the sites and important archaeological data. Pipari, 12 km east of Rudhauli is a single culture site of NBPW period with its cultural deposit of 37 cm. The site has been damaged due to floods in Ami. Orai, 15 km south-east of Basti has Kushan and Gupta remains with its cultural deposit of about 3 m. Red ware with typical shapes of the two periods and terracotta human and animal figurines and other minor objects were recovered besides a terracotta sealing with an inscription in Gupta Brāhmī characters reading *Śrī Gajāntasya*. Deoraon, 2 km north-west of Siswania revealed the same cultural sequence as noticed in the excavations at Siswania. Dharamsinghwa, 75 km north-east of Basti is an extensive Kushan site where the exploratory sounding revealed typical red ware and other minor objects of Kushan period. A very large Kushan tank was discovered at Mundiar, 33 km from Basti, exposed during the digging operation for a proposed modern reservoir by the local administration. Its exposed part of southern wall runs to a length of 60 m and the eastern wall upto 22.5 m suggesting its further extension. The exploratory sounding revealed twelve courses of its southern wall, constructed out of burnt bricks of the size 40 to 41x20 to 21x6.5 to 7 cm in the ratio of 1:3:6. The last two courses of the wall were found buried in the natural soil and the silt deposit was noticed over it upto the fifth course of the exposed part of the wall. The Sunga-Kushan habitation site at a distance of about 500 m towards south-east of the tank was discovered at village Dakharwa.

An important achievement of the exploratory survey was the discovery of Buddhist *stupas* at fourteen sites including the mounds of Mahjidia I, Ukada, Sevaidih, Hansudi, Barhari Gaura, Behil I, Baksari-Banni, Khajura Khurd, Katesar, Bhangura, Chetia, Bharat Bhari II, Thalapar and Rampur Reoti besides explorations at the *stupa* site of Birdpur. Carlleyle's description of the *stupa* site of Rampur Deoria wrongly identifying the same with ancient Rāmagrāma tallies with the *stupa* site discovered by us at Rampur Reoti and it would be not out of place to mention here that a village named Rampur Deoria also exists towards south of Basti but no significant archaeological remains could be located there.

The name of village Dharamsinghwa suggests its association with a lion capital of Aśoka. About 20 km west of it one such capital was found at Mahdeva which is preserved in the state Museum at Lucknow. A number of villages in Siddarthnagar district which were under the Sākyan territory still retain the ancient names or suggest their association with ancient cultural components. Some examples are chetia suggesting a *chaitya* or *stupa* which was also located there, Asogawa connected with Aśoka, Santha connected with Sansthāgāra of Sākyas and Gotihwa with Goshṭhāgāra, vihare near city site of Kopia with a *vihāra* and Devgah near Dharamsinghwa with Sanskrit Devagṛha or Pāli Devagaha.

The exploration work is under progress and further evidences are likely to throw fresh light on the problems related with movement of cultures in the region and identification of ancient sites with the archaeological mounds of the area.

REFERENCE

Dīghanikāya. I. 224

Lord Chalmers, 1932 *Sutta-Nipāta;* (tr. and ed.) London, 106-44.

Majjhimanikāya, II. 45 ff. and *Samyuttanikāya*, I. 34, 60 Pali Text Society, London; Malalasekera G.P., 1995: 951.

Malalasekera G.P., *Dictionary of Pāli Proper Names*, 1995 II, New Delhi. (Reprinted): 1121.

Mani, B.R. 1991, "Identification of Setavyā, the Ancient city of Kosala with Siswania and its Terracotta Art" *Puratattva*, 43-50.

Pali-Granthamala, (PGM). 1993. Dhammagiri 13, 56. Vol. 13, Igatpuri,

PGM. 12,73, 358

PGM 12, pp. 73, 358.

PGM 13, 28,71.

Rhys Davids (ed.) *Dīghanikāya:* 1911, II, by *et al.*, Pali Text Society, London, 349-74.

Sacred Books of the East: 10, II. 73.

Sarao, K.T.S. 1990, *Urban Centres And urbanisation As Reflected In The Pāli Vinaya And Sutta Piṭakas,* Delhi: 118.

Singh B.P. 1990. "Gulrihwa Ghat and Lohra Deva : Chalcolithic settlements in district Basti, U.P." *Prāgdhārā,* 1, 89-93.

Tewari R. and B.R. Mani. 1996. "Further Archaeological investigations in Sarayupar Area," *Prāgdhārā.* No. 6, 149-168.

Alagankulam an Indo-Roman Port: A Critique

K.S. RAMACHANDRAN*

Alagankulam was an ancient port on the mouth of the Vaigai River. Vaigai, the major river rising in the Varshanad valley in the Western Ghats, was perhaps a perennial river once upon a time, but now it is flush with water only in the rainy season and for the rest of the year it is almost dry (Ram. Gaz. 1972: 31-32). Further, although it might have joined the sea in the past, at present it gets lost in the big Ramanathapuram tank and a small overflow channel from it connects the sea. Incidentally, Vaigai, after filling up nearly 374 irrigation tanks in the Ramanathapuram District could hardly be expected to contain much water to join the sea; a parallel can be seen in the confluence of River Kaveri with sea which after irrigating the entire stretch of Thanjavur District is hardly ankle-deep channel at its joining the sea. On the north bank of this river Vaigai is situated Alagankulam; the mound here goes by the name Kottaimedu, apparently there must have been some sort of fort and this is strengthened by the presence of bricks at the periphery of the mound.

Alagankulam was excavated in 1986-87 and again in 1990-91 by the State Department of Archaeology, Government of Tamilnadu. The earlier excavation was by Nagaswamy, the then Director and the subsequent digging was carried by the present Director Shri Kasinathan Nagaswamy published his findings in the form of an article in *"The Indian Archaeological Heritage"* (Nagaswamy: 247 254); the results of the second season's work as well as the details of Nagaswamy's dig were published in the form of a brochure (Majeed *et al.* 1992)

Nagaswamy laid two trenches, one at the highest portion of the mound and called it AGM-1 and other in the slope designated as AGM-2. Later AGM-3/A1, AGM-3/A2 were laid to the east of AGM-1 while AGM-3/B1 was laid to the north of AGM-2/A1. Another trench AGM-4 was tackled 20 m. away from the main trench AGM-1.

The joint authors of the brochure Majeed, Thulasiram and Vasanthi do describe the composition, thickness etc. of layers encountered in the trenches AGM-1 and AGM-2. No description however, of the stratigraphy of other excavated trenches has been given. Hence while it could be possible to some extent to correlate the layers of AGM-1 with those of AGM-2; the stratigraphy in other trenches, perforce remain unrelated not only with AGM-1, (which I take as the index trench as it had provided the maximum habitational accumulation) but also between each other. Even between AGM-1 and AGM-2, description of the composition of the layers vary. In spite of this there is something to go by.

I am giving below the composition of layers embodied in the brouchure. Nagaswamy does not describe the stratigraphy in his article. He has only indicated the depth at which some of the important objects he had recovered from the digs. The data have been rendered here in a tabulated form.

Although the composition of the layers in AGM-2 is

* C3/305 A, SFS Flats, Pankha Road, Janakpuri, New Delhi 110058.

Layer No.	Composition	Thickness	Finds	Depth at which found	Remarks
1.	Grey, loose clay with sand	1.90	Three Roman copper coins– one good and two worn out. Rouletted ware Amphorae pieces.	–0.65-0.95m B.S	It is apparent that the exact depth at which the coin was found has not been measured. However, Nagaswamy says that the well-preserved Roman coin was found at a depth of 0.95 m
2.	Grey, hard clay with sand	1.10 m	Square copper coin and NBP	–2.75 m B.S	
3.	Grey, hard clay	1.10 m	Square silver punch–marked coin	–3.30 m B.S	
4.	Grey, loose clay with brick bats	1.10 m	NBP		
5.	Grey, loose sand	0.15 m			
6.	Yellow, hard clay	0.50 m	Lime mortar floor		
7.	Dust, grey in colour	0.50 m	earliest occurrence of NBP		
8.	Grey, loose clay	0.45 m			
9.	Loose sand	Natural	Below 6.05-6.30 m		

given, the thickness of each layer has not been provided. Thus layer 1 is grey loose soil with sand; 2 is brownish loose sand; 3 is brown hard sand; 4 is yellow sand, 5 yellow sand with brickbats; and 6 yellow loose sand. It will be seen that in AGM-1 the colour is throughout grey and the soil is sand and clay. In AGM-2 the colour differs and the clay is replaced by soil. I doubt very much that in AGM-1 also it has to be earth or soil but not clay. Forgetting the colour factor for a moment we may make a tentative correlation between the stratigraphy of both the trenches: layer 1 in both the trenches appear to be the same; layer 4 of AGM-1 may be correlated with layer 5 in AGM-2 since both contain brick-bats and layer 9 of AGM-1, loose sand may be related to layer 6 of AGM-2. Thus layers 2, 3 and 4 of AGM-2 stand aloof.

Ceramics

Alagankulam pottery consisted of a Black-and-Red ware, some with mat designs, of Iron Age affiliation, Rouletted Ware, a coarse red ware, a grey ware and some sherds of the distinctive pottery known as the Northern Black Polished Ware (NBP), usually assigned to the Mauryan times. Besides, sherds inscribed in Tamil Brahmi were also recovered, mostly from surface but two coming from actual digs. These inscriptions are in the nature of single line engravings, both before and after firing. So far they have been found on the Rouletted ware only. Of the six inscribed sherds two are from excavations and the rest from surface. The above are the cognizant ceramics of Period I.

In the succeeding period all the pottery of the earlier period continue. In addition amphorae pieces occur. A distinctive pottery having "a lustrous red surface manufactured from well-levigated clay, with generally a thin cross-section, was mistaken by us at first to be the "Arretine" Ware, known to occur in Arikamedu......... Dr. T.N. Potter of the Department of Prehistoric and Romano-British antiquities of the British Museum .... identified the pottery as "Late African slipped ware" its probable place of origin being Tunisia" (Nagaswamy 1991: 248). However, Begley swears that the "potterry marked 'Arretine ware' which I was shown in 1986, seemed to be yet another variant of the so-called rouletted ware fired red in core and surfaces in both form and decoration" (Begley 1991:193 as quoted in Begley 1994:320). Further on the authority of Prof. Kathleen W. Slanes a member of Pondicherry team who examined the pottery denies the lustrous red ware of Alagankulam as having anything to do with the Late African red ware. However, Begley, though reluctantly, does recognize the individuality of the ware when she says "One sherd with several rows of dot-like indentations from a pit in Trench VI of the Northern Sector (Arikamedu) in body and surfaces is very similar to the fine red ware from Alagankulam and may even be an import from there. Since the red variant of fine rouletted ware called "late African red slipped ware" is diagnostic of Alagankulam, it should be identified as Alagankulam red ware and not as import unless precise parallels in form and fabric can be demonstrated." (Begley 1994:320).

The Black-and-Red ware was numerically more in the lower levels i.e in Period I, However, in Period II and in the upper levels this ware diminishes in count. The coarse red ware becomes the predominant pottery. So is the case with the Rouletted ware and the amphorae. Stamped pottery was negligible; only four pieces being found.

Sherds bearing Tamil-Brahmi inscriptions either on Rouletted ware or grey ware are palaeographically assigned to 1st century B.C.– 1st century A.D. (100 B.C. 100 A.D.). (Majeed, 1992: 12-13)

Now Nagaswamy's observations when correlated with the description of layers provided in the brochure, the emerging picture shows that :

(a) The Black-and-Red ware occurs from the very beginning of habitation here i.e. layer 8. (I consider layer 9 loose sand–perhaps littoral sand-as Natural) together with coarse red and grey wares.

(b) The Rouletted ware begins to appear from a depth of 5.10 m from surface i.e. layer 6 on wards and continues till the end.

(c) Amphorae pieces are found from about 4.80 m from surface i.e. again from layer 6. Thus it would imply that both Rouletted ware and amphorae arrived almost at the same time or perhaps with a few years of negligible gap between them.

(d) As regards the NBP, they occur from a depth of 2.90 m upto a depth of 6m. It appears that the ten sherds found here are distributed between layers 2 and 7. This suggests its earlier appearance than the Rouletted ware as also from the very beginning of the habitation. It is a pity and is much regrettable that such an important evidence for fixing relative chronology has not been properly recorded. In fact the depth at which each sherd was found should have been properly noted down.

It has not been recorded either by Nagaswamy or by joint authors of the brochure at what level the so-called Late African red ware (Alagankulam ware) begins to appear. For, whether one accepts or rejects the identity of the ceramic with late African red ware, the fact remains that this pottery is a cognizant element ushering in a new phase in the cultural *milieu* of the site. This lack of observation, if not remedied from available records, or in subsequent excavations, the great lacuna in the Archaeological history of Alagankulam will haunt us forever.

As regards amphorae there is no doubt that they are 'shipping amphorae from Imperial Roman times'. (Begley 1994: 315). But regarding Rouletted ware Begley affirms that the ware is not an imported ceramic but of indigenous manufacture; the supply being from a common source, most probably, Arikamedu. On the chronology of the ware at Arikamedu she says that the earliest date could only be 100 B.C. while the terminal date A.D. 100. She also suggests that if Alagankulam Rouletted ware was earlier, then it should have been supplied from another source other than Arikamedu and which needs identification.

Begley is very much sure that, "None of the five wares, considered to be imports have so far precise parallels in the Roman world. To consider them as imports is unfortunate." Further, she adds, "Ever since Sir Mortimer Wheeler's excavation at Arikamedu in 1945, there has been a tendency to trace the provenance of fine pottery, specially fine red wares, found in early historical sites in south India to Roman world. None of the sherds of fine-grained clays known thus far appear to be from vessels imported from the Mediterranean region though they bear resemblance to fine *Roman wares in form and decorations or both"* (emphasis mine– Begley 1994).

The catch is in the emphasis. This raises some possibilities.

(i) The Indian Rouletted ware was patterned after an imported specimen;

(ii) The technique of manufacture was learnt from Roman craftsmen who were familiar with the manufacture of such wares; and

(iii) Some Roman craftsmen who had settled in India, specifically at Arikamedu taught this technique to the local potter before they left for their homeland.

Among these which is true cannot be asserted with any degree of truth. However, Wheeler is of the opinion that there was a Roman colony at Arikamedu.

Chronology

Coins

On the whole 10 coins were recovered from the digs and two from surface.

Three Roman copper coins were found here of which one is well preserved and the other two are worn out. The well preserved coin was picked up from Trench AGM-1 from depth ranging from 0.65-0.95 m below surface (There is a contradiction here. In the same paragraph Nagaswamy says that coin No. 1 occurs at a depth of 95 cm.). After cleaning this coin has been identified as that of the Roman Emperor Valentine II (A.D. 378-383) issued from the mint at Antioch. Of the other two copper coins, the less preserved one belongs to Theodosius II (A.D. 383-393) and the other to Arcadius I (395-408). Coin of Arcadius I was from AGM-3/A1. One square copper coin from AGM-1 was found at a depth of 2.75 m i.e. in layer 2 and silver coin from a depth of 3.30 m i.e. layer 3. The copper coin is highly corroded and the silver coin shows some punch-marks.

The Roman coins date in the 4th century A.D. The date of the punch-marked coin is uncertain.

Rediocarbon dates

Four radiocarbon dates (IAR, 1987-88: 149) are available for this site. All are charcoal samples coming from one and the same trench – AGM-2 and from different levels. Of these four, three pertain to Period II and one to Period III *(sic)*. These are uncorrected dates. Time span as per the ^{14}C dates is 160 years; the earliest date for this period is from layer 3 (depth–1.9) is 360 BC. (PRL 1298. 2310±130 BP) and latest 200 BC from layer 2 (PRL 1296. 2150±110 BP depth 1.40). The charcoal from the depth 1.55 m (the blackish layer-charcoal layer indicating conflagration) gives a reading 260 B.C. (PRL 1297. 2210+110 BP). The last sample from a depth of 2.8 m allegedly from Period III dates to 380 B.C. (PRL 1299-2330±110 BP).

The most interesting aspect is that the 'brochure' divides the cultural deposits into two and *not three* periods. It explicitly says, "The excavation at this site has revealed two broad cultural deposit i.e. period I and II". (Majeed, *et. al.:* 17-19) Here is a contradiction–which is correct – the details in his brochure or the data sent to PRL. This needs clarification. Incidentally this sample gives the earliest date to the site.

If we discard the date Period III (380 B.C.). as an aberration/we have a time range of 160 years for Period II spreading between 360 and 200 B.C. Even if we take into account the date of the dispute sample (380 B.C.) a couple of decades is not going to make much of a difference.

This date again is not reliable as will be seen from the ceramic and numismatic evidence.

Evidence from Pottery

According to Nagaswamy the site dates from 250 B.C. to A.D. 500, a life span of at least 750 years. However, the article avers the site was under occupation from 3rd century B.C. to 600 A.D. (Nagaswamy:). In the 'brochure' it is written, the site seems to have been in continuous occupation from at least 400 B.C. to 500 A.D.; a life span of 900 years. (Majeed, *et. al.:* 17)

Ceramics of Period I (400 B.C.-100 B.C) comprised Black-and-Red ware (some with mat designs), NBP, Rouletted ware, grey ware and a coarse red ware. Sherds with Tamil Brahmi inscription were also found. In Period II all the wares of the previous period continue. However, NBP is absent. Besides amphorae pieces and a typical pottery dubbed as 'Alagankulam ware' (Late African red ware of Nagaswamy) appears (100 B.C.-500 A.D.). The above is based on the details provided in the 'brochure'. The date assigned is 100 B.C.-A.D. 500.

Nagaswamy in his article declares that the Rouletted Ware "occurs from the beginning of the occupation and is found upto a depth of 5.10 m". Here, Nagaswamy intends to convey "by the words from the beginning" that the pottery was found from the top i.e. from the time of desertion of the site. Generally, archaeologists use the term 'beginning' to represent the earliest commencement of occupation represented by the first occupation of the site just above Natural. Hence it would imply from the top levels upto a depth of 5.10 m below surface (AGM-1) this pottery was encountered. This when compared with description and depth of layers given in the 'brochure' and Nagaswamy's statement would represent layers 1 to 6, just from above the mortar floor occurring in AGM-1 as also in other trenches, or just from below i.e. from layer 7.

The amphora also occurs from almost the top and is found upto a depth of 4.80 m in Alagankulam-I. This again would mean from layer 6 to layer 1. Hence amphorae and the Rouletted ware must have coexisted or came to Alagankulam at the same time.

The amphorae seem to be "shipping amphorae from Imperial Roman times" (Begley 1994). It would be worth-while to study them for fixing the chronological horizon. On the other hand the Rouletted ware in India is of the Roman times, some of which might have been imported and major portion imitated and locally manufactured. Rouletted ware dates from 1st century B.C. to 1st century A.D. To adduce an early date for this ware in India would be hazardous. Regarding the Rouletted black ware from Arikamedu, Krishna Deva observes. "The first appearance of the Rouletted pattern at Arikamedu is as early as the end of the first century B.C. or beginning of the first century A.D. while its terminal date is determined by the latest occupation in Southern Sector of the town, attributable to A.D. 200." (Wheeler, 1946:46)

Coming to NBP sherds. These sherds, numbering more than ten were found from a depth ranging from 2.9 m upto 5.6 m below surface (AGM-1) i.e. from layer 2 to 7. The ware as we know is attributable to the early historical times particularly the Mauryan times. This ware had been found earlier at Korkai (so far the southern most findspot) and now it is reported from Alagankulam also. At Korkai, on a single ^{14}C date is assigned to 805±95. (IAR 1969-70:68; Ramachandran 1975:74-75)

Now about the other wares. In the earlier layers before the advent of the Rouletted and the amphora, the basic pottery is the Black-and-Red ware of Iron Age affiliation which spreads from the lowermost strataum till the abandonment of the site. This happens to be cognizant pottery not only at Alagankulam but all over the entire Tamilnadu. Besides a coarse red as also grey ware and their variants form the local ceramic industry running throughout the life time of the site.

In fine the outcome of this exercise filters down to:

(a) Alagankulam is a single culture site with perhaps a couple of phases, the cognizant elements being Rouletted ware and amphore on the one hand and the Alagankulam ware on the other.

(b) The antiquity of the site is exaggerated. The Rouletted ware (1st cent. B.C.-1st cent A.D.) and the shipping amphorae both are contemporary, since both appears in the same level. This is supported by the inscribed Rouletted ware sherds bearing Tamil Brahmi script datable to 1st cent. B.C. - 1st cent A.D

(c) The earliest occurrence of NBP in layer 7 of AGM- It may perhaps be dated to late 2nd cent B.C. or early 1st cen. B.C.

(d) Ceramic and numismatic evidences do not lend any support to ^{14}C dates.

It would be worth while to ascertain the antiquity of the mortar floor which seems to be a universal occurrence and work back the antiquity of the site.

REFERENCES

Begley, V. 1991. Ceramic Evidence for pre-Periplus Trade on Indian Coasts in Begley, V. and De Puma, R.D. (eds.) *Rome and India*, 157-196 University of Wisconsin press: Madison.

____________1994. Are there imported fine wares at Alagankulan, South India in Kenoyer, Jonainan Mark. 315-322.

Indian Archaeology 1969-70 –A Review. Archaeological Survey of India, New Delhi.

Indian Archaeology 1987-88 –A Review. Archaeological Survey of India, New Delhi.

Majeed, A., Thulasiraman, D., and Vasanthi. S., 1992. *Alagankulam – A Preliminary Report,* State Department of Archaeology, Madras.

Nagaswamy, R. 1991. Alagankulam: An Indo-Roman Trading Port in Margabandhu, C. Ramachandran K. S. *et al.* (eds.). *Indian Archaeological Heritage,* Agam Kala Prakashan: Delhi.

Ramachandran, K.S. 1975. *Radiocarbon dates of Archaeological sites in India,* Govt. of Andhra Pradesh: Hyderabad.

Tamil Nadu District Gazetteers, Ramanathapuram, 1972 Govt. of Tamil Nadu, 31-32

Wheeler, R.E.M. Ghosh A. and Deva K. 1946. Arikamedu an Indo-Roman Trading Station on the East coast of India. *Ancient India* 2: 17-125.

The Raj Samudra Dam: A Milestone in Water-Management

RAMESH CHANDRA SHARMA*

The arid zone of Rajasthan warranted the conservation of water for irrigation and other purposes and this led to the construction of dams and reservoirs as part of efficient water-management during the medieval period. The rulers of Mewar took great interest in this work, as testified by surviving dams and lakes. But the available data — archaeological and otherwise– on these pre-modern dams appear to be very limited and insufficient (Khan and Kumar 1986:26). Although we have many epigraphic (Sharma 1983) and literary accounts of the dams and lakes of Mewar, enough information to enable a detailed study of the technique of dam-construction is lacking. Here, we shall attempt a study of the Raj Samudra Dam, built by the Maharana Raj Singh (A.D. 1629-1680), some sixty-four kilometres north of Udaipur (Shyamal Das 1986:112) near Rajnagar, to know about the technique of dam-construction and efficient water-management, on the basis of two contemporary works, namely, the *Rajprasastih* (Menaria 1973) and the *Rajvilas* (Bhagwandeen 1912)

The *Rajprasastih* is a poetical work in Sanskrit, composed in twenty-four *sargas* having 1106 *slokas.* (Menaria,: Bhumika) with a few addenda in Rajasthani by Ranchhod Bhatt (Menaria 1973) who started writing it on the bidding of the Maharana, when the work on the dam began.[1] Later it was inscribed on twenty-five marble slabs, and placed in the alcoves of the Nauchauki Ghat of the dam (Menaria 1973: Bhumika) by Raj Singh's son and successor, Jai Singh, some six years after the completion of the work (Menaria 1973: 5. 56). It is said to be the largest of the works inscribed on stone slabs (Ojha 1927: 311). The epigraph recounts in detail the construction of the dam, its consecration, the early history of Mewar, as well as the Mewar-Mughal conflict during Raj Singh and his son Jai Singh's, reign till the conclusion of peace (Menaria 1973: 9.23; Sharma 1971: 311) The *Rajvilas* is a historical poem by Man, in Brajbhasha after the style of the Rajput bards, in eighteen *vilasas* (cantos), begun in *Samvat* 1734 (A.D. 1677) and abruptly ended in Samvat 1737 (A.D. 1680) with the death of Raj Singh (Vyas 1983:136,8 and 68). It deals with the reign of Raj Singh and devotes a canto to the building and consecration of the Raj Samudra Dam. These two accounts, though primarily descriptive, give some technical details, of the careful planning and efficient execution of the project albeit poetical hyperbole, the admixture of the traditional lore with the historical, and certain factual inaccuracies .

Raj Sing, the last of the great Maharanas of Mewar, gave eighteen years of peace and prosperity to Mewar between 1662 and 1679, through his adroit diplomacy and generalship. The apex of his achievements was the construction of the Raj Samundra Dam.

In the year 1660-61, occurred severe drought and terrible famine. In order to relieve the people of their misery

*Department of History, St. John's College, Agra.

the Maharana decided to build a dam across the river Gomati at a gorge between two hillocks (Menaria 1973:8. 113-133, 136-138; Shyamaldas 1986: 12. 446) The site, it is said, the Maharana had already seen twice, once while going to Bundi for his marriage as a prince, and again while on a visit to Roopnarayan in 1661 after his accession to the throne. His advisers, priest and chief nobles were impressed with king's decision and pointed out that success would depend on the ruler's faith in the work, he coming into any conflict with the ruler of Delhi and his spending money freely. The king started the work on January 12, 1662 (Magh Krishna 7, Wednesday, *Samvat* 1718), and a large number of workers and beasts of burden and carriages were employed in this endeavour. Hectic activity began in digging, clearing the site, letting out water from it, cutting stones in an extensive area of some fifteen *kos* (48.27 km) in circumference enclosing boundaries of sixteen villages.[2] For the efficient execution of the work the Maharana himself supervised with capable noblemen. This work having been completed, the construction ceremony was held on May 8, 1665 (Baisakh Sukla 13, Monday, 1721 V.S.) Ranchhodrai, the elder son of the priest Garibdas, laid the first stone with five jewels, thus starting the masonry work with strong stone blocks and lime mortar (Menaria 1973: 9. 34-39, 96-98) The boat-floating ceremony was performed on June 30, 1671 (Asadh Krishna 4, 1727 V.S.). On the completion of the dam, water from three rivers-the Gomati, the Tala and the Kelva, began collecting in the lake.

The dam was completed in 1676 and the consecration of the lake (8.3668 sq km in area) took place on January 25, 1676 (Magh Sukla 10, 1732 V.S.) and completed by February 1, 1676 (Magh Sukla 15, 1732 V.S.). Rich and munificient *danas* were given to the brahmans and others by the Maharana and his queen, his chiefs and the priest. Invited guests were presented with gifts and those who were unable to attend the ceremony gifts were sent . The cost of whole project was Rs 42, 64, 625 and annas 4 for first stage, and Rs 1,05,07,608 or the second stage[3] and the total worked Rs 1,51,72,233 and annas 4. The overall expenses, however, must have been much more, as is clear from Ranchhod's statement. The lake was named Rajsagar as its first name and Rajsamudra its second name. The palace, built at the time, was named as the Rajmandir and the city as Rajnagar. (Menaria 1973: 18.16,194)

Now let us turn to technical data available on this big project, which should give some idea of the process of construction of such big dams and management of water resources available efficiently. For this we are indebted to the Maharana and his successor for having directed the poet Ranchhod Bhat to compose the *prasasti* of the inscription and getting it engraved on marble slabs which had been fixed into the Nauchauki, the main bund of the dam. It appears that the poet, though a layman had full knowledge of the plans and outlay of the dam including all technical details.

Raj Samudra Dam is a fine example of an exquisite combination of stability and utility. The dam, divided into six *setus* (bunds) –the *mukhya-setu,*[4] the *nimba–setu,* the *bhadra-setua,* the *kankroli-setu,* the *setu* near the village Asotiya, and the one near the village Bahsol– measures 6413 yards (5413. 9144 m),[5] and forms an irregular segment of a circle. It encircles the northwest and the northeast points. It contains a sheet of water about twelve miles (17.76923 km) in circumference. The *setus* have twelve of *Koshthas* (chambers) in all. The three on the *mukhya-setu* were *burij-koshtham*[6] (vaulted chambers); the one of the *nimba-setu* was square; the three on the *Kankroli-setu* were of varying breadth but of the same *nirgama* (outlet); of the two on the *setu* close to the village Asotiya one was octagonal and the other name *ardhachandra* (the crescent); of the three on the *setu* near the village Bansol, two were square and the third octagonal, named Kamalburij (ornamented with the lotus motif) (Menaria 1973). The *setus* were adorned with twenty–one *mandapas* (pillared pavilions) of different types. Of the forty-eight big *mandapas,* some of fine awning and some of wood, only two built of stone were extant till the composition of the *prasasti.* Of these the most notable were the one with nine *chaukis,* two excellent royal pavilions and the one with six *chaukis* on the *mukhya-setu,* and the one of white-stone, ornamented with eight figurines *(ashtaputrika).* There were four platforms and two *rahants,* one of which supplied water to the Rajmandir palace-fort. The lower portion of the dam had three *mekhalas* (girdles rotating around the dam), three *tilakas* (lower mouldings), and four *stharas* (traditional mouldings of the *pitha* of the Hindu temple) with nine *sopanas* (steps) each, thus making the total thirty-six. There were three *otas* (spill ways) in the dam with their lengths varying between 250 and 300 yards (228.6 and 274.32 m), breadth 10 yards (9.144m) and height from 1 1/2 to 2 1/2 yards (1.3716 to

2.288 m), with three *mandapas* over them, from which water was taken to the villages for irrigation. The dam, thus, was a diversion dam, which was also used as a pleasure resort by the Maharana and his noblemen. The lake, formed by damming the waters from three rivers, submerged six villages, periphery of seven other villages and thirty reservoirs, wells etc. of three villages (Menaria-1973: 12.,5,; 9, 124)

Selection of a suitable site is of utmost significance for dam-construction. The site chosen for the Raj-Samudra testifies the truth of this statement. The way the decision of the Maharana to dam the river in the gorge has been recorded might not show it clearly. But when we consider the failure of two earlier efforts — those of the Maharana Udai Singh and of the Maharana Amar Singh to construct a dam on the site, we can very well appreciate the sagacity, foresight and determination of Raj Singh as well the technical skill of his engineers and architects. In fact, a dam must be designed to suit the special condition of the site and foundations (Bourgin 1953:9) That the dam could withstand the floods in the Tala and the Gomati, while the work on it was still going on and that the lake has lasted so long— and still in use— without much damage, show that the engineers and architects of Raj Singh had established the watershed before constructing the dam, which is said to be the foremost consideration in water-storage construction in an arid zone (Zimmerman 1966:65). The initial diggings to reach the firm ground beneath the sub-soil water level for the dam in order to determine the stratum strong enough to ensure the stability of the structure over it, and the elaborate arrangements for draining the sub-soil water-the *rahants* and *dhenkulis,* besides all other means pointed out by the skilled architects and others, before the foundations for the dam were laid and the flooring of the reservoir started, (Menaria 1973; Bhagwandeen 1912), again, prove the skill of Raj Singh's engineers and architects in the efficient ground and water management. This is further proved by the fact that water thus available was taken to villages through canals and used for irrigating the fields.[7]

The dam was constructed in two stages. At first the *Saribandh* (earthen dam) was built and then the strong *Senbharonbandh* (masonry dam), the space between the two being filled with earth obtained from diggings in the area to be inundated.[8] The *Saribandh* was constructed by earth filling - actually a mixture of earth, pounded reeds and *kankar.* The *Senbharonbandh* was constructed with *sangikarya* (stone-work), for which huge blocks of the dressed white-stone were used both for the dam and the flooring of the lake (Menaria 1973; Bhagwanden 1912). The lime mortar with a mixture of glass powder was used for strengthening and fastening the joints. The most beautiful example of stone-work on the dam is the Nauchauki built of white marble, which provides a very enchanting sight of the lake. The use of hewn stones as a veneer to the steep sloping sides of earth dams had evolved in India, reaching its climax in the Veernam Dam, Tamil Nadu, built between A. D. 1011 and 1037. (Encyclopaedia of Britannica 1987).

So far as the personnel employed for the planning and execution of the project are concerned, the information available is insufficient; not even the name of the architect-in-chief has been mentioned. The entire credit has been given to Raj Singh. The Rajasthani addenda to the *Prasastih* do give names of the administrative staff as well as the architects.[9] Names of a few administrative supervisory staff appointed by the Maharana and designated as Thakurs or Shahs holding charge of the different divisions of the work appear in connection with the amount spent and also at the end about their presence along with the names of architects at the time of laying the foundation. *Daroghas* were appointed for watch and ward. The personnel who actually carried out the work of construction may be divided into three categories, namely, skilled workers, semi-skilled workers and the unskilled labour. The first category included architects and masons, who were called the *gajdharas* (wielders of the *gaj,* i.e. the measuring yard), *sutradharas* (wielders of the string), and *silpakaras* and *chejagaras.* Of these the first two were superior and more skilled, i.e. architects having precedence over the second, while the third signified a stone mason and the fourth a stone/brick layer.[10] Some of the last two could have formed part of the semi-skilled workforce along with the *beldars* (diggers of earth). The term *majur* signifies the large unskilled workforce. The number of all categories of the personnel must have been quite large, even if we may not accept the numbers given in the texts. The large number and variety of carts, carriages and beasts of burden, which were employed, are also mentioned. So far as mechanical devices are concerned, none is mentioned except the *rehant* and the *dhenkuli,* used for draining the water, as pointed out earlier.

It should not, therefore, be misconstrued, if we regard the Raj Samudra Dam as a remarkable feat of successful and efficient water-management. The available information, though inadequate and scanty, is sufficient to give us an idea of the achievements of the Rajasthani architects and workers in the seventeenth century. In view of its long life–it being still in use— the Raj–Samudra Dam may be regarded as a milestone in the technique of dam-construction in India.

NOTES

1. *Rajprasastih.* 1.10.15. Although at one place the poet says that he composed the work for the instruction of his brothers-Lakshman and Bharat (24.16.258), yet the way he explains the benefits that his readers would get on reading it (24.17-24.259-260) makes it clear that the work was composed for all and on the orders of the Maharana.

2. Ibid. 9.4-7.90-91, the names of villages are Dhoyanda, Sanvad, Sivali, Bhigvada, Morchana Pasund, Khedi, Chhaparkhedi, Tasol, Mandavar, Bhana, Luhana, Bansol, Ghushali, Kankroli and Madha. For the circumference cf. *Rajvilas,* 8.142.140

3. Shyamldas has given the figures as Rs. 1,05,47584 and 39,64,623 and annas 12 as the expenses on the II and I stages. He thinks the first figure to be total expenses, but in footnote no. 1 he adds up the two and surmises that even this total should not be surprising. *Vir Vinod,* 1.2:451. The *Rajvilas* mentions only the cost of pumping out the water as more than one lakh *dinars* –8.146.141, and that on the palace as Rs. 9,00,000– 8.152.143. Ojha gives the expenses as Rs. 1,05,07,584. *Rajputana ka Itihas* 1: 310. Braj Mohan Javalia in his paper on "Raj Samudra Jheel ke Nirman-Vyaya se Sambaddh Ek Sanskrit Kavya", has published the text of a contemporary anonymous Sanskrit poem of 34 *slokas,* which gives the expenses on the construction of the lake as Rs. 44,25,838- *Majhamika,* 1979-80, Udaipur: 15-22.

4. The dimensions of the Mukhya-Setu as given by the poet are :

   Length at the foundation: 515 yards (471.916 m)

   Length at the top: 585 yards (534.924 m)

   Width at the foundation: 55 yards (50.292 m)

   Width at the top: 10 yards (9.144 m)

5. *Rajprasastih* 12. 11-14.125 The length thus calculated would be 3 miles, 5 furlongs and 33 yards (5.4139144 km). *Rajvilas* says that the *pat* (extent) of water to be controlled was very wide being eighteen *doris* in measurement.– 8.18.140.

6. These comprise three large sections of the main dam projecting into the water accommodating in each an underground vaulted chamber and a pillared *mandapa* over it–*Rajprasastih* 11.7-10.113-114.

7. The depth of the foundation is given as 22 yds. (20.129978 m) and above the surface to the top 35 yds (32.024965 m), the total being 57 yds (52.15493 m)– *Rajprasastih* 9.30.96.

8. These two terms used for the dam appear to be local terms– *Rajprasastih* 9.45.99; 10.18.105.

9. The names of the Administrative staff present at the time of the foundation ceremony given are Ranavat Mahasinghji, Ramsinghji, Chundavat Dalpatji, Mohansinghji, Ravat Lunkaranji, Chundavat Mokamsinghji, Manjavat Narsingdasji, Garibdasji, Rathodsinghji: Ramchandji; Hamiji, Mokamsingh Chitgara, Ramchand Chechani Shah Kalu Pancholi Jagmalot; Sah Mukanddas Pancholi; Harram Seghvi; Lakhu Pancholi– *Rajprasastih, Rajasthani* addenda : 264.

   The names of the architects mentioned are *Gajdharas:* Mukund, Urjan, his son Kalyanji, and his son Jagnath, Urjan, brother of Jagnath and his sons Lala, Lakha, Jasi, Harji, Megho, Sukhdev, Keso, Sundar, Lala, Mohanji, Bagh; *Sutradharas:* Keso, Sundarram, Lado, son of Mohanji Sukhji. Their caste has been given as Sompura, *gotra* Bharadwaj and residence Udaipur *Raj-prasasti Rajasthani addenda.* 28, 56, 78, 89, 264; *Maharana Raj Singh and His Times,* p.46

10. The terms *Gajdhara* and *Sutradhara* deserve our attention. The *Gajdhara* appears to be a regional term while the *Sutradharas* appears in the hierarchy of the builders in ancient Indian architecture, which is as follows:

    Acharya, who planned and designed the building theoretically and also supervised its construction without himself working on it.

Sthapati who carried out the plan and design of the *Acharya* into actual form and participated in its day-to-day working, taking measurements and handling such other eight instruments as prescribed by the *sastras.*

Sutradhara, who actually built with the help of brick, stone and mortar in proportionate measurements under the overall guidence of the *Acharya* and the *Sthapati.*

Takshaka, though technically a carpenter as he was in Vedic age, when wooden architecture was in vogue, in the later period he became the mason, stone artisan, and carver, under the overall guidance of the *Sutradhara.*

In the course of its developments the place of the *Acharya* and the *Sthapati* was taken by the *Sutradhara,* who took over the supervisory function of an architect, under whom worked a number of skilled masons and unskilled workers enagaged in construction work. In the present context, however, arises the question of his relationship with the *Gajdhara.* It appears that the *Gajdhara* was superior in rank to the *Sutradhara.* We may, thus, regard the *Gajdhara* as the Architect and the *Sutradhara* as the Assistant Architect. This becomes clear from the way their names have been mentioned in the *Rajasthani addenda* of the *Rajprasastih.*

The number 1000 given for the *Gajdharas,* employed for the dam, by the poet Man (*Rajvilas,* 8.141.139) is obviously an example of the poetic hyperbole.

11. The *Rajvilas* gives the number of workers employed as (a) 1000 *gajadharas* with 100 *silpakaras* under each, the total thus coming to 1,00,000; (b) 2,00,000 beldars, and (c) 4,00,000 *majurs*– 8.141-142. 139-140.

12. Rajeev Sharma, in his paper "Raj-Samand Dam-An Achievement of 17th century Civil Engineering" presented at the 53rd session of the Indian History Congress, Warangal, February 1993, has shown that "the anonymous architects and engineers who accomplished this job, had full knowledge of the basic mathematical and hydrodynamical principles involved" by examining the "structure measurement *vis-a-vis* mathematical and hydrodynamical parameters essential for the stability of a dam" Volume of Papers on Indian History by Members of the Centre of Advanced Study in History, Aligarh Muslim University (mimeographed), pp.209-218.

REFERENCES

Bhagwandeen (ed) 1912. *Rajvilas,:* Kashi,.

Bourgin, A. 1953. *The Design of Dams,* F. F. Fergusson, (Transl.) London: 9.

Khan I. A. and Kumar. R. 1986. The Mansagar Dam of Amber in A. Roy and S.K. Bagchi (eds), *Technology in Ancient & Medieval India,* Delhi : 26.

M. Menaria (ed), 1973. *Rajprasastih Mahakavyam,:* Udaipur,

Ojha, G. H. 1927. *Rajputana ka Itihas.* i, Ajmer,

Shyamaldas, 1986. *Vir Vinod,* Delhi Reprint, : 112.

Vyas, R. P. 1983. *Maharana Raj Singh,* Jaipur: 136.

Sharma, G.N., 1983. *Rajputana ki Itihas Ke Srota.,* Jaipur: 41-235.

Medieval Water Supply System in Burhanpur Town, Madhya Pradesh: A Review

D.P. KAMBO, J.D. CRUZ AND JAVED ASHRAF*

Governor of the *Subah* of Khandesh during the reign of Jahangir, with Burhanpur as his capital, Abdurrahim Khan-i-Khanan got an underground canal built in the vicinity of the said city in A.D. 1615 to augment potable water supply of the city. Entire expenses on this construction was borne by him out of his personal income. The canal was constructed under the supervision of *Tabaqat-al-Ardh* or the Department of Earth (sciences) of the times that looked after such constructions. Once constructed, the structure as such could be maintained by the Department of *Auqaf* or personal charity, the appropriate authority for such charitable purposes.

Being a utilitarian structure for the use of everybody without distinction, let or hindrance, the canal was dedicated to the people in general, as mentioned in the inscription, and bequeathed by him for posterity. This point is underlined by the fact that since the inception all the channels of this canal entering the city were taken to places of public use of comfort like mosques, rest houses of *sarais, hammams* etc.

No other urban centre in India is known to have anything resembling this canal at Burhanpur.

Throughout its existence, according to *Tarikh-i-Auliya-i-Burhanpur,* the canal is known to have suffered twice. first at the end of the nineteenth century, when it was repaired by the British who, instead of cleaning the system, closed some of the channels and blocked some of the pipes, replacing the passage with metalic pipes for the length thus blocked. These replacements can be seen even now. The second instance occurred some years back due to which the present group went to inspect the system. In fact it was this closure during the last century that must have made some sections disfunctional and the people must have responded to this new reality by further augumenting the filth that has accumulated in the system due to lack of periodic cleaning over a long period of time.

It seems the canal also suffered seriously due to heavy deforestation in its catchment area which today is devoid of all trees or shrubs and presents a picture of bare rocks covered with just some grasses which also disapear with the withdrawl of the monsoon rains. Obviously this removal of the forest cover must have affected the water content as well as the quality of the water intake as plants affect both these aspects of the subsoil water in the area.

Ownership and Custody of the Canal Today

Except for the technical custody of the District administration, and within the Muncipal limits of the city

*D. P. Kambo, Conservation Architect, Indian Heritage Society, J.D. Cruz, Former Chief Engineer (Water Supply), Delhi and Javed Ashraf, Department of Life Sciences, Jawaharlal Nehru University, Delhi.

Muncipal Committee/Corporation, today no body looks after it or has any responsibility for its upkeep. The District and Municipal administration neither have resources nor expertise for maintaining the system in working condition.

Present status of Canal Functioning

It should be noted that the blocked channels yet show substantial amount of moisture in their mud content, underlining the fact that water seepage is still taking place in its blocked portion, and also that the channels can yet be reopened if these are properly cleaned and repaired.

As the entire system is for public utilisation without any distinction, people traditionally use it all along the path, using the aeration towers or *kundis* in the manner of a well.

It goes without saying that the level of purity of water in the channels, though not yet surveyed properly and systematically, would vary from point to point, being better at the start and not so good in areas where large volume of extraneous material is added to it due to sheer neglect and abuse.

The data-base so far available suffers from extreme skewness. It seems all the data on chemical composition, microbial quality, visual observations for salt deposition inside the channels etc. is from one point only – from Sukha Bhandara– which by now has become the main attraction for the visitors and we were taken there only for internal observations as facilities were created only there.

Sub-Surface soil Structure in the Region of the Canal

Surface soil of the region is typical of the Deccan Trap. Burhanpur lies at the junction of the Deccan Trap with that of northern India of the Vindhyan system; it is broadly where the boundaries of the ancient Gondwana land meets the region formed due to the upliftment of the Himalaya. Highest point in the vicinity, Asirgadh, is 667.2 metres at the point where the river Tapti flows. In other words this is the surface gradient or slope in this part of the Satpura ranges on which the city is located.

Soil cover is about 30-40 m in thickness under which the hard basalt rocks are to be found. Such a situation prevails for about 200 sq.km around the city. Under this rock– cover, exposed on the mountains and on the banks of the river Tapti, lies the lava sheet that is superbly impervious to water. Eventhough Tapti otherwise is quite deep at this point where Burhanpur is located, Tapti, during the medieval times, appears to have been fordable so that stationing of a permanant garrison was a necessity of the times to look after the boundaries with Deccan and cross the river without building a bridge.

Available rainfall in the region is about 808.8mm. Ground water formation in the region is probably due to percolation of overground water into the soil and its flow into the river due the natural gradient of the region. This process is facilitated by the impervious nature of the underground rocks over a large part of the area which is almost breakage and fault free.

Hydrological Features of the water Supply to the Canal

This unique system in India, and even otherwise rare in the whole world, is based on the ancient water supply system which in Arabic is called *qunnat,* and is characterised by the presence of a large number of aeration towers that, like poles, blemish the entire system as if holding a canopy.

The catchment area in our case, extending from Asirgarh, provides for the recharge of ground water system. A number of streams and nalas originating in the Satpura range carry the surface run-off to the Tapti river through the catchment area of the underground canal system during the monsoon season and through percolation also contribute to the recharging of the canal itself.

The water recharging system devised for the canal is based on the principle of intercepting the run-off in the subsoil groundwater level through underground channels, and collect it in structures, partly underground and partly overground, called *bhandaras* through a system of underground channels and gallaries. The ground water thus collected is stored in sump-wells called *karanj*, from where it is further distributed through quaternary channels throughout the major consumer points in the residential area of the city of the medieval times.

Geological structure shows that the subsoil water in

the region is available in the calcareous bed lying in the inter-trappeans consisting of rock of volcanic origin. Earlier also these beds were used for underground storage of water. At the base of the Satpura range these calcarious beds are almost on the surface or very near from it. Sukha Bhandara is located in the areas where such structures are very near the surface; Mool Bhandara and Chinta Haran are located right on these beds. Large area of such rock round the canal acts as "collector wells" where, due to large area of exposure and contact, the aquifer collects water through wall seepage. Impervious basalt rock form the base that stops further downward movement of water. This collected water is simply carried to the users through channels; first to the *Karanjas* or water tanks and then further into the city.

Components of this unique water supply system

The unique water supply system at Burhanpur essentialy consists of the following:

1. Collecting ponds/ reservoirs,
2. Aqueducts carrying water from these collecting ponds,
3. Service reservoirs,
4. Pipelines connecting the service reservoirs to the city of Burhanpur , and
5. Distribution system within the city.

One of the wings of this entire system at Burhanpur was abandoned during the late last century while two wings are yet in operation though with modifications and repairs done during the recent past.

Collecting Reservoirs

The collecting ponds or reservoirs receive water from low level springs situated in the Satpura range hills in the north-west of the town.

One of the components of this system is known as Sukha Bhandara; it is also known as Satpura Bhandara. This is a huge hole, e[illegible]d very deep in the soil till it reach an undergroun[illegible]. From this reservoir Trikuti aquaduct, which is about 8000 feet long, starts. This aqueduct was mostly constructed by tunneling. However, at some places it is made up of mosonary channel below the ground and is arched over with stone massonary set in lime mortar. A number of brick masonry air shafts provide air to the tunnel. These are raised 2 to 3 feet above the ground level. These air shafts also act as silt traps as the their level is below the level of the conduit.

This aqueduct discharges into the Trikuti Bhandara through an open mouth. It was subsequently tapped for giving water supply to the railway station and for watering the Lalbagh gardens.

The other collecting reservoir system is the Mool Bhandara or the Phutta reservoir. This reservoir collects water from a stream running down the hills. The water is passed through an underground channel which is called the Phutta Aqueduct. As in the case of the Trikuti aqueduct, a large number of air shafts projecting a few feet above ground were constructed. This aqueduct discharges into the Khuni Bhandara and is about 9,600 feet long.

The Khuni Bhandara is a masonry tank with approximately 44 x 40 feet on plan and has a depth of 30 feet 9 inches, out of which 29 feet is below ground.

From Khuni Bhandara, a Phutta aqueduct after a distance of 2830 feet discharges into Jali Karanj which is a service reservoir feeding the city. This part of the conduit is partly through a masonry channel and partly by four sets of earthenware pipes.

These earthenware pipes were subsequently replaced during the last century/beginning of the present century by the British administration by cast iron pipes. Unlike the Trikuti service reservoir, the Jali Karanj reservoir is a circullar well and the water from Khuni Bhandara comes under its floor and overflows from the top or from openings in the wall of the tank. From Jali Karanj, the water was supplied by earthenware pipes to the city but was subsequently substituted by 9 inch CI pipes during the British period.

Some time during the year 1880, in order to increase the water supply to the town, a 3 inch pipeline was laid down from Trikuti Bhandara which was connected to the 3 inch CI pipe supply from Jali Karanj to the town. This 3 inch pipe was replaced by a bigger pipe around in the year A.D. 1890.

Another tank, known as Chinta Haran receives water from a seasonal nallah. Two conduits also originated from Chinta Haran; one which supplied water to Rao Ratan's palace. At the beginning of this century, a new connection (Chinta Haran) was constructed to add water to the city and was connected to the Phutta Aqueduct. This system has now fallen into disuse.

Distribution system in the town

The water supply from Jali Karanj is brought to the Shaniwara Gate of Burhanpur. A water tower or *Bamba* is constructed and the feeding main to the city takes off from the bottom of this tower. The head is caused by heading the water in this tower. Two outlets were subsequently provided at a higher level in this water tower to allow supply during the night to the places where it is required.

The water supply in the town was originally from the shallow masonry tanks at varying levels. The inhabitants drew water from these tanks as also from the draw–wells. The original pipes feeding these tanks were of earthenware and were gradually replaced by CI pipes.

The medieval water supply system was based on gravity-flow towards the city from *Bhandaras.* Its uniqueness consists in the fact that no source of energy is required to keep it functioning. The entire system is based on selection of suitable gradient which ranges from 1:245 to 1:324. Such variation in the gradient is sufficient to allow the flow of water under the force of gravity throughout the system and even now it is functioning.

However, these days the system is under considerable stress and its efficiency has been reduced due to: (1) The instalation of tube-wells for irrigation purposes right in the vicinity of the water carrier tunnels that augment their water through constant and continuous percolation and seepage of the subsoil water ; (2) Reduction of the amount of water in the carrier tunnels due to blocking of weep-holes because of calcium deposits in certain sectors lying close to the mountainous water sources; and (3) Collapse of some of the shafts due to aging, poor construction as well as due to absence of maintenance of the system as a whole. Some damage to the system has also been caused by heavy vehicular traffic in some sectors, especially near to the city itself. This traffic includes heavily loaded tractors as well as trucks loaded with harvest or such other material as lime etc.

Identification of Present Problems of the Canal and Their Possible Solutions

PHASE -1

In all probability the collapse has taken place in areas where heavy-duty transport, probably by trucks or heavily laden Jeep-trollies; one such area of damage to the channel was located next to a cement depot and the other on the road on the side of which banana fields are located. It needs detailed investigation to identify probable reasons for this collapse.

Because of constant seepage, large amount of salt has got deposited both in the inner surface of the brick–line in the starting sector of the canal as well as in the outside area adjoining the bricked channel, as later shown by our observations on the damaged sector on the spot. Weep-holes in the underground channels have almost clogged with salt at some places. Naturally this situation is met with more in regions nearer the sources that are predominantly not covered with agricultural fields. It is here that the seepage has been its highest and formation of salt on the surface is most. Once this salt is scraped off carefully, the weep-holes and general seepage on which the water supply in the whole system is based, is restored, water supply to the canal shall substantially improve and the canal restored almost to its original capacity, The damage due to removal of vegetal cover shall take quite some time till the plants grow.

Hence among the first steps to be taken for restoration of normal functioning of the channels is to carefully remove the accumulated salt through scraping with care taken for avoidence of strong vibrations; mechanical removal seems to be the best method for reducing the salt layer. Weep-holes in their original position can then easily be opened to augment the water supply.

On the basis of the above one can state that in Phase-1 the present structure of the canal as its exists today can be restored back to normalcy and the system made to function in the manner it was intended to function when the canal was dug *ab initio.*

PHASE-II

It seems that the aeration towers, or *kundis,* in the original planning are more than sufficient. As quite a few *kundis* today are in the residential areas, it is reasonable to assume that these are acting as sources of dumping filth in the system.

It is desirable that the *kundis* falling within the residential parts of the present day city be closed from within, and if necessary, their outer surface appearance obliterated.

Under changed cultural conditions we have to follow the spirit and not the word of conservation practices in archaeology. Moreover, in their present form these *kundis* are open to sky. It advisable that these structures, while being kept in their present place and height in accordance with the norms followed by the Archaeological Survey of India, be closed at the top and openings be made on the side so that these *kundis* do not act as chutes for addition of refuse to the canal system.

Major problems in the foreseeable future shall appear only in the process of restoring the channels that have been non-functional for quite some time now.

We have mentioned that the deposit in the closed channels shows mud even now, i.e. the deposit is yet soft and wet. There seems to be no problem in getting this mud removed.

Once the channel is repaired and cleaned, it can be reconnected with the traditional alignment and the openings in the tanks and again made functional in the same manner as it was designed originally.

With the completion of the second phase the canal, within a short period of probably two years, should be able to begin functioning normally in its original form.

PHASE–III

This phase primarily deals with steps to be taken to augment water holding capacity of the soil on which basically the structure is based, leading to in practice of the past and of the present increased seepage into the canal system for transport which ultimately results in the use by consumers in the city.

In order to visualise what steps have to be taken, one has to first assess that ecological changes that have taken place between the period of the canal construction and today. The canal was originally based on ecological principles that scholars like Khan-i-Khanan understood well. It has changed since then rather drastically. Information regarding the original ecological situation to some extent can be had from contemporary and immediately following records spanning right upto the time of the British rule.

Ecological Restoration of Catchment Area and Augmentation Resources

Gardens and orchards around Burhanpur produced all sorts of fruits, vegetables and medicinal herbs including bananas, pomegranates, all types of citruses, mangoes, guava, ananas, local fruits like *gurhal, burhal, tari, khajur,* etc. Jagri made out of *khajur* has been admired by a number of European travellers passing through Burhanpur to the northern parts of India. Other floral and agricultural details are available in literature.

Agricultural fields here produced in the olden days what they produce today; jowar, cotton, pulses, sugarcane, rice, wheat and vegetables of various types. Because of the good quality of cotton produced in the region, Burhanpur developed as a big centre of textile production, the produce of which used to be sent to near and far places all over the country besides being exported.

Some European sources mention large amount of *Tadi,* or Toddy, of very good quality. However, by now such palm trees, have disappeared due to the policy of the government.

As the city earlier was known for its various annual and perennial flowers, it would also be a viable proposition to revive this aspect if the logistics of marketing or other usages, like perfumary, cottage or small scale industry, turn out to be viable.

Burhanpur lost its significance under the British when it ceased to be a stagging point for the British army. In due course prosperity here was replaced by relative poverty and the skills declined due to migration of the skilled workers to other industrial centres.

Today the ranges are completely devoid of any tree cover. Gardens and orchards are no more. The land is virtually denuded of all trees and large tracts sometimes are left uncultivated so that they recover the loss due to earlier cash crop cultivation. Land virtually lies exhausted and the mountain ranges are completely denuded and destroyed due to removal of the vegetal cover.

Restoration and augmentation of the canal system. and solving problems related to it, are intimately linked with the complex and sustained improvent in the region.

Conclusions

The underground canal system at Burhanpur is unique in the whole country, and perhaps in the whole world. It is a national cultural heritage. Hence its preservation is morally, culturally and patriotically imperative.

Steps should be taken to get his underground canal, and the area around it over ground, declared as National Heritage of India zone under suitable law of the land and efforts be made to put it on the national tourist map of the country in the same manner as Roman aqueducts. The canal system falls in the same category . With the emergence of thematic tourism, there are good chances that substantial number of general as well as specialised tourists would start visiting Burhanpur. However, side by side with other steps, facilities for proper stay in the city are to be developed as these are nil today.

Not withstanding the above suggestion its utilitasion value as a civic infrastructure makes it obligatory to conserve, restore and supervise its upkeep. It is advisable that a control body be created to lookafter it after it has been restored so that it does not fall into disuse and disrepair as in the past when there was no body to look after it and competent enough to either do it or get it done. It may be a trust or other similar organisation involving representatives of the society as a whole, which is judicially recognized and created not only to mobilise public opinion but also to collect funds and proper expertise required for its upkeep and maintanence either partially or wholly.

Technically the structure can be taken over by the Archaeological Survey of India as a medieval monument– and they are in a legal position to do so– and maintain it along with a number of other monuments that they are looking after in Burhanpur. This possibility is to be looked into *vis-a-vis* the concept of public trust with an idea to improve management and wider involvement of local people in the affairs related to the upkeep and securing benefits from the canal.

The canal served public purpose in a given social context. In the changed context public purpose would mean relating the total water supply to the needs of the region including the city. If the canal can contribute sub–stantially to this effort at augmenting the water supply without any investment in energy costs, then besides being a national heritage it becomes an important contribution to our thinking about resource management in various fields.

Canal is complex system that involves not only its structures but also its catchment area. Without catchment area structural restoration will not serve any purpose. Hence, with canal as a focal point, the entire complex is to be first visualised and then put in place that makes the canal's revival as also its continued functioning in the development of the economy of the region as a whole. In the given setting it is not only desirable but feasible.

Restoration of the damage done either in the recent past or during the British rule is feasible. However, the entire process of restoration shall need verification under working conditions. Hence, one should think in terms of a five year period of restoration, when not only the canal will be restored but its functioning will be tested but the essential ecological prerequisites are put back on the rails and the catchment area is also revived that feeds the entire system.

In is necessary that certain steps be taken to safeguard the whole area for future. These steps are:

Heavy duty traffic be prohibited on the *kuchcha* roads that are located in the vicinity or the traffic that crosses over in the vicinity, or that crosses over the canal structure.

Tube wells and other such heavy extraction systems should not be allowed within certain limits on each side of the entire length of the canal at all points to allow for normal and uninterrupted seepage of the soil water into the system.

Peasants and farmers be advised not to cultivate corps that take large amount of soil moisture away so that normal functioning of the soil is not affected. This is especially the true of banana and sugarcane; both these crops requiring heavy duty transport for their post harvest disposal.

While the road leading to various points on the canal system as a whole does require improvement and up grading as well as upkeep, it is not necessary to construct metalled road for this purposes as it will add to actual and potential load on the underground canal structure and weaken it.

Steps be taken to develop the canal-complex so that the local people feel the cultural benefit and get involved in observing the norms that give them benefits from the project and observe the welfare fall out. In this context one is reminded of a *Firman* of Akbar asking for the plantation of fruit trees along the embankment of a canal so that people may have the incentive of coming there for free fruits and report if they see any abnormality on the banks.

This attitude should be the guideline for the management of the canal– complex in order to have timely information from the people who have to be involved themselves.

In order to achieve the above at this stage it is necessary that an expert team be sent to Burhanpur in order to:

1) Assess that underground damage to the canal– system and structure as a whole at various points;

2) Estimate the cost, duration of each step as well as number of persons required to complete the job in hand within the given time frame;

3) To assess if any material is to be analysed in order to get the same quality produced as per special order and quality control to match the original material used in the construction of the canal; and

4) To explore the possibility of creating a body that shall take over in future the repaired structure of the canal after its restoration and maintain it. With the prospect of the Panchayati Raj emerging in future, including in the area of planning at the district level, it should not be a serious problem to involve the Panchayats in the looking after of the canal including its development in the various phases of their own district plan.

The underground canal built by Khan-i-Khanan at Burhanpur is an example of an extremely eco-friendly structure of immense utilitarian nature that has expansion capacity on these very lines virtually without limits. Under present conditions of water shortage it is most important that not only we restore one of the finest example of our heritage in the field of underground water utilisation means but also to put it as an example of environment management in a eco-friendly manner at very low cost that is based on local resources and avoidance of use of any energy other than locally available renewable resources.

Some Thoughts on Indian Art and Architecture (from the earliest Times to the 12th Century)

M.N. DESHPANDE*

After the decline of the Harappan Culture around 1700 B.C. there is a gap of over thousand years till the dawn of the historical period. The iron technology, in both north and south India, had developed around the 10th century B.C. and the production of a variety of tools, both for offence and defence as also for clearing forests and use in agricultural operations and craft activities had facilitated commerce leading to the emergence of a merchant class and semi-urban centres for collection and distribution of surplus produce. This development led to the formation of as many as sixten States known as the *Mahajanapadas,* each with its capital .

This process, called the *"Second Urbanization"* by archaeologists, gave rise to further proliferation of arts and crafts, with *Śrenīs* or guilds of organized craftsmen. This was also a period of great philosophical and religio-ethical upsurge and the 6th century B.C. witnessed the coming of two great personalities, Buddha, the founder of Buddhism and Mahavira, the 24th Tirthankara of the Jainas, both of kshatriya origin. These two religious movements were of the nature of reaction to the Brahmanical supremacy over other castes and their domination in almost every sphere of religious and mundane life. The new religious leaders talked to the people in their spoken language *(Prakrit)* as opposed Sanskrit, which was the language of the elite.

The rise of urban centres heralded the beginning of the classical Indian civilization on a grand scale. Around 326 B.C. there was temporary intrusion in the form of an invasion of north-west India by Alexander the Great but the situation underwent a complete change with the establishment of the Mauryan empire towards end of the 4th century B.C. when Chandragupta Maurya consolidated his position and usurped the throne from the Nandas in 321 B.C. His grandson Aśkoa ascended the throne in 273 B.C. and his empire consisted of almost the whole of northern India and parts of south India. It is about this time that we have evidence for the production of steel which contributed to the tremendous increase in art, architecture and sculpture especially rock-cut architecture on a monumental scale. Aśoka is credited with the excavation of caves for the Ājivika sect of monks in the granite outcrop of the Barabar hill (district Gaya, Bihar). Excavation in granite, the hardest of the rocks, was possible because chisels of steel were by that time available for the purpose. It will not be an exaggeration to state that Indian architectural and artistic activities received a great boost with Aśoka's conversion to Buddhism. For the next two centuries it was primarily Buddhism which dominated the art-forms, though Jainism and Brahmanism equally contributed. Aśoka was also responsible for introducing the construction of stone structures, as miners were now able to quarry the sandstone from the mines of Chunar and turn out tall monolithic pillars which in their roughly finished state were rolled down from the hill-side to the nearest tributary of the Gaṅgā for being transported

*D-25, Press Enclave, Saket, New Delhi.

to distant locations on the banks of the Gaṅgā and Yamunā, and installed at different places connected with the life of Buddha or places of religious importance like Sarnath where Buddha had delivered his first sermon, Rummindei in the Tarāi region of Nepal where the Master was born, or Kausāmbi, near Allahabad, where Buddha had delivered sermons during his ministry. Aśoka had inscriptions carved on the rock-face where he styled himself as Devānampiya Piyadasi and, in a few cases, his name, Aśoka also finds mentioned. These pillars and rock-edicts are found in far-flung areas and at once provide evidence of the extent of Aśoka's empire and the spread of the Buddhist faith. Of the thirty or so pillars set up by him and which were 10 to 15m high, ten were inscribed with his edicts.

It is traditionally believed that Aśoka opened eight of the ten original *stūpas* built over the body-relics after the *parinirvāṇa* of the Master and distributed the relics to devout followers and over these relics eighty-four thousand *stūpas* are alleged to have been built throughout the country. He also sent emissaries to different parts of the world to spread the Buddhist faith and his inscriptions in Aramaic and Greek at Kandahar in Afghanistan bear witness.

Among the Aśokan pillars, the one at Sarnath is one of the finest examples. It is a tapering monolith with an inverted lotus capital, crowned by four finely carved spirited lions once supporting the *Dhamma-chakka* or the Wheel of Law, which is missing now. Its abacus bears in relief an elephant, horse, bull and lion, each separated from the other by *Dhamma-chakka,* below which is an inverted lotus looking like a "bell". The entire pillar is highly polished, and is characterised by high finish, triumphant execution and symbolical significance. Among other pillars, the one at Rampurva with its bull capital is exceptional for its naturalism, depiction of nervous tension and anatomical details. The Lomasa Rishi cave at Barabar has a carved rectangular entrance set in a slightly projecting horse-shoe arch bearing a sculptured frieze of elephants and *stūpas.* The cave is almost a copy in stone of a circular hut and an ante-room with an ornate frontage. Its facade including the interior walls had mirror-like polish, a characteristic feature of Mauryan art whether it be a sculpture, pillar or cave.

During the Aśokan period Buddhism had absorbed in its pantheon popular indigenous deities like *Yakshas, Yakshīs, Nāgas* and *Nāgis;* their function being to bestow plentitude to the worshippers, protection of devotees and places of worship. The image of *Yakshī,* well-known as Didārganj Yakshī, nearly life-size, carved in the round was found in a suburb of Pātaliputra. It is an exquisite piece imbued with great beauty and charm. It has the usual Aśokan polish and the figure exudes feminine grace and vitality, all its own.

During the period of Aśoka, the Third Buddhist Council met at Pataliputra under the chairmanship of Moggaliputra Tissa and the Council decided to send religious emissaries for the spread of Buddism, among whom was one, by name (Yavana) Dharmarakshita , who was sent to Aparanta (the northern part of west coast). He started his religious activity from Sūrpāraka (modern Sopara, District Thana), a flourishing port-town and the findspot of an Aśokan edict. Perhaps taking cue from Aśoka and his grandson who has carved out monastic retreats for Ājivika monks in the genissic rock of the Barabar and Nagrjuni hills in south Bihar, the Buddhist monks might have felt that western India was ideally suited for a similar purpose.

The perpendicular cliffs of the amygdaloidal trap formation of the Sahyādri with horizontal beddings provided a hospitable place and convenient medium for the excavation of monasteries and prayer-halls and out of desire to create something more enduring and monumental than ordinary buildings, they zestfully exploited this medium. Of the nearly 1200 rock-cut excavations in India, about 800 are situated in western India.

The earliest caves in the Deccan belong to the Hīnayāna faith and were excavated in the wake of the spread of Buddhism during the two centuries before and after the Christian era. Their beginning coincides with the rise of the Sātvāhana dynasty which had its capital at Pratishthana (modern Paithan) about 50 km south of Aurangabad in modern Maharashtra. Among the earliest caves of this period mention may be made of the *chaitya* cave at Bhaja, at the end of the Borghat, and a *chaitya* hall at Kondivite (in the present limits of Bombay), and at Kondane at the northern end of Borghat and others on the trade-route passing from Desha to Karnataka, through Karahataka (modern Karad), Brahampurī (near Kolhapur) leading to port-towns of lower Aparanta region. Among other caves which can be attibuted to the 2nd century B.C. are those at Ajanta (Cave 10) and Pitalkhora (Cave 3). These were followed, in the first century B.C., by a cave at Ajanta (Cave 9) and those at Nasik, Karla and Kanheri. The early *chaitya-grihas* were apsidal on plan, spacious and imposing, having a central nave separated from the aisle, on either side, by a row of octagonal pillars. A *stūpa* was carved at the rear end of the apse facilitating circumambulation. The inner vault was originally fitted with a network of curvilinear wooden beams and rafters in imitation of contemporary brick and timber *chaitya*-halls and supported on stone pillars with a prominent inward rake. The horse-shoe opening above the entrance allowed light in the interior and helped, in no small measure, to ehance the grandeur of the edifice. The excavations undertaken by the author at Pitalkhora, a rock-cut monastery, about 60 km north-west of Aurangabad, revealed the forecourt of a *chaitya-griha* (Cave 3) and the rock-cut basement of a grand *vihāra* (Cave 4) provided with a spectacular entrance flanked by a standing *dvārapāla* dressed like a warrior, on either side, and the whole *vihāra* supported by a row of nearly life-size elephants each mounted by a *mahout.* In the foreground of the *chaitya*-cave were found two *yaksha* images, one of which bore a *Prakrit* inscription in Brāhmi script of 2nd century B.C., stating that it was the handiwork of a goldsmith *(hiranakāra).* The sculptures from Pitalkhora constitute the earliest artistic achievements of the Deccan sculptors, who till then were working either in gold, ivory or timber like the north-Indian craftsmen. However, the work of excavating large cave monasteries, *chaitya grihas* and *viharas* was entrusted to a special class of artisans styled in inscriptions as *saila vardhakins* (carpenters who had taken to stone-cutting.)

The Satavahana royalty and devout merchants with the riches obtained from trade with the Mediterranean countries were busy excavating monumental Buddhist cave-monasteries along trade-routes in the Deccan. About the same time in Orissa Khāravela, king of Kalinga, a contemporary of Pushyamitra Sunga, excavated caves, in the sandstone outcrops on the twin-hills of Udaigiri and Khandagiri, near Bhubaneshwar around 100 B.C. These caves ware retreats for monks of the Digambara sect of the Jainas. The entrances of some the individual cells were provided with *toranas* with the capitals bearing addorsed animals. The upper friezes of the *toranas* were decorated with fanciful vegetal pattern and sculptures depicting mythological stories, among which the story of Udayana and Vasavadatta has been identified by scholars. Iconographically we meet with early forms of Surya, Lakshmī and *vrikshakas* carved on the lintels of some caves. Among these caves, the double-storyed cave, Rānī Gumpha is noteworthy for its sculptural wealth alongside the semi-circular *toranas* resting on pillars with capitals of animals like those at Bhaja and Pitalkhora in western India. The Manchapuri-gumpha is equally important for its sculptural wealth. Stylistically these early Orissan sculptures are similar to those on the Buddhist *stupa* at Bharhut of the Sunga period.

In central India two early Buddhist establishements namely those at Bharhut and Sanchi, are of singular importance. They represent artistic creations of the Sunga-Satavahana period portrayed on the railings around the *stupa.* Bharhut was discovered by Alexander Cunningham in 1873 and the surviving monumental remains from the site are now preserved in the Indian Museum, Calcutta. Fortunately, an inscription of the 2nd century B.C. on one of its pillars records that the *torana* gateway of the *stupa* was executed during the reign of the Sungas. The pillars and the railings carry life-size carved figures of *Yakshas* and *Yakshis, Devatas* and *Nagas,* together with bas-reliefs depicting *jataka* episodes, each with a label-inscription. The sculptures represent the first indigenous expression in stone of an earlier tradition of carving in wood and ivory, and an indomintable urge for recreative expression of the people and, therefore, represent a landmark in the story of Indian artistic tradition uninfluenced by the Mauryan court-art.

The Buddhist *stupa* at Sanchi near Vidisha in Madhya Pradesh, with temples, monasteries, *stupas* erected from the Mauryan to the medieval ages, is a monument of great architectural, archaeological and artistic interest. The principal *stūpa,* attributed to Aśoka, was presumably enclosed by a wooden railing and an Aśokan pillar was planted near its southern gateway. This original brick *stupa* was enclosed and enlarged by stone-casing in the Sunga period. The enlarged *stupa* measured 36 metres in diameter and 16.46 metres in height, forming almost a hemispherical dome surmounted by a square *harmika* crowned by triple umbrellas. The Satavahana kings who ruled the Deccan were responsible for adding the lavishly carved gateways in the four directions providing entrances for circumambulation of the *stupa.* The gateways are carved on both the sides with *jataka* tales, secnes from the life of Buddha, and represent one of the magnificent architectural edifices erected at the beginning of the Christian era. The lively narrative scenes contained in the *jatakas* represent a development from the more static manner in which similar *jataka* tales were carved on the railing of the Bharhut *stupa*. Sanchi also has the distinction of having a few more *stupas* of about the 2nd century B.C., erected at a time when the principal *stupa* was enlarged in the Sunga period. One of these *stupas* yielded caskets containing the relics of Sariputra and Maudgalyayana, principal disciples of the Buddha. The site also has one of the earliest temples of the Gupta period, besides ruins of monasteries for the residence of a large community of monks. Not far away from Sanchi there are also other monasteries among which one at Satadhara on the bank of the Bes river is noteworthy for it contains the body-relics of the two desciples of Buddha, Sariputra and Maudgalyayana mentioned above.

Before we move to later developments in the field of art and architecture, it would be essential to take note of some mural paintngs of *ca.* 2nd century B.C. in one of the earliest *chaitya-grihas* (Cave 10) at Ajanta. Here, a very interesting rock-inscription came to light as a result of calculated removal of a small portion of unpainted plaster from the left-side wall. The record refers to the donation of the cave-wall by one Kanhaka, a resident of Bahada. It appears that immediately after the cave was completed, the architect decided to use the wall-space as a carrier for mural paintings. The walls were plastered with mud and eventually painted. One of the subjects shows a prince (with a parasol held over his head by an attendant) proceeding with his retinue of musicians for worship of the *Bodhi* tree, which in the early stages of Buddhist art represented the Master. In continuation of this painted scene there are multilated remains of paintings where a *torana* - entrance, like the one at Sanchi, can be discerned. Further, there is the depiction of seven kings riding elephants and recently Dr. Schillingloff has identified the subject as a pictorial episode depicting the transport of the relics of Buddha after his *parinirvana* at Kusinagara, the *torana* being that of the city of Kusinagara. On the right-side wall are remains of Saddanta and Syama *jatakas*. In the adjoining *chaitya*-cave (no.9) which was excavated in first century B.C., there are paintings assignable to the beginning of the Christian era. Both these caves, however, contain later paintings on pillars which are considered to be contemporaneous with the Vakataka period paintings (*ca.* 5th cen A. D.). However, there is reason to surmise that some of these paintings representing standing figures of the Buddha in *udichya* dress may be a century earlier. The drapery with heavy folds worn by the figures is similar to that depicted on Gandhara sculptures. This would suggest that Ajanta which lay on an ancient trade-route attracted artist-monks from the Gandhara region, whose disciples in the 5th-6th century decorated the cave monasteries at Bamiyan with mural paintings and this innovative artistic practice gained popularity and spread to Central Asia along the Silk Route up to and beyond the Thousand Buddha grottoes of Dunhuang in China.

The first few centuries before and after the Christian era, Amaravati together with other sites like Jaggayyapetta and Nagarjunakonda, in the Krishna delta of Andhra Pradesh, which was anciently under the Satavahana rule, developed into a flourishing centre of Buddhist art with relief carvings of narratives drawn from the *Jataka* tales decorating the *stupas* and railings for which local white limestone was used. The elongated and delicately modelled groups of sensuous figures, male and female deveotees and semi-divine beings decorating the *stupa* reliefs of the Amarvati school influenced the pictorial art of the Vakatakas at Ajanta.

During the rule of the Kushanas, Mathura which was a meeting place of several trade-routes emerged as a very important urban centre for the dissemination of sculptural art. In fact, Mathura had inherited the art-legacy of the Maurya-Sunga age and during the Kushana, rule, its ateliers produced Buddhist, Jaina and Brahmanical icons in hundreds. The early Buddha and Bodhisattva figures from Mathura constitute a special product of the indigenous tradition derived from pre-Kushana *yakshas* which are masculine in character with broad shoulders, the robe leaving the right shoulder bare and the drapery clinging to the body and arranged in schematic folds. The nimbus is plain or scalloped at the edge in low relief. It is thus unrelated to Hellenistic or Gandhara images of this class. The museums at Mathura and Lucknow contain a very rich collection of the Kushana art consisting of sculptural railings which once enclosed Buddhist or Jaina *stupas*, pillars with inscriptions of Kanishka and Huvishka, large figures of standing Buddha, Bodhisattva and *yakshis*. The sensuous nude or semi-nude female figures and Bacchanalian scenes found at Mathura bespeak of the contemporary fertility beliefs and are excellant examples of the Kushana art of Mathura. The product of Mathura ateliers were in great demand and many images were exported to adorn the sacred sites like Sarnath, Lumbini, Sravasti and Rajagriha. Recently a very spectacular discovery of 177 Mathura Kushana sculptures was made at Sanghol in the Punjab.

It appears that this artistic treasure entirely manufactured out of the typical Mathura sandstone was hurriedly buried, beside the *stupa,* perhaps to save them from destruction at the hands of the Huna hordes who were overrunning the country in the 5th century A.D. This indeed is a very fortuitous and momentous discovery which has placed Sanghol on the map of Mathura art.

At the ancient site of Sonkh, 22 km north-west of Mathura was uncovered an apsidal brick temple devoted to *naga* cult, in the upper phase of which was found a stone lintel in typical red sandstone assignable to the period of Kanishka and bearing a very intresting panel of Nagaraja and Nagini with two attendants carrying the royal emblems, *chauri* and an umbrella. Further, it contains a scene showing three *brahamanas* and ascetics making an offering of a necklace to the *nagaraja.* In the same horizon was also discovered a sculpture of *śalabhanjika.*

The period from 4th to 6th century, starting with the accession of Chandragupta I and the establishment of the Gupta dynasty, is considered as the Golden Age in Indian history. As a result of economic prosperity resulting from internal and external trade, there was efflorescence in the field of arts and letters. The hallmark of this period was the emergence of structural temples as places of worship, although rock-cut activity like the Brahmanical caves of Udayagiri near Vidisha and the Buddhist Gupta-Vakataka caves of Ajanta were also excavated. The structural temple (no. 17) at Sanchi, Tigowa (District Jabalpur), Eran (District Sagar), the Śiva temple at. Bhumara and Parvati temple at Nachna, both in District Panna, are examples of the emerging classical style of temple-art. The Sanchi temple was a shrine for a Buddha image and shows departure from the concept of a *chaitya*-cave as a place of worship. In fact, in the *chaitya-grihas* at Ajanta (Caves 19 and 26), the standing figure of Buddha was set against the *stupa* and the ground plan of the *adhishthana* for the *stupa* followed the layout of the Gupta temples with offsets of *rathas* and *anurathas* marked on the floor in relief. The structural temple, however, to begin with was of modest dimensions consisting of a square *garbhagriha* with an entrance doorway and a pillared portico. The *sikhara* had not developed and the roof was flat. The Nachna temple, however, was provided with a storey over the flat roof of the sanctum. Very soon, the idea of a spire (*sikhara*) over the sanctum was felt essential and the first examples of such a class were the Dasavatara temple at Deogarh (District Lalitpur) and the entirely brick-bulit temple at Bhitargaon in District Kanpur. To the same class would also belong the Maitraka period temple at Gop in Saurashtra where the receding *sikhara* courses were decorated with trefoil arches a feature derived frm the *chaitya* window motif of the Buddhist caves. It has been suggested that the flat-roofed cella was derived from the megalithic dolmen and the placement of the object of worship against the back wall shows a distinctive departure from the layout of the *chaitya* hall where a circumambulatory path around the *stupa* was provided. Perhaps, the idea of placing the object of worship against the backwall of the cella was the result of shrine- *cum-vihara* (caves 1 and 2) at Ajanta where the object of worship was located against the back wall of the *garbhagriha.* The Dasavatara temple at Deogarh referred to above was provided with a *tri-ratha* sanctum . It has beautiful sculpured compositions in niches on three sides of the shrine, provided with graceful pilasters and architraves and containing images of Vishnu Seshasayi, Gajendra-moksha and the penance of Nara and Narayana. These are among the noblest specimens of Gupta art characterized by grace and sublimity.

Reverting to the Buddhist art of the Gupta period, the Buddha figures of the Sarnath school are unparalleled in regard to execution and delineation of sublime and serene expression. The Gupta art of Mathura is equally impressive; some of the Buddha figures being of exceptional quality.

In the sphere of plastic arts and paintings of the Gupta period, we have to take congnizance of the world-famous sculptures and paintings Ajanta executed during the Mahayana phase when the Vakataka kings ruled over the Deccan from Vatsagulma (Vasim, District Akola). A princess of the Gupta family, daughter of Chandragupta II, by name Prabhavati Gupta, was married to Vakataka king Rudrasena II and as a result of this matrimonial alliance, we find that the Gupta idiom had influenced the local artistic expression which has its roots in the Satavahana art of the Vengi School and the Deccan cave-art. The product of this fusion is best reflected in the cave paintings and sculptures in Caves 1,2,16,17,19 and 26. The style of paintings follows the aesthetic norms laid down in *Chitrasutra* section of the *Vishnudarmottara,* forming an appendix of *Vishnu-Purana* assignable to 4th-5th century A.D. The Subject matter of the paintings is drawn from the *Jatakas, Avadanas* together with scenes from the life of Buddha. Thus, the whole gamut of life of contemporary India came to be depicted in vivid colours, from kings and princes to beggars, Bodhisattvas, monks and ordinary persons in a variety of settings, palaces or common man's residences and forests, including facets of animal and plant life. Among the mural paintings, the one on the rear *vihara* -wall of Cave 1, shows what is popularly described as Bodhisattva Padmapani. It is considered as a masterpiece of Asiatic art. The Mahajanaka *Jataka* on the left side wall, depicts the story of king Mahajanaka wanting to follow the path of renunciation, where each incident is separated from the other by suitable architectural motif. In Caves 2 and 17, scenes from the life of Buddha are painted.

Although there is an overall predilection for paintings in the Vihara caves, the *garhbagriha,* door-frames of the shrines and facades of caves were replete with excellent specimens of sculptures. The highly ornate facade of the *chaitya*-cave 19 has a wealth of sculptures, affording an opportunity for the study of those of the classical period. The facade was artistically conceived with a view to achieving an aesthetic unity by harmonius blending of architecture and sculpture. The upper part of the facade is relieved by a central *chaitya*-window of an elegant design with a figure of richly-bedecked and majestically standing *yaksha* on either side. For wealth of sculptures and their judicious placement, the facade of this cave is indeed an exceptionally fine example of the classical period.

Along with the developments outlined above, the region of Aihole, Badami and Pattadakal (District Bijapur) under the Chalukyas of Badami provided an ideal area for experimentation in the format of a temple. The kings of Chalukyan dynasty, founded by Pulakeśin I (A.D. 550-556), were great patrons of art and the region around their capital came to be described as a cradle of early temple architecture.

We have three temple styles in India, namely the *Nagara, Dravida and Vesara,* of which the *Nagara* temple are to be mainly found in the North while the *Dravida* style was prevalent in Tamil Nadu. Andhra Pradesh and Karnataka, and *Vesara* temples are generally to be found in the Mysore region of the Decccan. At Pattadakal the *sthapatis* experimented with temples of the *Nagara* and *Dravida* styles while the Sangamesvara, Virūpāksha and Mallikarjuna temples exhibit many elements of the Dravidian *vimana.* The Sangamesvara, the earliest of the three, built by Chalukya Vijayaditya (A.D. 697-733), is almost akin to the Pallava form. The Virupaksha temple, which is much larger, is square on plan from base to *sikhara* and has many features common with the rock-cut temples of Kailasa at Ellora. It is an extensive complex consisting of *vimāna* and axial *mandapas* and peripheral sub-shrines around a court enclosed in a *prakara* with *gopura* entrances in front and the rear.

At Aihole, the typical *mandapa*-temple is exemplified by the Lad Khan, Konti Gudi and Meguti temples. The Lad Khan temple contains massive columns of the cave-temple type and consists of a rectangular hall with four tall pillars supporting a flat roof which is surrounded the peripheral rows of 12 and 20 pillars of lesser and lesser heights supporting a sloping roof. Thus, the central bay is enclosed by double aisles. The central aisle in the rear side of the temple is converted into a shrine. This appears to be the first experiment of converting a square hall meant for the gathering of village elders into a temple. The Konti Gudi complex, consisting of three temples, has, in each case, a shrine-cell at the rear like the Lad Khan temple. The Jain temple, the Meguti temple precisely dated to A.D. 634 is more evolved.

The Durga temple at Aihole is a square structure provided with an apsidal cella and is the only temple of this type at Aihole and stands on a high moulded *upapitha* apsidal on plan and carrying a peripheral row of columns on its edge.

At Badami, the capital city of the Early Chalukyas, there is group of Brahmanical and Jain caves. Cave 3 of this group is a Vaishnava cave, dated to A.D. 578, which contains grand sculptured figures of Vishnu seated on Ananta and Narasimha in the varandah, besides bracket figures of graceful females and *mithunas.* The eaves of the cave contain remains of paintings showing a court scene.

The Elephanta Caves, off the sea shore, near Bombay is a group of which the large principal cave contains some of the finest sculptures of post-Gupta period (*ca.* 6th cen. A.D.) depicting *lila-murtis* of Siva, besides a *sarvatobhadra* linga-shrine. The three-faced image of Sadasiva in the back-wall is both majestic, collossal and awe-inspiring and is considered to be one of the finest specimens of Indian plastic art. This cave provided a model for the Dumar Lena Cave of Ellora where the monolithic linga-shrine, located opposite the entrance, is the chief object of worship.

Orissa with a glorious art-tradition, became a thriving centre of temple activity during the post-Gupta period. Bhubaneshwar contains hundreds of temples and provides a continuous history of the regional style of temple architecture from the mid-7th to the 13th centruy; the great Sun temple at Konarak marking the culmination of the grand architectural movement.

This regional building style is characterized by a sanctum with a tall curvilinear *sikhara,* called *Rekha-deul.* Preceding the sanctum and joined to it is an astylar *mandapa (Jagmohana)* with a pyramidal roof of horizontal tiers *(pidha-deul),* although in the early temples the *mandapa* was a pillared hall covered by a low flat roof of two sloping tiers with a clerestory in between. The Parasuramesvara temple, built towards the end of the 7th century, represents the earliest temple of Bhubaneshwar. It has a pillared *mandapa* in front of the *triratha* sanctum surmounted by a low curvilinear *sikhara.* The second stage is provided by the Vaital Deul, the sanctum having a wagon-vault roof locally known as *khakhara*; its *mandapa* being similar to that of Parasuramesvara temple. It is dedicated to Chamunda and belongs to the close of the 8th century. The Muktesvara temple at this place is considered to be a gem of Orissan architecture. It is surrounded by a low enclosure wall and is approached through an ornate *makara-torana.* The sanctum is *panchratha* on plan and the *sikhara* has a rounded contour with its base figuring an elborate *chaitya* window flanked by a pair of grinning *yakshas* (dwarfs). From the 10th centruy onwards the typical Orissan style underwent further development represented by the Lingaraja temple, dated to 11th centruy, which is the tallest (45 metres) and grandest structure in Bhubnashwar. It has a sanctum, *Jagmohana, Natamandira* and *Bhoga-Mandapa* all standing on a common platform and studded with intricate ornamentation and sculptures. The Raja-Rani temple is unique in that its *sikhara* has clusters of miniature *sikharas* like the temples of western and Central India.

The great temple at Puri dedicated to Krishna, Subhadra and Balarama follows the style of Liṅgaraja but is larger and loftier. The last of the series and built in the 13th centruy is the Sun temple at Konarak. It was conceived as a gigantic chariot of Sun god with twelve pairs of exquisitely ornamented wheels, yoked to seven rearing horses. The curvilinear *sikhara* over the sanctum which was presumaly 68 metres high has since fallen, but its *Jagamohana* (38.8 metre square and 38.8 metres high) and a detached *nata-mandapa* are still extant. Well known for its intricate sculptured wealth, including erotic figures, this majestic temple is one of the grandest achievements among Indian temple edifices.

Among temples of north India, the temples in Himachal Pradesh at Brahmaur and Chatrarhi, attributed to the dynasty established by Meruvarman around A.D. 700 are architecturally important. Many of these temples were constructed in wood with intricate carvings and wooden sculptures. The monolithic temple-complex at Masrur of *ca.* 9th centruy A.D. is also a fine example of monolithic complex in the *Nagara* style, which is a little later in date than the monolithic temple of Kailāśa at Ellora in Maharashtra.

The medieval temples of Central India built during the rein of the Kalachuris, Chandellas, Kachchhapaghatas and Paramaras consist of a fascinating variety. Progressive development of temple architecture can be seen in the temples of the period of the Paramaras. The Paramara king Bhoja (*ca.* 1010-1080) was a great patron of art, architecture and letters and the author of *Samarangana-sutradhara,* a manual on temple architecture. The temple built by him at Bhojpur, although incomplete, demonstrates how ancient temples were built with the help of ramp, so that heavy architectural members could be carried to great heights. Near this temple are also preserved line-drawings on the rock showing plan and elevation of the temple and its constituent members. Stone for this temple was also quarried and sculpted locally and, therefore, this temple is very interesting in several ways. The Udayesvara temple at Udaipur, attributed to the Paramara king Udayaditya (1059-1080) is an exquisite example of the developing style and distinctive on account of great size, elegant design of its *sikhara* and sculptural ornamentation.

Khajuraho has the distinction of possessing the finest and best-preserved group of Chandella temples. Except half-a-dozen temples assignable to the ninth century, all the temples of Khajuraho date from the tenth to the twelfth century and pertain to the typical Chandella style. Affiliated variously to the Saiva, Vaishnava and Jaina sects, these temples are of a congnate style and share certain pecularities of plan and elevation. They are compact and well-knit structures, some comprising an entrance-porch, a *mandapa*, a *maha-mandapa* with lateral transepts, a vestibule and a sanctum enclosed by an ambulatory with rear and lateral transepts. Erected on a lofty platform-terrace, the temples have an emphatically high *adhisthana*, consisting of a series of ornamental mouldings which grip the platform-terrace. Over this stable and ornate base rests the *jangha* which consists of solid walls alternating with the voids of the inner compartments. The balconied windows canopied by overhanging eaves provide ventilation to the interior and form beautiful openings for the inner compartments. The solid wall-spaces between them are studded with two to three horizontal bands of statuary of exquisite grace which constitute the most attractive feature of these temples. The deep shadows cast over the whole composition by the beautiful balconied windows and the light and shade falling over the sculptural bands following the alternate projections and recesses of the indented plan indeed produce a highly picturesque effect. Over the central zone of the *jangha* rise the individual roofs on the several compartments in a modulated crescendo, from the lowest over the entrance-porch to the loftiest over the sanctum.

The developed Khajuraho temples are characterized by an intricate arrangement of subsidiary *sikharas* of diminishing sizes attached to the main *sikhara* at graded heights. The clustering together of subsidiary peaks to the main peak and the progressive ascent of the roofs converging to the highest pinnacle lend a peculiar vertical quality and rhythm to the temples. Their interior too displays an amazing exuberance of decorative details, sculptural wealth, largely found on the doorway, pillars, architraves and ceilings. Particularly remarkable are the female bracket-figures of the interior, which, with the sensuous modelling, charming postures and exquisite finish, constitute masterpieces of medieval sculpture. With their compact but elaborate plan, vertical accentuation of each constituent of the elevation and plastic exuberance, combined with a harmonious integration of sculpture with architecture the Khajuraho temples mark the culmination of the Central Indian architectural style.

The sculptures adorning the temple walls at Khajuraho comprise figures of higher gods, various minor deities and demi-gods including *ganas, gandharvas, vidyadharas* and *surasundaris;* secular sculptures including erotic figures, and birds and animals– both real and legendary. The sculptures of *surasundaris* and females revel in admiring the charms of the human body from the most fascinating angles and excel the contemporary schools of Indian art in the vivid portrayal of human moods and fancies through the medium of provocative gestures and flexions.

The developed Khajuraho style of art and architecture was ushered in by the Lakshmana temple (A.D. 950), which was followed by the Parsvanatha, Visvanatha (A.D. 1002), Jagdambi and Chitragupta temples, marking successive stages in the efflorescence of the local style. The peak is reached in the Kandariya Mahadeva temple (*ca.* A.D. 1025-50) which represents the grand finale of the architectural and sculptural activities at Khajuraho.

BIBLOGRAPHY

Agrawala, V.S. 1965. *Indian Art,* Varanasi: Prithvi Prakashan.

Basham, A.L. (ed.). 1975. *Cultural History of India,* Oxford: Clarendon **Press.**

Coomaraswamy, A.K., 1927. *History of Indian and Indonesian Art*, New York.

Cunningham, A. 1879. *The Stupa of Bharhut,* London.

Cunningham, A. 1892. *Mahabodhi.* London.

Deva, Krishna. 1969. *Temples of North India.* Delhi National Book Trust.

____________1990. *Temples of Khajuraho,* 2 vols. Delhi. Archaeological Survey of India (ASI)

Fergusson, J. and Burgess, James . 1880. *The Cave Temples of India.* London,

Ghosh, A. (ed.) 1964. *Archaeological, Remains Monuments and Museums.* 2 Parts. Delhi: ASI.

____________1967. *Ajanta Murals,* Delhi: ASI.

Majundar, R.C. and Pusalkar A.D. (eds). 1951. *The Age of Imperial Unity,* Bombay: Bharatiya Vidya Bhavan.

Marshall, John and Foucher Alfred, 1940. *The Monuments of Sanchi,* Calcutta and London.

Meister, Michael W. *et al* (eds) 1988. *Encyclopaedia of Indian Temple Architecture. North India. Foundations of North Indian Style,* Delhi: American Institute of Indian Studies.

____________1991. *Encyclopaedia of Indan Temple Architecture. North India. Period of Early Maturity.* Delhi: American Institute of Indian Studies.

Percy Brown. 1959. *Indian Architecture (Buddhist and Hindu Periods)* 4th edition, Bombay: D.B. Taraporevala & Sons.

Sivaramamurti, C. 1972. *Mahabalipuram.* Delhi: ASI.

____________1979. *Chitrasutra of the Vishnudharmottara,* Delhi: Kanak Publication.

The Concept of Bodhisattva Avalokitesvara in Ancient Thailand and its Iconographic Forms

BACHCHAN KUMAR*

This paper makes an effort to evaluate the concept of Bodhisattva Avalokitesvara through analysing the distinguishing features of the various images found in different parts of Thailand. Avalokitesvara, a Bodhisattva, especially associated with the principle of compassion, is the most popular deity in Mahayana Buddhism. Worshipped and invoked in both male and female forms, he is considered as a potent saviour in times of life-threatening dangers. He watches over all beings and heeds to their cries of suffering and distress. He responds directly to the pleas of those in great need, while also serving in symbolic manner as the embodiment of the principle of compassion, a fundamental aspect of the Buddhist way of life. Not only was he represented as the symbol of mercy or *karuna*, it was given to understand that he was so much moved by the pangs of the suffering humanity that he declined to accept *nirvana* until all sentient beings could be elevated to that state, and thus he emerged as a very effective deity who played a significant role in distinctive local traditions throughout Buddhist Asia.

At present Hinayana form of Buddhism is practised in Thailand. Hinduism probably appeared into Thailand during the early century of the Christan era. After the advent of Hinduism, Mahayana Buddhism entered into Thailand and worship of Avalokitesvara became popular.

Much has been written on this deity but very few have worked on his iconographic details in Thailand. References have been made in several texts. Nandana Chutiwongs has contributed a voluminous work entitled Avalokitesvara in the Mainland Southeast Asia. In her work she has contributed a chapter on Avalokitesvara of Dvarawati period in Central Thailand. Her work is commendable from the point of view of descriptive iconographic motifs of the deity of Dvarawati period. The worship of Avalokitesvara was not confined to Dvarawati period alone; it continued even longer upto the fourteenth century A.D. A large number of images has been found from the peninsular region of Thailand which have their own significance.

Sanskrit treatises mention many eminent Bodhisattvas e.g. Manjusri, Avalokitesvara, Samantabhadra, Gaganaganja Vajrapani, Vajragarbha, Sarvanivaranaviskambhi, Kshitigarbha, Khagarbha, Vyuharaja, Indrajali, Ratnagarbha etc. But, among them, Avalokitesvara was the second popular Buddhist deity. Scholars have different views on the meaning of the word Avalokitesvara. Avalokitesvara is a compound of Sanskrit words *avalokita* and *isvara* which has been translated in several ways, emphasizing his sovereignty over the material world and his responsiveness to the call of suffering humanity:

"The Lord, who sees, or looks down."

"The Lord, who is seen or manifested, or is every-

*Indira Gandhi National Centre for the Arts, New Delhi.

where visible."

"The Lord of what is seen, of the visible world."

"The Lord, who is seen from the height" (i.e. by Amitabha Buddha, as a small Buddha-figure is often placed in the head of the statues of Avalokitesvara).

"The Lord, who looks from height" (i.e. from the mountains, where he lives, like Siva).

"The Lord of View." "Lord of compassionate glances."

"The Lord of the dead and the dying."

Some scholars do not agree on the significance. According to them, Avalokitesvara means either 'the lord of what we see', i.e. 'of the present world', or 'of the view', or 'the lord whom we see', "the lord revealed', 'the master who is or was seen'. But the Tibetans took it to mean 'the lord who looks'; for their translation 'Spyan-ras-gzings" appears to dispense with the idea of "visible lord' (Sarat Chandra's Dictionary, Burnouf, Introduction: 226).

Lokesh Chandra opines that the suffix *"isvara"* in the word Avalokitesvara is the only conspicuous Saiva element (1988: 14). However, the images have been sometimes found wearing *yajnopavita* and the antelope-skin. For instance, a bronze image of this deity (now in the Somdat Phrai Narai National Museum, Lopburi) of sixth century has been found wearing the *yajnopavita* as a shawl and his hair is arranged in *jatamukuta* like Siva. Another stone statue of late sixth century has an antelope-skin flung over the left shoulder (Chandra 1988: 14). These images reflect the combination of the features of Buddha and Siva.

Origin of Bodhisattva Avalokitesvara

The origin of Bodhisattva Avalokitesvara is obscure. Scholars have different views. Saunders thinks that he is a Sun god of Central Asia (1928: 71)). Har Dayal concurs with this view. He states that the name Avalokitesvara, his association with Amitabha, his lordly and leisurely movements throughout the Universe, the stress laid on his "eyes", his capacity for illuminating the world, and his epithet of Samantamukha, all point to a solar deity. The worship of Avalokitesvara seems to be a Buddhist adoption of the Sun worship of the *Sauras* and *Magi* (Dayal 1978:48). However, we do not find reference to any solar deity in any Buddhist text. Oskar Von Hinuber opines that Iranian influence, to some extent, is found. Although his image was widely worshipped in India, they are profusely found in Central Asia (Von Hinuber 1984:104). No doubt, the worship of this deity originated in India then spread to Tibet and China where it became more prominent. R.C. Majumdar opines that the local traditions in Yunnan affirm that Avalokitesvara came from India and converted the entire region to Buddhism (1963: 256). Etienne Lomotte suggests that Avalokitesvara was dwelling on the Mount Potalaka before manifesting himself in China in the form of female deity, Kuan-yin (1984: 92). Potala has been identified as a mountain in south India and is regarded as the seat of Tibet's patron Bodhisattva Avalokitesvara (Per Kvaerne, 1984: 265).

The Subjugation of Siva and his Retinue by Buddha

A mythological story narrates the subjugation of Mahesvara (Siva) and his retinue by Buddha in *Sarva-tathagata-tattva-sangraha* (Lokesh Chandra 1987: 56-58). It states that when Siva was not accepting the doctrines of Bodhisattva, Buddha's followers went to Vairochana (a stage of Buddha) and complained about Siva. Keeping in view of the anxities of his followers, he sat in meditation in order to acquire more power. The other Tathagatas also went to mount Sumeru for penance. They thought, the anger of the wicked can only be pacified by means of *karuna.* There all the Tathagats entered into the body of Vairocana in order to give him enhanced power. After accumulating all the strength, he sat in meditation known as *Vajra.* Afterwards, Vajrapani's body turned into a ferocious holding *vajra, ankusa, kosa* and *pasa* in his hands. Then Vajrapani sat in meditation known as *vajradhithanam.* As a result, a power emerged from his body called as *Hung.* The Vajrapani then uttered the following Sanskrit tantric verse:

Om sumbha nisumbha hum! Grihan Grihan hum!
Grihnapaya hum! Anaya hon bhagwan!
Vajra hum phat.

Then, *Hung* asked Vajrapani, what is expected from him. Vajrapani ordered him to bring Siva. Siva and his retinue soon after appeared in front of Vajrapani, and Vajrapani asked them to understand the doctrines of Buddha. In reply, Siva asked Vajrapani, how can we understand the doctrines of Buddha? Vajrapani advised them to go to *Buddha, Dhamma* and *Sangha*. You will get supreme knowledge there. Siva and his retinue then became angry and refused to do so. They said that I am lord of three *lokas* (worlds). Also I am creator and destroyer of all beings. I am also a lord of all the *devas* (deities). I can not accept your doctrines. Hearing their reply, Vajrapani warned them. "If you do not accept Buddha's doctrines, I shall destroy all of you". Siva answered with great anger, "no I shall not accept your doctrines as I am superior than you all." Then Vajrapani asked them, "how do you consider yourself superior to us?" You cannot be. You live in the cremation ground, smear with ashes of human being and eat their fleshes and drink blood. In spite of this, Siva refused to obey the order of Vajrapani. Then Vajrapani addressed Tathagat as and explained them that Siva and his retinue are not accepting the doctrines of Buddha because of false pride. He then asked Tathagatas, what to do? The Tathagatas earnestly prayed him to do something. Afterwards, Vajrapani uttered the same *mantra* (Tantric verses) as stated above. As a result, Siva and his retinue fell down at the feet of Vajrapani and prayed for their rescue and died. Because of *karuna*, Vajrapani pardoned and then Siva with his retinue woke up and accepted the doctrines of Buddha.

The supreme form of the Bodhisattva Avalokitesvara is described in the *Karanda-vyuha*. The deity has been personified as the symbol of mercy. He abrogates and nullifies the old law of *Karma*, as he visits the purgatory and *avichi* and makes it a cool and pleasant place. He also goes to the realm of *pretas* and gives them plenty of food and drinks in order to regain normal figure. The beings, liberated from these realms, are reborn in the paradise of *Sukhavati* (*Karanda-vyuha:* 6 and 43). It is also mentioned that numerous divinities have emerged out of this supreme Buddhist deity. From the eyes of the god emerged the Sun and the Moon, Mahesvara (Siva) from forehead, Brahma from the shoulders, Narayana from the heart, Sarasvati from the two rows of teeth, Vayu from the mouth, Prithvi (Earth) from the feet, Varuna from the abdomen, Vahni from the navel, Lakshmi and Sri from the left and right thighs respectively, and many other deities from the body of lord (Kamleswar Bhattacharya 1964: 77).

Introduction of Avalokitesvara in Thailand

The worship of Avalokitesvara may have been introduced in Thailand directly from India by sea route by the traders. From the beginning of the Christian era, Indian traders embarked on their journey to Suvarnabhumi and carried such images for the safety of their voyages. As a result, a large number of images has been found in peninsular Thailand. In the beginning, images of Avalokitesvara came with the traders; later they were locally made.

It is very difficult to say when the worship of Avalokitesvara was introduced into Thailand. The earliest known image is a bronze statue of sixth century A.D. (Piriya 1979: 78-79). No doubt, the worship of this deity must have been introduced in Thailand by the beginning of the sixth century during Pre-Angkorian period, just after the fall of Funan Kingdom. Afterwards, we find a number of images from the area of Dvarawati as compared to other images of divine personages. It indicates that he was the most favourite deity worshipped by the Mons of Dvarawati Kingdom and may have enjoyed special veneration.

Images of Avalokitesvara in Thailand

Numerous images of Bodhisattva Avalokitesvara have been found in various parts of Thailand. Based on art styles, these images can be broadly categorised in to three different art styles i.e. Duarawati, Srivijaya and Lopburi art styles.

The images of Avalokitesvara found in Thailand a are two basic form of the *Saumya* (benign) and the *Raudra* (wrathful). The *Saumya* motif signifies the deity bestowing kindness and benevolence on the devotees while the *Raudra* chastises them if need be. In Thai iconography, these images have been represented both as an independent deity as well as associated with the Buddha. He has been represented as a young male.

Dvarawati Period (6th–11th Century)

Due to internal problems, the Funan empire, in the later part of sixth century, began loosing its hold on the outer reaches of its empire. The lower Chao Phya River Valley was inhabited by the dominant Mon people. The

Mons took advantages of this internal problems and asserted their independence and founded the Dvarawati kingdom. The account of the Chinese pilgrim Hsuan Tsang (Coedes 1968: 76) and inscriptions on silver medals testify to the historical existence of Dvarawati kingdom (Boeles 1964: 101-103).

It is strongly believed that Theravada Buddhism predominated the intellectual life of Dvarawati and played an important role in the development of artistic activities. Chutiwongs opines that this doctrine remained important in central Thailand throughout the entire Dvarawati period and even beyond. It survived till the Khmer occupation which brought into Thailand a strong Hinduism and Mahayana Buddhism during eleventh century (Chutiwongs 1984). No inscription of the entire Dvarawati period mentions the prevalence of the worship of Avalokitesvara. However, a large number of images of Avalokitesvara of this period found from the different parts of the area points to the popularity of the worship of this deity. It extended fairly over the entire Dvarawati domain. During the period a unique Buddhist art-style developed which was inspired by Indian schools of art. This style existed from the sixth to the beginning of nineth century A.D. and even to the later part of the same century. The images of this period are of two-armed, four-armed and twelve-armed varieties.

A two-armed image represents simplicity in art style which reflects the characteristics of the Indian art of Sarnath school. The image has flowing locks and flexion of the hip and the garment is tied on the left side. It is of early Dvarawati period (sixth century A.D.) when Mahayana Buddhism was introduced in Thailand. Another two-armed image from Surat Thani province is plain and smooth. It is in a pose of with one leg slightly advanced. The image has rounded face, jointed eyebrows, almond-shaped eyes, smiling mouth and thick lower lip. The earlobes are elongated. The headdress reminds the *jata* of Siva.

Four-armed images of this period are less in number. Chutiwongs (1984; 235-256) has reported a nice four-armed bronze image which is now in the British Museum, London. The Bodhisattva stands in the static pose of *sambhanga.* He wears a simple diadem in his high-piled up *jatamukuta* which contains a indistinct Buddha figure. His attire is rich. The lower part of his legs, the upper hands and the attributes in them are missing. The broken stem of a *padma* is seen in his first right hand, and a *kamandalu* in his first left.

Another a fine image of twelve-armed Bodhisattva of the 8th century has been reported from the province of Prachinburi in east Thailand. It is generally assumed that this was brought from Malayan archipelago. The body of the image is slender and attenuated, displaying– even in its flexed position– a certain stiffness and static austerity which characterise many images in the Dvarawati style. The elongated form of the *jatamukuta,* the *ajina* skin on his shoulder and the pleated *dhoti* represent the features of indigenous origin. In the right hands, from front to back, are seen a lotus bud, a *kamandalu,* an object like a *pasa* or *ankusa* or a *gada* (club), another *kamandalu,* a raised hand which holds an object and a book. His left hand displays the *abhayamudra* and holds a *tridanda* and an *akshamala.*

The images of this period represent a calm and benign attitude. The ascetic aspect predominates in these images, as indicated by their regular display of the *jatamukuta,* extremely plain attire, the *ajina* skin and a sacred thread. Tantrism is clearly seen in the images of this deity and this is because of introduction of Tantrism in the Mahayana Buddhism. No doubt these images were made for the purpose of invocation of the deity during calamaties for peace and prosperity for the state. However, we do not have any epigraphic confirmation.

Srivijyaya Period (8th to 13th Century)

Between 8th and 13th century, Srivijaya was dominant force in the peninsular Thailand. A group of scholars suggest that the southern part of Thailand was the cultural centre of Srivijaya. Beek is of the view that during five centuries of rule, Srivijayans have changed their capital several times. Probably it was due to economic or strategic reason (Beek 1991; 73-75). The southern part of Thailand might have been the capital of Srivijaya during 8th to 9th century A.D. The Srivijayan kings were patrons of Mahayana Buddhism and Avalokitesvara was worshipped by them. It is because of the popularity of the deity, a large number of images have been found influenced by Gupta, post-Gupta and Pala Sena styles.

A stone figure of Bodhisattva found in a Chaiya of

early Srivijaya period of 8th century A.D. has *jata* like headdress bearing Amitabha in the front. It is decorated with lot of jewellery. Both hands of the image is broken.

A bronze image of four-armed Avalokitesvara dated to 8th–9th century has been found from Betang in Yala (Pl. II. 2) . The image is in standing posture showing baey seriousness in the face. Behind the head is a *chakra*. The image is richly attired and bejewelled. The left anterior hand is missing while the posterior hand shows *vitarka-mudra* holding rosary. The left hand is partly broken but is in *varadamudra*. The posterior hand has a lotus bud. The figure of Amitabha adorns the centre of the crown.

It is a stylised Chintamani chakra Avalokitesvara. The name Chintamani chakra is composed of two words i.e. *chintamani* meaning 'wish-yielding gem' and *chakra* means 'wheel' which are his two principal attributes. The lotus is of course the most distinct cognizant of Avalokitesvara while rosary becomes a common emblem in his tantric manifestations. In exceptional cases the image is found in standing posture. In a scroll painting of A.D. 864 standing figure of Chintamani chakra Avalokitesvara in *samapadasthanaka* pose has been found from Tun Huang (Pal:41). In Japan, Chinatamani chakra Avalokitesvara is called as Nyoirin Kannon and is one of the most popular form of Kannon in Japanese art. He is one of the six Kannons, especially venerated by the Tendai sect during Kamakura period. Numerous temples have sprung for his worship (Pal: 39). His special attributes are compassion and protection from life-threatening dangers (Weinstein: 159).

Another four-armed image, (provenence unknown) has a smiling face. The Bodhisattva holds a rosary in the right posterior hand, the lotus in the right anterior, the nector-vase in the left anterior and a book in the left posterior hand. The sacred thread is in the form of a shawl, while the hip scarf is tied in a bow at the sides.

The best sculpture of this period is a bronze image of eight-armed Bodhisattva of late 8th or early 9th century found from Chaiya. The figure is richly attired. All its arms are broken. The ornaments are florid which has resemblence with the four-armed Avalokitesvara from Wonogiri, Central Java. Such figures are very rare in Thailand.

Of late 9th or early 10th century A.D. a bronze image has been found from Phunphin District in Surat Thani province. Both arms are missing. The image is well-dressed wearing a *dhoti* with a frontal medium pleat folded in front as a lower garment. The facial expression is calm and the headdress is like the *jata* of Siva. Another image of the same period is a two-armed bronze Avalokitesvara. The left arm is in *abhayamudra* holding rosary while the right hand is missing. The lower garment is *dhoti* tied at the waist. The image is in *Dhyanamudra*, and reflects *karuna* in its face.

The worship of Bodhisattva attained great popularity in Thailand during 8th to 13th century A.D. Priya believes that upon the invocation of his very name, the deity would guide the souls of the departed to Sukhavati, the "land of bliss" in the western paradise of Amitabha and utterance of the phrase "reverence, reverence to the giver of safety," Avalokitesvara, the great being, prevents from misfortune such as fire, missiles, armed robbery, witchcrafts, demons, wild beasts, snakes, thunderbolts, shipwreck and mishaps while climbing mountains. Adoring him would accrru more merit than worshipping incalculable number of Buddhas.

The bronzes were generally used by the royal court as it was costly. The existence of various images of this deity well attired and bejewelled shows that these were intended for the worship by the royalty. The images of this period, no doubt, represent tantric manifestation and were also worshipped by the royalty for the welfare and prosperity of state. Perhaps, influenced by the mysticism of Vajrayana, popular in Bengal from the middle of eight century, Srivijayan emperors introduced the worship of this deity. The sources mention the construction of the sanctury of Bodhisattva at Ligor by the royal court (Coedes: 96).

Lopburi period (10th to 14th century)

In the central, eastern and north-eastern parts of Thailand, there existed a style of art, termed as "Lopburi Art" which shows affinities both in sculpture and architecture with the Khmer art of Cambodia. It is believed that the town Lopburi was under the Khmer rulers. Many rulers of Angkor empire were Mahayanist. Kavindrarimathana, *Rajakulamahamantri* (the great adviser of the royal family) of Rajendravarman, was a

Buddhist and he under his supervision founded a monument of Bat Chum for the Buddha, Vajrapani and Prajna (Coedes: 116). Suryavarman II who was the builder of Angkor Wat propagated Mahayana Buddhism. Thus the worship of Avalokitesvara must have been popular in the area. Of this period, a large number of images has been found in this area.

Worthwhile mentioning is a rare bronze figure of *Ekadasamukha* (Eleven-headed) Avalokitesvara of 10th century discovered in 1979 during the course of digging a tank in the village Wat Khanun in Muang district, Songkhla province. It is the image of Samantamukha Avalokitesvara who looks in every direction to save all the living beings. The image is standing on the stalk of a lotus with only one row of petals placed on a circular base. The ten extra heads are arranged above the primary ones in two tiers, three heads on the upper tier and seven on the lower. The main two hands are missing while the other ten pairs exhibit the *abhayamudra.* The figure wears a short garment, pleated with a loop on the left side, with the upper pleat shorter than the lower one. Priya is of the view that this image belongs to Khmer's Koh Ker style but its base which is of different bronze compound clearly relates to some of the bases of images found at Sathing Phra. This form of Avalokitesvara with eleven heads and twenty-two arms reappeared later at Banteay Chamar of the late twelfth century A.D., along with seven other forms having four to thirty-two arms and from one to sixteen heads (1980: 66).

Another nice sandstone eight-armed image of Avalokitesvara has been found from Prasat Muang Singh in Kanchanburi (now in Bangkok National Museum). The image expresses cheerful mood . All the arms are broken. It has three eyes *(tri-netra)* and numerous Buddhas on the body. The headdress is like *lata* and has a figure of Ambitabha at the centre. The earlobes are elongated. The lower garment is tied by a belt. The figure is called as Radiating Buddha which symbolises compassion.

Votive Tablets

Numerous votive tablets depicting Avalokitesvara have been recovered. Two types of Bodhisttva images: one showing a seated four-armed figure and the other standing twelve-armed form have been noticed.

The four-armed seated figure from Khao Khao, Trang province, is now in Bangkok National Museum. The Bodhisattva is shown in *padmasana* posture with the posterior right hand holding rosary, the posterior left hand a book, the anterior right hand in the *varamudra* and the anterior left holding a stem of lotus. Another four-armed image of the 10th century A.D. found from Yala province (Pl. II. 3) seated in the *maharajalilasana* (royal ease) recalls the iconographic details of Avalokitesvara figure on a terracotta plaque of Mainamati, Bangladesh. The worksmanship of these images is of highest order, especially in the refinement of the images pulsating with life.

The twelve-armed form of votive tablet of Bodhisattva, in standing posture, has been reported from Trang province which is a rare one so far as the art style is concerned. The image is attended by two unidentifiable figures, one on each side.

Avalokitesvara: an associate of Buddha

Avalokitesvara has been represented as an associate of Buddha in various tablets. A terracotta discovered from Yala province of late 8th or early 9th century A.D. represents Buddha Amitabha in meditative mood in the centre while on his left side is Avalokitesvara and on his right side Bodhisattva Mahasthamaprapta. It is believed that Dhayani Buddha Amitabha presides over Sukhavati in the western paradise and bestows immortality on the departed souls.

A bronze votive tablet of late 13th or early 14th century represents Mahayana theme the *tri-ratna* (three gems) has also been discovered. The image of Bodhisattva Avalokitesvara is shown on the right side of Buddha. The central Buddha figure is under a *naga* while on his left side is the figure of Prajnaparamita (Diskul 1991: 14). It is believed that they were produced according to Mahayana tenets. After the remains of dead monks or larymen had been cremated, the ashes would be mixed with clay and then moulded into the figures of Bodhisattva for the merit to the dead.

No sculptural remains of the deity from 14th century onwards has been found. It seems that the popularity of this deity ceased soon after a century of the arrival of the Thais. It is very difficult to attribute reason. Perhaps it is due to the Hinayana Buddhism appealing to a large portion of the local people.

Conclusion

The Bodhisattva Avalokitesvara was the most popular deity in Thailand from the pre-Angkorian period to the 14th century A.D. The images, no doubt, convey compassion. They were primarily made for the worship in the royal court for the welfare of the state. Later, Avalokitesvara was invoked by the common people at the time of crisis, suffering or distress. Also, he was worshipped for guidance of the departed souls in Sukhavati, "the land of the bliss." Mahayana Buddhism mentions that all the Brahmanical deities have emanated from Avalokitesvara while the iconography of the image found from Thailand gives prominence to Saiva and tantric cult.

REFERENCES

Beek, Steva Van and Tettoni, Loca Invernizzi 1991. *The Arts of Thailand,* London.

Bhattacharya, Kamleswar 1964. 'Hari Kambjendra,' *Artibus Asiae,* XXVII, No. 1-2.

Boeles, J.J. 1964. 'The King of Sri Dvaravati and his Regalia,' *Journal of the Siam Society,* 52, pt. 1, pp. 99-110.

Chandra, Lokesh (ed.) 1987. *Sarva-Tathagata-Tattva-angraha* Sanskrit text with Introduction and Illustrations of Mandalas, Delhi.

– 1988. *The Thousand-Armed Avalokitesvara,* Delhi.

Chutiwongs, Nandana 1984. The Icognography of Avalokitesvara in Mainland South East Asia, unpublished thesis, Leiden.

Coedes, G. 1968. *The Indianized States of Southeast Asia,* Honolulo.

Dayal, Har 1978. *The Bodhisattva Doctrine in Buddhist Sanskrit Literature,* Delhi.

Disku, M. C. Subhadradis, 1991. *Art in Thailand: A Brief History,* Bangkok.

Hinuber, Oskar Von, 1984. 'Expansion to the North: Afghanistan and Central Asia', in Heinz Becert and Richard Gombrich, e (ed) *The World of Buddhism,* London.

Krairiksh, Piriya, 1979. *The Sacred Image: Sculptures from Thailand,* Koln (Museen der Stadt Koln).

Lamotte, Etienne 1984. 'Mahayana Buddhism' in *The World of Buddhism,* London.

Majumdar, R. C. 1963. *Hindu Colonies in the Far East,* Calcutta.

Pal, Pratapaditya. 'The Iconography of Cintamani Cakra Avalokitesvara', *Journal of the Indian Society of Oriental Art,* II, pp. 39-48.

Per, Kvaerne, 1984. 'Tibet: The Rise and Fall of a Monastic Traditon' in *The World of Buddhism,* London.

Samasrami, S. B. 1873. *Karanda-vyuha,* Calcutta.

Saunders, K. J. 1928. *The Gospel for Asia,* London.

Weinstein, Stanley 1983. 'Bodhisattva' in *Kodansha Encyclopedia of Japan,* I, p. 159.

Maradharshana Episode : A Unique Representation

SHASHI ASTHANA*

Maradharshana is one of the most important events in Buddha's life. The subject has been continuously exploited by the artists for a variety of compositions right from the 2nd century B.C. to the 12th century A.D. Whenever this theme is depicted in sculptural art, Buddha Sakyamuni has been treated as a focal point; the whole event revolved around him as narrated in Buddhist literature (Buddha; Lalita). But that is relevant only to the extent that iconography was to be strictly adhered to. Here the Buddha is shown seated on *vajrasana* or the diamond throne under the Bodhi tree in *bhumisparsa mudra.* Mara and his daughters along with the host of demons are always present on the scene emulating a battle scene in which Mara assaults Buddha sitting resolutely. He along with his daughters attempt to seduce him, all in order to shake the resolve and the will of Sakyamuni to attain the position of universal sovereignty through *nirvana.* While Mara is usually depicted in an attacking posture, ready to shoot the arrow at the body of the Buddha, the daughters are always in dancing pose, apparently to lure Him. Mara's host is represented attacking with various types of weapons. Goddess Earth, who witnessed the Enlightenment, is always shown appearing from the earth and leaning against the pedestal. This is the usual setting of the Maradharshana episode. There is, however, a unique stone sculpture housed in the National Museum (NM) representing the theme of Mara attacking where, most surprisingly the Buddha is not figured in human form or even symbolically (Pl II. 1). He is conspicuously absent from the scene. Instead, he is replaced by a four-armed Buddhist deity to which we will return shortly.

The sculpture was brought in the year 1966 from a dealer. Its exact provenance is not known. Stylistically, however, it can be dated to the 8th century A.D. and assigned to eastern India. This too will be discussed later.

The sculpture presents a four-armed Buddhist male deity seated cross-legged, holding a rosary and an indistinct object in the upper hands and a *kamandalu* in the lower left hand. His lower right hand, on the lap, displays the *chinmudra.* He is dressed in *ekansika sanghati* and a lower garment. The sacred thread is visible near the shoulder. The deer-skin is flung our the left shoulder. His hair is arranged in a typical manner–parted in the centre and then combed back on either side and tied on the top of the head in the form of a bun. The curls of hair are shown falling on the sides of the head. A beaded nimbus or *prabhamandala* is shown adorning his head. The branches of the *Bodhi* tree surround the whole image and form the background. Half embedded female is shown in *anjali mudra* near his right thigh. The pedestal presents a flaming wheel flanked by two deers, symbolising the moment of First Sermon.

Below this is a representation of a male figure in a ferocious form, holding a bow and arrow in hand and standing in *pratyalida* posture against the *Bodhi* tree. He is shown ready to attack as he has picked up an arrow

*National Museum
New Delhi.

from the quiver. *Makara's* mouth has been used here as quiver. In front of this ferocious man there stand three beautiful females in dancing pose. They are adorned with *ekavali, patra kundalas,* bangles etc. The hair of all these images are set alike, combed back and tied on top chignon. All of them appear to be dressed only in the lower garment secured at the waist with a beaded girdle.

The sculpture is made of black basalt. Its composition is balanced with human figures arranged one behind the other in groups with visual weight divided equally over the whole picture. Although it is crowded, yet the human beings have been generally imbued with animation with diagonal arrangement of the axis of figures. It is indeed a technically perfect and aesthetically charming work of art.

A casual look at the sculpture recalls to the mind the usual Mara-attack scene, a recurring theme in Buddhist art. But a careful study of the details reveals altogether a different context in which Mara appears on the scene.

The details of the lower half of the sculpture clearly attest to the image of Mara and his daughters. The man with a ferocious face and armed with a flower-bow and arrow is no other than Mara, the god of death and desire, mentioned frequently in the Buddhist texts. For example the flower-bow has been assigned to him in the *Buddhacharita* (13:7) as his special weapon. Just at the back of Mara, *makara* or crocodile with open mouth is represented. *Makaradhvaja* is the standard assigned to Mara and is frequently shown in this context in Buddhist art. However, here the *makara* figure has been used as a quiver, which is indeed at once a very pleasant variation and an interesting artistic device, besides being symbolically meaningful in the present context - death and desire rest in Mara as well as *makara* with equal emphasis. Its very presence substantiates the proposed iconographcal identification and the concept Maradharshana. The three female figures, represented here in dancing pose, are clearly the daughters of Mara - called Rati, Arati and Trishna in *Lalitavistara* (Maradharshana: iii) an early Buddhist text. They helped their father at the time of the attack by trying to lure the Lord.

This subject is vividly narrated in Buddhist literature. In the Mara–attack scene, usually the army of Mara also appears on the scene. However, none of the demons of his army is present here. The goddess Earth is also present here half-embeded in the earth, but her posture and placement both are different from the usual manner. Normally, she is shown on a pedestal emerging from the earth, holding a pot. However, here she, displaying *anjali mudra,* is shown on the right thigh of the male figure.

The presence of Mara, his daughters, the *makara* and *Prithvi* help us in the identification of this panel as the scene of Maradharashana.

Nothing would have been unusual if Buddha Sakyamuni had been depicted in *bhumisparsa* or earth touching pose in upper panel. However, neither the Buddha is here nor his earth-touching attitude. Instead, in his place is shown a four-armed male deity and that has made this sculpture unique in the realm of Buddhist art.

Buddha has never been shown with more than two hands and the only attribute which he holds sometimes in his hand is his alms bowl. Therefore, the identification of this male deity with Buddha is completely ruled out. Further, by this time the iconography of the Enlightenment of Buddha had been stabilised. Therefore, his identification with Buddha is also impossible. Hence, here we have undoubtedly an altogether a different deity, other than Buddha, the Sakyamuni. The identification of this deity of course depends upon the attributes. Two of the attributes *askshamala* or rosary and *kamandalu* or water vessel are clear and distinct while the third one is not clear which is a curved object which appears like a snake. It has three small offshoots also. The identification of this object is difficult.

Here, two stone sculptures, otherwise Brahmanical, may be referred to. A sculpture representing Parvati from Mundeshwari cave (Ghosh 1980: iii, 36) presently housed in Patna Museum, shows a similar attribute in one of her hands. Here this has been identified as *Tridandi.* Another goddess from Central India dated to 6th century A.D. is also holding the same type of object in her upper left hand (Pal 1978). It is common knowledge that Buddhist goddess Bhrikuti invariably holds a *tridandi* in one of her hands as mentioned in literature and reflected in her images (Ghosh 1980: iii, 52). On the basis of these similarities this attribute may be identified as *'tridandi'*.

Coming back to the main image, we find rosary, pot

and *tridandi* as attritubutes. All these and the deer skin reveal his identity as Sugatidarshana Lokesvara a form of Avalokitesvara to whom all these three attributes are assigned in the *Sadhanamala* (42). According to this text, he is six-armed, displaying *varada* and *abhaya mudras* and carrying rosary in the three right hands and holding lotus, water pot and *tridandi* in the three left hands. He is adorned with jewelled ornaments and sacred thread and a crown of matted hair. He stands on the moon over lotus and is peaceful in appearance. However, there are some problems in accepting this image as the image of Sugatidarshana Lokesvara. The present image is only four-armed and holds rosary, *kamandula* and *tridandi* and displays *chinmudra.* While the rosary, *kamandalu* and *tridandi* are the attributes of this deity, *chinmudra* is never associated with this deity. Instead *abhaya* and *varada mudras* which are mentioned in the *Sadhana* are absent here. And, on top of these, the contextual reference is a problematic issue. Neither Sugatidarshana Lokesvara has ever been found represented in the narrations of the Mara-attack episode nor there is textual sanction for this. Mara's presence is mentioned in Buddhist literature at various places and several times but always with Buddha Sakyamuni, for example at the time of *abhinishkramana* or Great Departure also Mara comes to persuade the Lord to return to the Palace. However, the author fortunately could lay her hands only on one reference where the fight of Mara's army is mentioned with some one else too, i.e. the army of Maitreya, the Future Buddha.

There is a Chinese inscription at Bodhgaya. (Cunningham). This inscription was set up by the priest Yun-Shu in A.D. 1021 and it records the hymn of praise in honour of the body and throne of Buddha. In one of the stanzas while praising the triple body, he eulogises the shrine of *Nirmana kaya* and there in the last line he mentions fight between the arimes of Maitreya and Mara.

> "I proceeded to eulogise the shrine of the Nirmana Kay as follows:
>
> There are wondrous footprints in the heavens
>
> Produced with the limits of the six cardinal points
>
> In depth descending to the bottom of the golden chakra
>
> In height reaching to the surface of the earth
>
> Never do any mortal caves mingle there
>
> For how can fire and water blend?
>
> Sometimes the armies of Maitreya and Mara fight
>
> Until the latter are quelled by the roar of the lion."

Now this inscription gives us the real clue: it is the Chinese Buddhism in which existed an added tradition, i.e. besides the Mara's attack on Buddha, there was Mara's attack on Maitreya also. This deity may, therfore, be identified as Maitreya.

Let us consider it in greater detail. Normally Maitreya is shown two-armed; but his four-armed images are not unknown in Buddhist art. We do find four-armed images holding rosary, *kamandalu,* and *nagakesara* from south India. *Sadhanamala* (Ramachandran) and *Nispannayogavali* (50, 68) also prescribe four arms for Maitreya. With two main hands he displays *vyakhyana-mudra,* the remaining two hold the *kamandalu* and *nagakesara.*

Rosary and *kamandalu* are the well known attributes recommended for Maitreya but *tridandi* has never been found associated with him. As far as the deer-skin is concerned, normally it is shown placed on the shoulder of Avalokitesvara. However, there are some images of Maitreya where one finds the presence of deer skin. An image of Maitreya from Kashmir can be cited in this regard (Pal 1975). Getty has also mentioned images of Maitreya with deer-skin (Getty 1928).

While *Sadhanamala* (28) allots the *vyakhyana mudra* to Maitreya, *Nishpannayogavali* (50) mentions the *dharmachakra mudra* as one of his features. However, in this image we find the *chinmudra* though it is depicted in the lap in very unusual manner. It is generally shown against the chest. It also carries the same meaning, i.e. preaching. This is further substantiated with the wheel-and-deer motif which stands for the First Sermon in which Buddha is always shown in this posture.

In the final analysis, this image may most logically be identified as that of Maitreya, even though there are some minor variations between the texts and the actual image, but this is equally true of many examples.

As far as its dating is concerned, it appears to be the product of 8th century A.D. The hair style, which became a very distinctive feature of the Kashmir sculptures, was not unknown in eastern India. This hair style, one comes across in 6th cent. A.D. in Central India. A number of early Pala sculptures are characterised by this type of hair style. The hair curls remind us of the legacy of the Gupta art and so the face of the deity too. The hairdress of Mara and his daughters, their *patrakundalas, ekavalis* and their lower garment all reflect early features. However, the flaming wheel and the *Bodhi* tree both are very typical and parallels for these could not be traced in the Pala art. Similarly, the Earth goddess is also shown in very crude form.

The sculpture is not like the typical Pala steles made in eastern India. It is slightly oval in shape at the back.

Post Script

This paper was presented at the Annual Conference of the Indian Archaeological Society held at Kanyakumari in November 1990. On its presentatation, Dr. Chandrashekhar from the Nagpur University tried to identify this sculpture as the image of Siva. According to him the episode presented here is as follows: once on the persistance of gods, Kamadeva, the god of love, shot an arrow at Siva to disturb him from his penance. Obviously, his identification is based on the attributes which this image has : *kamandalu,* rosary and snake or trident and deer skin. *Chinmudra* also goes with Siva in his Dakshinamurti form in which he sits under a tree. The image shooting the arrow has been taken as an image of Kamadeva. Surprisingly, he missed a few points which are absolutely essential for this episode but are absent here.

1. Siva was seated in meditation while this event occurred which is not the case here.
2. Siva's third eye, which played the vital role in this episode, is completely absent here on the forehead.
3. Kamadeva is never mentioned along with his three daughters in the Hindu literature and that is also in a dancing poture. He is always accompanied by his two consorts only.
4. Siva is never shown wearing the typical Buddhist robe called *sanghati* in which this image is dressed.
5. *Dharmachakra* flanked by two deers has never been a part of Saivite iconography. It appears with Buddhist and Jaina images only.
6. There is hardly any representation of this episode in the Indian art.

REFERENCES

Buddhacharita, Sarga 13, *Slokas* 1-73;

Cunningham, A. *Mahabodhi.*

Ghosh, M. 1980. *Development of Buddhist Iconography of Eastern India: a study of Tara, Prajnas of Five Tathagatas and Bhrkuti,* New Delhi.

Getty. A. 1928 *Gods of Northern Buddhism.*

Lalitavistara, Maradharashana Parivarta,

National Museum, New Delhi, Acc. No. 66. 224

Nispannayogavali,

Pal, P. 1978 *The Ideal Image,* Cat. No. 46

__________ 1975. *Bronzes of Kashmir,* Cat. No. 38

Ramachandran, T.N. *The Nagapattinam and other Buddhist Bronzes in the Madras Museum,* Bulletin of the Madras Govt. Museum,N. S. Vol. VII, no. 1, Pl. VI.

Sadhanamala

Saivite Art and Thought in the Literature of Kerala: A Survey

B.S. HARISHANKAR*

Literary Tradition

The development of Saivite art in Kerala was inspired by early and late literary works. In other words, literature has inspired art and art has kept alive the flames of literature through the ages as in other parts of India.

In south India, the Sangam literature datable to late B.C.s and early A.D.s was authored by different poets and gathered in anthologies. It is from some of these works like *Padirrupattu* and *Silappadikaram* that we get a glimpse of early Kerala. By the time they crystallized, the Saivite pantheon had taken deep rooted influence in south India. Siva is referred in *Silappadikaram* in His various aspects with the primordial Mother Goddess. He is the Lord of the Great Goddess who vanquished the demon Mahisha and who is clad in lion's skin and is the sole witness of His cosmic dance. Unlike the concept of Vaishnavi Durga who is independent or sometimes treated subordinate to Vishnu Narayana, the concept of the Mother Goddess was considered equal or even higher than Siva in south India.

Oral tradition in Kerala is essentially associated with the cult of Kali Bhagawati, the Great Mother Goddess. The *Sanghakkali*, *Theeyattu* and *Kalampattu* belong to this tradition. The *Panarpattu* is a song centred around Siva and Parvati, sung by a nomadic group known as Panas. Similarly, the *Velarpattu* and *Malayarpattu* are also dedicated to Siva. *Teyyam* or corrupt form of *Deivam* is a popular ritual dance of north Kerala. The cults of the Mother Goddess and Siva have an important place in performing art.

The early Tantric literature in Kerala which evolved by the eleventh and twelfth centuries were essentially based on Saivagamas. *Prayogamanjari,* an abstract of the Saivagama written by Ravi during the eleventh century is considered to be the earliest of its kind. Another comprehensive Tantric treatise *Isanasivagurudevapaddhati* consists of nearly eighteen thousand *slokas* based on the Saivagamas. By the thirteenth century, the Saivite tradition was further enriched especially by the *kavya* and *stotras* in Sanskrit. *Tripuradahana* a *yamaka kavya* by Vasudeva Bhattathiri and *stotros* like *Dakshinamurtistava, Mahakalashtaka* and *Kalavadhakavya* composed by Vilvamangalam Swamiyar are some of them.

Fourteenth century marked the growth of vernacular as well as *manipravala* literature. The latter was a blend of Sanskrit and Malayalam. Although there was no spectacular development of classical Sanskrit and literature, there were works like the *Sivavilasa,* a poem on the Kandiyur Siva temple composed by Damodarachakkiyar which throws light on the society and culture during the

* Sree Sailam, Pattom,
Thiruvananthapuram.

period. Ramananda's commentary on *Tripuropanishad* belongs to the fourteenth century A.D.

Malayalam literature was enriched by Rama Panikkar who belonged to Niranam in Thiruvalla taluk of Alappuzha district. He composed the *Sivaratri Mahatmya*, a poetic work of great literary excellence. Krishna Panikkar who belonged to his lineage composed the *Trikkapalisvarastotra*–eighteen songs in praise of Siva, the presiding deity of Trikkapaliswara temple in Niranam. *Pasupatastralabham pattu*, an anonymous work belonging to this period has Kiratarjuniya episode as its central theme. *Thirukkaniyalannansthuthi* is another hymm to Siva by another anonymous author.

The greatest contribution to Malayalam literature came after the sixteenth century with the revival of Bhakti movement by literary luminaries like Thunchathu Ramanujan Ezhuthachan, Punthanam Namboodiri and Melpathur Narayana Bhattathiri, to name of few. Ezhuthachan initiated the *Kilippattu* tradition in Malayalam literature, a form where the parrot narrates the story. After Ezhuthachan, the *Kilippattu* legacy was inherited by Gopalan Ezhuthachan, the author of *Paravti Svayamvaram kilippattu..*

The oral and written literature in Kerala is not exclusive to Saivite tradition. Siva is represented in early literature as Dakshinamurti, Kiratamurti, and Umamahesvaramurti.

Archaeological Evidence

Although early archaeological evidence for Saivism in Kerala are the rock-cut cave–temples, scholars have attempted to correlate megalithism with Saivism. It has been observed that a number of megalithic sites in Kerala are located near Saivaite temples, a fact pointed out by Robert Sewell (1882), Alexander Rea (1910-11), and Aiyappan (1933). K. A. Nilakanta Sastri (1966) has pointed out the association between the megaliths and the Saivaite pantheon on the basis of antiquities excavated from Adichanallur in Tamil Nadu. Asko Parpola (1973) has emphasised the relationship of *Vratyas* with *Rudra-Siva*, a fact of much importance. Megalithic antiquities like the iron trident, Black-and Red Ware, and Black Ware have been viewed as having symbolic relationship with Saivism. Heesterman (1962) in his study of *Vratyas* points out that their rites represent an earlier form from which the classical Vedic ritual developed. Although archaeological evidences are not that abundant, the unearthed megalithic artefacts, as pointed out by I. K. Sarma (1982) clearly suggests a diffusion of cults and practices in the South during the pre-Mauryan period. Allchins (1996), too have contended that the megaliths are to be associated with the Saivite cult. However, nothing definite can be postulated from the above .

Early Cave–Temples

The cave-temples belong to the type popularly as *mandapas* with shrines in the midst, lateral or hind position. The cave-temples came into existence under the Pallavas and Western Chalukyas—Mahendra Pallava and Chalukya Mangalesa.

The Pallavas and their successors who pioneered it plastered the interior of these as seen from the cave-temples at Thirunandikkara and Kaviyur. Unlike the cave-temples at Kottukal and Kaviyur, the pillared frontage is absent at Irunilamcode cave-temple in Thrissur and Bhrantanpara cave-temple in Palakkad districts. The single-celled shrine seen at Kottukal is similar to the one at Vizhinjam in Thiruvananthapuram district. All these temples are dedicated to Siva.

Soundara Rajan (1978) has pointed out that the *linga* in Kerala has two distinct characteristics. The cave-temples at Trikkur and Kaviyur have detachable *linga* on a monolithic *pitha.* At Ayirurppara, the *linga* is of the *arsha* or archaic type.

At Kaviyur, the *dvarapalas* on the walls of the *ardhamandapa* reflect the Pallava influence. Siva referred as *Jagradubhyah* in *Satarudriya* traces the beginning of *dvarapala* and Vishvaksena. The *dvarapalas* of the Pallavas are differentiated by their locks of hair in large mass resting on the shoulders, adorned with thick necklace, armlet, bracelet, and waistband. The hands are placed on a heavy club encircled by a snake. These features are very much present at Kaviyur. H. Sarkar (1978) observed a close resemblance between the *dvarapalas* at Sevvalpatti and Thirumulapuram in Ramanathapuram and Thirunelveli districts of Tamil Nadu with that of Kaviyur. The *dvarapala* at Kuttalanatha temple at Kuttalam in Tirunelveli district is much more similar to the one at Kaviyur.

However, the roots of the Pallava style can be traced in the Chalukyas of Vengi, who exercised great influence on the cultural life of Andhra and a *dvarapala* figure recovered from Vijayawada is preserved in the Madras Government Museum.

The next stage in the development of Saivite cave-temple, can be traced in the *dvarapala* from Vizhinjam, with two arms, one in the posture of wonder and the other in defiance (Sivaramamurti 1961). H. Sarkar (1978) has ascribed this to the Pandyas. However, the inscriptions on the northern base of the Vishnu temple at Trivikramangalam in Thiruvananthapuram district mentions that it was founded during the period of Chola domination of Vizhinjam. Similarly, the Tirupptisaram Vishnu temple in Thovala taluk of Kanyakumari district in Tamil Nadu has an inscription on the west base of the second *prakara.* It records that Vizhinjam was renamed as Rajendrasolapattinam and continued to be called by that name. In the light of these evidences it is difficult to accept Sarkar's view that the Siva figures at Vizhinjam are defenitely of Pandya origin.

Then we have Saivaite art in the wood carvings. Stylistically, these images cannot be dated before the Vijayanagara times. They can be ascribed to the 16-17th century A.D.

Kerala has a few bronze images of Siva, some of which are in the collection of Harry Lenart and preserved in the Los Angeles County Museum of Art. These bronze images represent the Hoysala and Chola styles.

The third type is the murals of Kerala. The murals seen in temples and palaces are of gods and goddesses and are drawn using colour of five varieties. This traditional art–form of Kerala termed as *Kalamezhutthu* in Malayalm is based on *dhyanaslokas* (meditational hymns) describing them from the forehead to the feet in all their splendour. The murals have distinct art form developed along with the growth of structural temples in Kerala. They were earlier associated with cave-temples as seen from the mural of an *apsara* at Thurnandikkara. The colour of the murals represents symbolically the qualities of the painted figure. Siva in his various manifestations is white, while along with the *ganas* etc. he is depicted in golden colour. A significiant feature regarding the murals is their spatial distribution. The Pallimana Siva temple at Kumbalanad and the Sankara-Narayana temple inside the Vadukkannatha temple–complex in Thrissur gives 1691 and 1731 as inscriptional evidence for dating the murals.

Let us examine some of the important forms of Siva represented in the art of Kerala.

Kiratamurti

The manifestation of Siva as *kirata* in the Mahabharata, originates from concepts like *Vrikshapati, Vanaspati* and *Nishada* in *Satarudriya.* The deity is popular in Kerala. The earliest evidence of *Kirata*-Siva is seen in the Vizhingam cave-temple. However, the Kiratarjuniyam episode—Siva bestowing the Pasupata weapon on Arjuna is mainly depicted in wood carvings and murals in the temples of Kerala.

The Sattankulankara Narasimha temple at Chengannur in Alappuzha district, the Mahadeva temple at Vazhappalli and Ettumanur, both in Kottayam district, the Vishnu temple at Kadavallur and Madathil Appan temple at Peruvanam, both in Thrissur district portray Kiratarjuniyam episode in wood-work by an interesting series of bracket figures.

The murals of *Kirata*-Siva has been depicted at Panayannarkavu Sribhadrakali temple in Alappuzha district, the Vishnu temple at Trikkodithanam Sribhadrakali temple in Aalappuzha district, the Vishnu temple at Trikkodithanam, and the Mahadeva temple at Ettumanur both in Kottayam district, Pallimana Siva temple at Kumbalanad, Sri Rama temple at Triprayar and Siva temple at Chemmanthitta, all in Thrissur district have a touch of class with lively expressions. This is also obvious from the murals in Padmanabhapuram palace in Kanyakumari district and Mattancherry palace in Ernakulam district.

It has to be mentioned in this context that *Vettaikorumakan,* the son born to Siva and Parvati in their *Kirata* manifestation is one of the popular deities worshiped in the traditional sacred groves known as *kavu,* especially in north Kerala. He is depicted in murals found in Pandavam Siva temple in Kottayam district.

Sasta, another son of Siva and Vishnu (Mohini) according to the *uttarakhanda* of Brahmanda Purana, and one of the most popular dieties in Kerala is shown as a hunter at Panayannarkavu Sribhadrakali temple in Alappuzha district, Mahadeva temple at Ettumanur and Siva temple in Kottayam district and Thodikkalam Siva temple in Wynadu.

Dakshinamurti

The concept of *Jyestha* in *Satarudriya* is interpreted by Sayana as "one who imparts the supreme knowledge". Here lies the origin of the later concept of Dakshinamurti. Although this manfestation of Siva does not figure in literature nor is that widely worshiped in Kerala, it has acquired a prominent place in wood carvings.

The earliest evidence of Dakshinamurti is found from the reliefs in the cave-temple at Irunilamcode in Thrissur district. He is shown wearing the *yajnopavita* and surrounded by sages.

In wood carvings, Dakshinamurti is depicted in number of temples. The Sri Padmanabhaswami temple and Sri Narayana temple in Thiruvananthapuram district, Sri Vallabha temple and Kandiyur Siva temple in Alappuzha district, Vazhappalli Mahadeva temple in Kottayam district, Kadavallur Sri Rama temple, Thirukulasekharpuram Sri Krishna temple, both in Thrissur district and Kadirur Suryanarayana temple in Kannur district are some, where he is sculptured.

Dakshinamurti is not widely depicted in murals. Panayannarkavu Sribhadrakali temple in Alappuzha district, Pundarikapuram Vishnu temple in Kottayam district, Pallimana and Chemmanthitta Siva temples, both in Thrissur district and the Padmanabhapuram palace in Kanyakumari district bear murals of Dakshinamurti.

Although Dakshinamurti is depicted in various styles, in accordance with the *mudras and asanas,* like *Vyakhyanadakshinamurti, Jnanadakshinamurti, Vinadhara Dakshinamurti* and *Yogadakshinamurti* it is the latter which is popular in Kerala.

Uma-Mahesvaramurti

Siva along with his consort Uma-Haimavati has been a favourite theme in the art of Kerala. The earliest evidence of Siva and Parvati is found in the unfinished reliefs at the Vizhingam cave-temple in Thiruvananthapuram district. The most popular theme is Siva's marriage with Parvati. The bride and the bridegroom well adorned are flanked by gods and sages. The carvings are seen on the wall at Kandiyur Siva Temple in Alappuzha district, Perunayil Sri Subramanya temple in Kottayam district and Sankaranarayana temple in Palakkad district. At the Aranmula Parthasarathi temple in Alappuzha district, we find a panel showing Parvati being dressed by two female attendants along with Brahma and Vishnu in the Siva-Parvati marriage context. The Vishnu temple at Pundarikapuram in Kottayam district and Mattancherry Palace in Ernakulam district too portray murals Siva Parvati.

Ardhanarisvara

Siva-Parvati as Ardhanarisvara is depicted at Panayannarkavu Sribhadrakali temple in Alappuzha district and in the Vishnu temple at Pundarikapuram in Kottayam district, Mattancherry palace in Ernakulam district and Padmanabhapuram palace in the present Kanyakumari district of Tamil Nadu. Saktipanchaksharamurti is not much popular and is seen in Padmanabhapuram palace.

The mural of Paravti witnessing the dance of Siva and Vishnumaya, is portrayed in Mattancherry palace and Kottakkal temple in Malappuram district. This is a rare depiction found in Kerala.

A beautiful bronze image of Siva seated in *lalitasana* with Uma sittng on his left thigh datable to the 17th century is to be seen in the Los Angeles Museum of Art.

Natarajamurti

Siva *Tandava* is mainly depicted in murals. The *Tandava* is comprehensively discussed in the section on *Tandava lakshana* of *Natyasastra,* which describes the 108 *karanas* or the integrated movement of the hands and feet. Siva *tandava* scenes are found at Panayannarkavu Sribhadrakali temple in Alappuzha district, Vishnu temple at Pundarikapuram and Ettumanur Mahadeva temple, both in Kottayam district, Elankunnappuzha Subramanya temple in Ernakulam district, Pallimanna and

Chemmanthitta Siva temples in Thrissur district. However, the one in Ettumanur Mahadeva temple is remarkable since it is depicted in accordance with the *karana* termed *Talasanghattita* in Bharata's *Natyasastra* (4.124). The *shodasahasta* (sixteen-armed) Siva enclosed within a circular and trampling the Muyalaka holds musical instruments and weapons. The *kaparda* or matted locks are decorated with a variety of flowers. The great serpants of Indian tradition are shown adorning Him, while Bhadrakali, who according to Keralite tradition emerged from the third eye of Siva is shown sitting on a *Vetala* observing the dance with wonder and devotion. A host of gods and goddesses are shown playing musical instruments and observing the cosmic dance of the great god.

Sankaranarayana

Sankaranarayara or Harihara is a composite image like Ardhanarisvara. Sankaranarayana is depicted in a few murals in the Vishnu temple in Pundarikapuram in Kottayam district, Pallimana Siva temple in Thrissur district and Padmanabhapuram palace which deserves special mention.

Kalabhairava

This is another aspect of Siva with sharp protruding teeth and elephants for ear ornaments along with snakes which decorate the *jata.* Garlands spring from *makara* and form a large band along edge of Bhairava's flying hair. This piece belonging to the 17th century is at present kept in Los Angeles County Museum of Art.

Besides these, there are other forms of Siva like, Yogisvara, and Ekadasarudras which are not much popular.

REFERENCES

Aiyappan, A. 1933. Rock-cut cave tombs of Feroke, South Malabar, *Quarterly journal of the Mythic Society,* Vol. XXIII, No.3, Bangalore.

Allchin, Bridget and Raymond.1996. *The Rise of civilization in India and Pakistan.* Cambridge: Cambridge University Press.

Heesterman, J. C. 1962. Vratya and Sacrifice, *Indo-Iranian Journal* (6).

Pisharoti, K. P. Narayana (Transl) 1987. *Natyasastra,* Vol. I, Thrissur: Kerala Sahitya Akademi.

Iyer, Ulloor S, Parameswara 1974. *Kerala Sahitya Charitram* Vol. I, Trivandrum: University of Kerala.

Parpola, Asko 1973. *Arguments for an Aryan origin of the South Indian Megaliths.* Madras: Tamil Nadu State Department of Archaeology.

Pal, Pratapaditya 1978. *The Divine Presence– Asian Sculptures from the collection of Mr. and Mrs. Harry Lenart.* Los Angeles: Los Angeles Country Museum of Art.

Rea, Alexandar, 1910-11. *Madras Archaeological Department Annual Report,* Madras.

Sarkar, H. 1978. *Monuments of Kerala,* New Delhi: Archaeological Survey of India.

Sarma I. K. 1982. *The Development of Early Saiva Art and Architecture.* Delhi: Sundeep Prakshan.

Sastri, K. A. Nilkanta 1966. *A History of South India from Prehistoric times to the fall of Vijayanagara* Madras: Oxford University Press.

Sewell, Robert. 1882. *The list of Antiquarian Remains in Madras Presidency.* Madras.

Sivaramamurti, C. 1961. *Indian Sculpture,* New Delhi: Allied Publishers.

____________1976. *Satarudriya-Vibhuti of Siva's Iconography,* New Delhi: Abhinav Publishers

Soundara Rajan, K.V. 1974. *Temple Architecture in Kerala,* Trivandrum: Government of Kerala

Rock-Paintings in India: Decay and Control

Rashmi Pathak*

Rock-paintings have been found throughout India viz. in Mirzapur in Uttar Pardesh, Hampi in Karnataka, Alania, Parvati Valley, and Parwan Valley in Rajasthan, Bhimbetka, Hoshangabad, Pachmarhi in Madhya Pradesh etc. Surprisingly, very little attention has been paid so far for their proper care and maintenance. For the care of any type of art objects including rock-paintings, it is necessary to understand their process of decay so that a preservation strategy can be devised.

Decay

There are two main factors responsible for the decay of rock-art. First is vandalism and the other is environmental. These two factors function very differently. Vandalism is totally random and indiscriminate and affects all types of rock-paintings equally (subject to accessibility). On the contrary, the effect of environment differs according to the nature of rock, nature of paint material, age of rock-painting etc. In the present article, the rock-paintings in open air sites only have been taken into account and not others

Vandalism

The principal threat to rock-paintings is human vandalism. Paintings or carving of initials and dates, scratching the paint etc. by local public or tourists pose great danger to the rock-paintings. Tourists sometimes take casts or even saw off the whole painting for the museums or for their personal collection.

Tourists by their shoes can cause considerable damage on rock-exposures. Through ignorance, some rock-painting sites are frequently used by shepherds as shelter. Their animals rub their body on the painted surface. The smoke from their lighted fire deposit soot on the paintings defacing them.

The rock-paintings sites near roads are mainly victims of vandalism.

Other type of vandalism noticed is often intentional. For example, sometimes paintings are rubbed or dampened to increase their effect for photographic purposes or for better viewing. This action ultimately obliterates the surface and the risk from dampness is increased.

Some of the restorers believe in the application of chalk, water etc. on the rock-paintings for scientific purposes which is quite an ugly form of vandalism imaginable. Thus, we see that we, including researchers, are the greatest enemy of rock-art.

Environment

Environment is the second serious threat for the rock-paintings which slowly destroys them. There are various environmental factors like rain, wind, frost, ground-water seepage, biological growth, seasonal varia-

*National Research Laboratory for Conservation of Cultural Property, E/3, Aliganj, Lucknow.

tion in temperature etc. which contribute to the natural decay, also known as weathering of rock-paintings.

The environmental factors affect the art in two main ways: First, they cause instability of the actual rock-surface, and second they cause instability of the paint layer. In any case the paintings are affected in both ways.

Of environment, there are several components, like moisture, salts, temperature, microflora and microfauna. Their combined effect causes weathering and havoc.

Water

The first important cause of destruction of rock-paintings is the dripping or flow of water running from the rock-roof over the paintings. Since these paintings are not inside the caves, water coming down from top may flow through the front over the paintings and carry away with it the paint.

Moisture

Moisture is another major cause of rock-weathering. It is by capilary action, seepage or through condensation, encourages the disintegration or deformation of the rock-surface. Micro–organisms, mosses and vegetation become active in the presence of moisture. Movement of moisture on or within the rock from several sources like rain, ground, condensation etc. affects its pH, its soluble constituents and their distribution. Rain water is often slightly acidic and leaches out the most soluble contents of the rock (causing erosion of the surface) and thus reduces its strength and ultimately physical breakdown of the rock takes place.

Another effect of direct rain is patination, which consists of the formation of usually stable mineral accretion.

Salts

The root cause for the presence of salts on or within the rock is often moisture. Salt efflorescence has been reported as the most serious problem at many rock-art sites. Another possibility is that some paintings were executed on an already eroded (or eroding) surface; hence their life is relatively brief.

Due to salt efflorescence, the pigments may be dislocated by slow wearing, tearing or blistering of the surface. Paint layer may even flake off by salt efflorescence or sub-efflorescence. Salt decay has been noticed as a major problem in sandstone, causing surface erosion and on the sites situated in coastal areas.

Temperature Variation

Day and night temperature variation (freeze-thaw cycle) causes large flat plates from the rock to flake-off or exfoliate. Sometimes due to these thermal changes, stresses are developed within the rock as a result of differential expansion of its constituents and which ultimately result in the physical breakdown of a rock.

In some cases, an uneven rate of weathering may be observed over a rock-surface. A possible cause of it is that condensation takes place preferentially in small depressions already present on the surface which begin to act as foci for further accelerated weathering and thus the rock initiates self-destruction.

Hydration

Even under controlled temperature and humidity, dimensional changes in a rock can occur on hydration. In some cases, flaking and scaling of paint layer have been reported due to dimensional changes caused by hydration.

The hydration of anhydrite to gypsum develops high pressure causing the cracking and breaking of rock. The hydration of clay also causes significant dimensional change.

Microflora

Rock-paintings are easily affected by lichens, bacteria, fungi, mosses, algae and higher plants. Water and organic acids are produced by some biological species. Most soluble mineral elements are slowly leached away by those acids and a sound and hard rock ultimately converted into soft and weathered clay in due course.

Nitrogen bacteria which produce ammonia, nitrous and nitric acids provide a favourable condition for erosion of rock-paintings.

Oxidation of some sulpher minerals, such as pyrites, may be enhanced by the presence of sulphur producing bacteria. Iron bacteria (Ferrobacillus sp.) and sulphur bacteria (Thiobacillus sp.) promote oxidation of iron and may be potential threat to the colour of earth pigments in a rock–painting.

Iron fixing bacteria (Pseudomonas) are capable to transform iron from its ferric to ferrous state and back according to the humidity conditions and play a role in colour changes in earth pigments.

Several species of fungi are reported to be able to corrode silicates. Algae and lichens make colonies over the rock-surfaces and derive their nutrients directly from the rock and atmosphere. Apart from microflora, vegetal growth and roots of higher plants cause direct destruction of a rock-painting by masking them and developing pressure within the rock respectively.

Microfauna

Microfauna is rather a more serious and great danger to the rock–paintings. Termites, insects, birds and bats, larger animals etc. cause damage to the rock-paintings in various ways.

Some organisms like termites and mud wasps build mud structures over the rock surfaces.

Mudnests built by swallows can cause serious damage and are a significant problem in rock-paintings.

Bird and bat droppings and other organic debris are the possible sources of bacteria which is responsible for sulphur conversion. It may produce sulphuric acid providing corrosive conditions for the paintings. The combined effect of bird and bat droppings and water bleaches the colours.

Larger animals like cattles cause damage by rubbing their bodies on the painted surfaces or stirring up dust. The accumulation of excreta including urea may seriously damage the paintings.

Weathering of Painting

Apart from the damage to the rock support, durability of a rock-painting depends on several other factors like properties of pigments and binder, adherence and coherence of paint etc. On humid surfaces, pigments may easily be washed away or may spread over the surface. Some pigments are hygroscopic in nature and may flake off during alternate wetting and drying and this may result in complete removal of all traces of painting from the surface unless there is some penetration of pigments into rock pores. Under certain conditions, ultraviolet radiation may cause oxidation of mineral pigments. For example, ochres associated with some specific minerals which are susceptible to oxidation may easily be faded.

Silica or silcrete deposits which are often chemically stable, may be formed over the surface and the pigments become embedded within these deposits obscuring the paintings. Grain by grain attrition or dislocation of pigments may take place in presence of salt efflorescence, which is noticed to be a major problem in Indian rock - paintings.

The phenomenon of chromatic alteration of earth pigments may be promoted by the presence of some bacterial species.

Control

Thus we see that the causes of rock-painting decay are often complex, interrelated and not always fully understood. Remedies of some of the major problems are discussed below.

Moisture Control

To avoid dripping or flow of water coming from the rock roof over the painting, drip lines may be constructed. Silicone driplines have been suggested by many experts. Location of driplines position is decided in relation to the shape of rock, mostly the ideal position is at the junction between the vertical and horizontal planes at the outer edge, where water has its maximum vertical flow velocity. Where this position cannot be attained, the dripline can be moved towards horizontal planes. The effect of diverted water should also be considered as it may affect the adjacent rock or paintings.

Construction of gutters and flashings over the rock-top is helpful in protecting the site from direct rain or periodic water flow.

Control of ground water through capillaries is rather a more difficult problem. In some cases, the whole 'site' may be isolated from the internal sources of moisture by drilling or other means. In such cases, sealants and other water-repellent substances may be used at the rock-surface. But on the contrary, if the rock bearing the painting has not been isolated from its hydrological system, use of such substances may even be harmful in many ways like preventing the washing out of salts from the surface. They may accumulate behind the impervious surface and cause extensive spalling.

The third major source of moisture is through condensation, which affects the rock-painting in various ways. The ventilation at the site may be modified, by controlling the surrounding vegetation and a better ventilation will certainly lead to increased evaporation. On the other hand, increased evaporation will enhance crystallization of salts. Hence, all the possible effects of a remedial measure should be taken into account as control of one source may enhance the damage from the other.

Salt Removal

Poultices are commonly used for salt removal from the surfaces. Blotting paper poultices have not been proved to be very satisfactory. It is temporary remedy and it does not remove the source of salts, of course.

Consolidation

Detached parts of painted rock are generally fixed with epoxy resins after complete documentation. Epoxy resins are quite stable but discolour in ultraviolet (UV) radiation, hence they are preferably used on unexposed areas. The essential qualities of a consolidant to be used are good penetration, good adhesion to the rock-components, chemical stability and resistance to moisture, biological attack and UV radiation. The resin must also be clear and colourless.

Some of the commonly used consolidants and water repellents are methyl methacrylate, silicone used products like silicone esters, silanes, acrylics etc. Methyl–methacrylate discolours and becomes brittle after UV exposure and also it is difficult to remove after discolouration. Most of the products form an impervious layer over the rock-surface hence their indiscriminate use is to be avoided.

The use of resins in spots is preferred as glueing the whole area promotes sealing effects.

Mudnest Removal

Mudnest removal programme, once decided must be thorough to check the likelihood of reinfestation. Knives and brushes are generally used for mudnest removal. Where clay is humid, the treatment is added with water and non-ionic detergents. Use of insecticide is not a permanent remedy for rock-art sites. However, dieldrin spray, dichlorovos and chlordane have been reported to be used at several places.

Lichen Control

Lichens play an active role in rock-weathering. Hard scrubbing and non-ionic detergents are in common use to remove any lichen growth on a hard and sound rock. But both are not advisable when the rock is already weathered, fragile and weak as it may cause further damage. In such cases, use of fungicides is recommended. The selection of fungicide depends on the nature of rock and painting, fungal species present and environmental conditions. Ortho-phenyl phenol, ammonium hydroxide, zinc or magnesium flourosilicate are some of the commonly used fungicides although each of them has its side effects.

One must be careful while using o-phenyl phenol although its long-term effect is not yet known. Zinc and magnesium flourosilicate have been noticed to form a hard crust on calcareous rocks which discolours the surface.

Ammonium hydroxide causes discolouration of rocks which contain iron oxide in it and can not be used on rocks and pigments with iron base.

Conclusion

Thus we see that determination of all causes of decay and their interrelated effects is essential before any attempt at conservation is taken up. Each site presents a unique combination of problems which demand proper consideration and interpretation before any step is taken to limit the decay process.

Detailed and complete documentation of the site is always recommended before applying any treatment. One must always try for a reversible treatment, wherever possible.

The major factors of decay like flow of water, vegetal growth etc. must be removed before the chemical treatment.

The management of the site after the conservation is a much more important aspect in rock-art conservation. Vegetal management, installation of driplines, study of behaviour of materials used in conservation require long-term monitoring of the site. Continuous recording of microclimatic data, removal of fire hazards, installation of grills and screens, dust depression measures etc. must also be taken into account.

Apart from that, some public awareness programmes may also be organised. Some important rock-painting sites may be sign-posted.

Research in the direction of study of micro-climatic behaviour of the site may be carried out and accordingly the recommendation from such study may be implemented afterwards.

BIBLIOGRAPHY

Dolanski, J. 1978. 'Silcrete skins, their significance in rock art weathering' in Pearson C. (ed) *Conservation of Rock Art,* 32-36, ICCM, sydney.

Hughes, P.J. 1978. "Weathering in sandstone shelters in the Sydney Basin and the survival of rock art' in Pearson (ed) *Conservation of Rock Art,* 36-42, ICCM, sydney.

__________ Hughes, P.J. and Watchman, A.L. 1983. 'The deterioration, conservation and management of rock sites in Kakadu National Park' in Gillespie D. (ed). *The Rock Art sites of Kakadu National Park,* 37-86, ANPWS, Canberra.

Lewin, S. Z. 1982. 'The mechanism of masonry decay through crystallisation,' in Baer N.S. (ed.) *Conservation of Historic Stone Buildings and Monuments,* 120-144, National Academy Press, New York.

Mathpal, Y, 1978. 'The technique of reproducing rock paintings,' *Bulletin of the Deccan College Research Institute,* Poona, Vol. 37, 68-70.

Naumann, I.D. 1983. 'The biology of mudnesting Hymenoptera (and their associates) and Isoptera in rock shelters in the Kakadu region, N.T., in Gillespie D. (ed.) *The Rock Art Sites in Kakadu National Park,* 127-189, ANPWS, Canberra.

Neumayer, E. 1983. *Prehistric Indian Rock Paintings,* Oxford University Press, 2/11 Ansari Road, Daryaganj New Delhi.

Schaffer, R. J. (1932) 1972. 'The Weathering of Natural Building Stone', *Dept. of Scientific and Industrial Research Special Report No. 18 1932* (Reprint Fascimile, 1972).

Wakankar, V. S. and Brooks R.R.R. 1976. *Stone Age Paintings in India,* D.B. Taraporevala Sons & Co Private Ltd., Bombay.

Webley, D.M., Henderson, M and Taylor, I.F. 1963. The Microbiology of rock and weathered stones,' *Journal of Soil Science,* 14(1), 102-112.

Illicit Trafficking In Indian Antiquities: Problems and Challenges

C.B. Patil and C.B. Misra*

The cultural heritage of India in its grandeur is unique and at the same time diverse in character. This cultural wealth of immense value has been raped, ravaged and depleted by explorers, conquering hordes and the alien colonists, particularly the English. The pre-Independence time was no exception to such plundering; in fact it was more systematic and intense. The same scene continues to be enacted even today in the international art markets of the affluent countries. They lure of Indian objects of artistic, of traditional and antiquarian interest which are much in demand, leads to the adoption of clandestine methods for the plunder and illicit export.

The recent sensational journalistic coup of Peter Watson from London revealing his investigative acumen in penetrating the fort of art smugglers is narrated in the *Sotheby's: Inside Story* (Watson 1997: 109-197; 273-278; also available in the form of video tape) and has been telecast by the BBC as a documentary under *Despatches* programme on its Channel Four. This portrays the present situation vividly. He has shown how regularly and methodically Indian antiquities and art objects are being smuggled out only to surface elsewhere in the world, either in the private collections or in the art markets. At the same time, the alarming increase in the theft, vandalism and illicit trade and traffic of cultural property has become a great threat to our priced heritage demanding immediate attention of the authorities.

The present paper seeks to examine the roots and causes of the issue, the existing legislations, their inadequacies etc. The paper also attempts at suggesting some possible ways and means to tackle this ever increasing menace.

Modus Operandi

Theft and vandalism of antiquities resulting in smuggling and clandestine trade are closely interrelated. Such an operation is always preceded either by blatant robbery/thievery or wanton destruction of cultural property. The next step obviously is to sell them at high price and this in most cases, happens in the international art markets where it fetches a fabulous price. The whole process, however, involves: the source, the local elements, the receiver, the middleman and the final purchaser. The *modus operandi* involves persons of rank, influence and immunity, diplomatic or otherwise. To illustrate we would like to quote Watson who comments on Lot No. 119 put to auction in April 1996 in London by Sotheby's. In reply to Watson's question 'How did you manage that ?' He (the smuggler) 'made dismissive motion with his hand. The diplomatic bag' (Watson 1997: 197).

The unprotected monuments and sites, particularly in remote places of central and north India and the religious institutions (temples) of south India, especially in Tamil Nadu are more prone to such acts. Both, Centrally pro-

*Archaeological Survey of India, New Delhi.

tected and State Government monuments are not immune from such thievery and vandalism. Yet, a little vigilance by the watch and ward staff have kept it low. Museums to have not escaped the long hand of these anti-social elements.

There seems to be no particular preference; anything ranging from sculptures in any media and other objects of plastic art, miniature paintings, illustrated or painted manuscripts or leaves taken out of them, coins and medals, arms and armoury, watches and clocks and jewellery - many of which belong to the notified category of antiquity declared under the Antiquities and Art Treasures Act, 1972 come within the clutches of these persons who mainly operate under the guise of handicraft traders; individuals not excluded.

Some of the examples of the smuggled antiquities and art objects are; Nataraja from Sivapuram, Tamil Nadu (1956); Buddha–head from Government Museum, Mathura, Uttar Pradesh (1961); sawn stucco heads from Nalanda, Bihar (1974); terracotta figure from Bhitargaon, Uttar Pradesh (1982); bronze images from the Archaeological Museum, Nalanda, Bihar (1961-62); Tara from Mahant Ghasidas Memorial Museum, Raipur, Madhya Pradesh; embroidered costumes and a gunpowder receptacle in the form of horn of jade from the Archaeological Museum, Red Fort, Delhi; Amin pillars, Amin, Haryana; and terracotta Yakshi from Tamluk, West Bengal and Yogini from Lokhori, district Banda, Uttar Pradesh (1987). Pink mottled Kushana pillars probably from Central India put to auction recently in 1996 by Sotheby's in London and subsequently withdrawn are the latest in the list.

Genesis of the Antiquarian Laws

The cultural renaissance that began with the establishment of the Asiatick Society in 1784 heralded an era of new found interest in Indology and Indian Archaeology which subsequently paved the way for the genesis of antiquarian laws in the beginning of the nineteenth century. Consequently, a series of legislations were enacted to preserve and protect the cultural wealth of our country both by the constituent States and Central Government. They include; (i) The Bengal Regulation XIX (1810); (ii) The Madras Regulation VII (1817); (iii) The Act XX (1863); (iv) The Indian Treasure-Trove Act (1878); (v) Ancient Monuments Preservation Act (1904); (vi) the Antiquities (Export Control) Act (1947); (vii) The Ancient and Historical Monuments and Archaeological Sites and Remains Act (1951); and (viii) The Ancient Monuments and Archaeological Sites and Remains Act (1958).

A New Act

The inadequacies of the Antiquities (Export Control) Act, 1947when put-into actual operation was inadequate to cope with the alarmingly high incidence of theft and illicit traffic in antiquities. A new comprehensive legislation was felt urgent. Besides, in pursuance of the UNESCO Convention (Paris, 1970) urging the constituent States to adopt preventive measures to safeguard their cultural property was under active consideration. The outcome was 'The Antiquities and Art Treasures Act, 1972' and the 'Rules' thereon framed in 1973. This Act of 1972 replaced the Antiquities (Export Control) Act, 1947.

Since the paper concerns with illicit traffic in antiquities etc. only we will confine ourselves to the revised legislation concerning them. The Antiquities and Art Treasures Act, 1972 (AAT Act, 1972) along with Rules came into force with effect from 5th April, 1976 and deals exclusively with movable cultural property of two broadly different categories - Antiquities and Art Treasures. This Act, has as many as thirty-three sections dealing with the subject and provides for: (i) compulsory registration of notified categories of antiquities; (ii) regulating the export trade in antiquities and art treasures; (iii) prevention of smuggling of, and fraudulent dealings in antiquities; (iv) compulsory acquisition of antiquities and art treasures for preservation in public places; and (v) certain other matters 'connected therewith or incidental or ancillary thereto'.

Global Concern

The international communities are evincing deep concern in the preservation and protection of world's cultural and natural heritage. Consequently, world bodies like UNESCO, ICOM and ICOMS became pivotal in promoting global awareness for the preservation and propagation of cultural heritage. An array of documents of Recommendations and Conventions, with useful guidelines brought out by these bodies amply demonstrate their concern and the immediacy (UNESCO 1985:8-9).

In the present context, however, the document entitled 'Convention on the Means of Prohibiting and Preventing the Illicit Import, Export and Transfer of Ownership of Cultural Property (1970),' has greater relevance as it embodies provisions for the repatriation of cultural property exported illegally.

The General Conference of UNESCO adopted 'Recommendations on the Means of Prohibiting and Preventing the Illicit Export, Import and Transfer of Ownership of Cultural Property' at its 13th Session in Paris on 19th November, 1964. In order to develop the principles and standards set forth in this 'Recommendations' and to make them binding on the State Parties these 'Recommendations' were adopted later as 'Convention on the Means of Prohibiting and Preventing the Illicit Export, Import and Transfer of Ownership of Cultural Property' at its 16th Session, Paris on 14th November, 1970 (UNESCO 1985 : 57-73; Sarkar 1981: 189-198). The Convention came into force with effect from 24th April, 1972. Although India ratified this Convention on 24th January 1977, most of the countries are yet to ratify this Convention.

This historic document has as many as twenty-six 'Articles' dealing with the subject. The importance of this Convention, however, is the provision it has for repatriation of cultural property exported illegally. The request by the State parties for such repatriation has to be made under Article 7 (b) (ii) of the Convention (UNESCO 1985 : 65; Sarkar 1981: 193).

India's concern in the international scenario will be incomplete without a reference to repatriation of the cultural wealth that has been taken out clandestinely. India is urging fellow countries to dispense with free flow of cultural heritage and also pursuing various problems connected thereof, particularly the repatriation of stolen/illegally exported cultural wealth through the international for a and conventions viz; (i) restrictions on the liberalised import policy towards illegally exported cultural property; (ii) ratification of the of 1970 UNESCO Convention, which most of the countries have not done as yet–a major hurdle in the restitution process; (iii) encourage bilateral agreements as they impose obligations on States in view of the expensive and time consuming Court litigations in retrieving the heritage; (iv) proper verification of the antecedents of the objects like stolen/exported illegally before they are acquired by the individuals and museums or put to auction/sale by the auction houses; and (v) the compensation to be paid to 'an innocent purchaser' or 'to a person who has valid title to the property'.

In spite of these constraints, some of the art objects have been retrieved. The significant ones are; (i) sawn stucco heads from Nalanda, Bihar (UK and France, 1976); (ii) Nataraja of Chola period from Sivapuram, Tamil Nadu (USA, 1986); (iii) terracotta Yakashi of Tamluk, West Bengal (UK, 1986); (iv) Nataraja of Chola period from Tiruvilakkudi, Tamil Nadu (USA, 1986); (v) Nataraja of Chola period from Pathur, Tamil Nadu (UK, 1991); (vi) terracotta figures from Bhitargaon, Uttar Pradesh (USA, 1991); and (vii) Amin pillars, Amin, Haryana (UK, 1979-80). The details of these have been given in the appendix.

Problems and Solutions

While implementing the AAT Act, 1972 and the Rules framed thereon, we observed several shortcomings which had been and are being exploited by the illegal traders and smugglers of antiquities and art treasures. To obviate such a situation some suggestions are being made in the following pages.

To begin with, the inadequacies to be tackled are: (i) the term 'Antiquity' defined in the Act includes only certain notified categories of objects. There is an urgent need to make the definition of antiquity broad-based and artifacts recovered from marine expeditions etc. should also be brought within its ambit. Items like arms and armour, seals and sealings, Jewellery, coins and textiles etc. also need to be registered.

(ii) The production of replica of an antiquity in the same size, material and fabric is not prohibited. This lacuna has greatly facilitated replacement of several original objects with replicas. The originals went out and the replicas took their place (Joshi and Ramachandran 1980:298). Countries like Pakistan and Iraq have already enacted regulatory restrictions on production of replicas of antiquities (Sarkar 1981: 75). It is high time India also imposed such restrictions.

(iii) The Act is silent on the import of antiquities in the country. Regulatory provisions regarding imports of antiquities deserve our due attention since India is a signatory to the UNESCO Convention of 1970.

(iv) Provisions for issue of 'Non-Antiquity Certificate' (NAC) for export should be regulated in such way that the objects once presented for obtaining 'NAC' to a particular Advisory Committee of Archaeological Survey of India (ASI) is not allowed to be re-presented before any other Advisory Committee of the ASI without mentioning the fact and along with the earlier committee's observations. To have an effective control over this malafide practice, the decision of one Advisory Committee should be circulated among other such Committees.

(v) The clandestine trade of antiquities is also carried out through misdeclaration of items in the export consignments like 'handicrafts' etc. The Customs Department can be motivated to make suitable amendments to their 'Rules and Regulations' and any laxity be dealt with firmly by imposing heavy penalties so that the menace of misdeclaration can be done away with.

(vi) There should be adequate provision in the Act so that no transfer of ownership of a registered antiquity is effected in favour of foreign nationals particularly who come as tourist, as the existing provisions in the Act are silent on this vital issue.

(vii) The Archaeological Survey of India is the custodian of the cultural wealth of the country and the Director General, is the prime regulatory authority of the Act. But after obtaining necessary authorization, the investigating agencies do not keep him informed about the progress of the cases from time to time. These agencies should maintain a close liason with the Director General during prosecution of the law breakers. They should also take his concurrence before finally closing the cases where further investigations is not possible and this should made mandatory. Suitable amendments are therefore, required to be made in the Act so as ensure adherence of above mentioned procedures.

(viii) The penal provisions in the Act are too mild to deter the bad elements violating the Act. The provision of heavy penalties/longer period of imprisonment etc. would be an effective deterrant.

(ix) Individuals and the licensed dealers found guilty of violating antiquarian legislations should be listed and circulated globally. Besides, denying visas to them for travel abroad since their involvement in the illegal export and arranging sale of antiquities cannot be ruled out, would be another hurdle in their nefanious activity .

(x) In the event of theft of cultural property, the look-out notices deserve a global circulation, instead of merely circulating them in India so that the museums, Art-auctioneers, and the purchasers outside India are aware of the stolen property and desist from acquiring them.

Under the prevailing conditions, the task of ensuring safety and security of our cultural heritage against vandalism and illicit traffic has become a fairly perplexing issue. It requires a multi-pronged strategy to erase this menace, a major challenge before the present generation. It would be contextually relevant to advert to some of them:

(i) Human factor is fairly vital so far as safeguarding the nation's heritage is concerned. There is hardly any substitute to the active participation of masses in preserving our heritage. People are still ignorant about their own invaluable heritage, not speak of the legislations. The poor and innocent villagers have been enticed in helping the educated thieves in their illicit operations, obviously without knowing the irreparable loss being perpetrated by them. Secondly people do not come forward to register antiquities they possess because of the apprehension that the Government will acquire these once they are registered. The need of the hour is public awareness - to educate people by instilling in them a sense of love and pride for their cultural heritage and to make them understand the importance of the legislations in preserving our heritage for posterity.

(ii) India being a grand repository of rich cultural patrimony, the vestiges of the bygone ages can be seen strewn all over the country. Except for the monuments under the protection and control of the Central and State Governments, no serious attempts so far have been made, to document and to prepare an inventory of these relics of the past which are neither under the protection of the

Central or State Governments, lying uncared for in remote villages, thick forests and hilly tracts which also incidentally are the open gold mines for idol lifters and smugglers. A time, therefore, has come to photo-document besides preparing an inventory of this cultural wealth of loose and scattered sculptures, architectural fragments apart from the dilapidated monuments/structures. Such inventories will be of immense help in establishing the titles to lost cultural property and their retrieval.

(iii) As a corollary to the photo-documentation, the creation of sculpture-sheds and museums in rural and urban areas would further strengthen the efforts in safeguarding the scattered archaeological wealth in a specified area which can easily form the nucleus for a future museum there. However, rare and outstanding antiquities from these sculpture-sheds should be transported to museums in the urban and district centres till adequate security arrangements are made in the rural areas. The village Panchayats in the rural areas and at the urban level the corporate bodies like Muncipal Corporations, District Authorities, if not the voluntary organisations, should be entrusted with this task and should be made accountable to the appropriate authorities.

(iv) Paucity of adequate funds, trained, personnel, vigilant watch and ward, latest equipment and safety devices are the other factors giving impetus to the illicit trade in cultural wealth.

Establishment of the 'National Cultural Fund' by the Government of India is a welcome step in this direction. The availability of sufficient funds will enable strengthen ing infrastructural set up besides providing a viable solution to the arising problems on account of fund crunch.

(v) ASI is the prime regulatory authority so far as the antiquarian laws are concerned. But it does not have a legal cell of its own. The constitution of legal cell in the ASI will augment the organisation particularly the court litigations pending in various Hon'ble Courts within the country as well as abroad more efficiently and also to pursue the cases of retrieval of cultural property back to India.

(vi) The incentives and rewards for persons giving information concerning cultural heritage and antiquarian offenses should also be considered as in the case of other investigating agencies like the Directorate of Revenue Intelligence and Customs Department who have this kind of provisions.

(vii) The retrieval of cultural property is yet another serious problem, It has several constraints and deserves a global thinking. No doubt Article 7(b) (ii) of the UNESCO Convention of 1970 has provision for repatriation of cultural property exported illegally. It has, however, certain drawbacks like paying compensation to the owner of the object. Added to this, non-ratification of the above referred Convention by most of the countries, absence of restrictions on the import of cultural property of other countries, lack of uniformity in the definition of antiquity and cultural heritage etc. add to our woes Moreover, court litigations are too expensive and time consuming. In view of the above constraints, bilateral agreements appear to be more viable for restitution of cultural heritage. These bilateral agreements are the legal bindings which impose obligations on the nations and, therefore, must be encouraged.

Yet, disputes may arise while negotiating either through the bilateral agreements or other arrangements like Article 7(b) (ii) of UNESCO Convention, 1970. In such circumstances, the retrieval cases may be taken care of by International Court of Justice preferably by a Special Bench to be constituted for the purpose, instead of knocking the doors of the Hon'ble Courts in the respective countries.

(viii) The definition of the term 'Antiquity' has been found lacking precision and varies from country to country. A widely acceptable definition should be worked out by member countries. In case, this is not possible the definition of the country of origin should be honoured by the other member country while negotiating the retrieval issues.

The aspiration for heralding a new era, absolutely free of clandestine dealing in the cultural patrimony will merely be a dream till active public participation with a firm commitment of denouncing shady dealings in antiquarian wealth reinforced with effective regulations do not become a reality.

APPENDIX

Nataraja, Sivapuram: This famous bronze image of early Chola period, originally found as Treasure Trove along with five other images in 1951 and kept in the Siva temple at Sivapuram, district Thanjavur, Tamil Nadu was replaced by a **replica** when it was sent for repairs in 1956. After changing several hands and varied costs, the image finally, reached the private collection of Mr. Norton Simon, Los Angeles, USA on a foreign airliner through Palam Airport, Delhi (1969) who purchased it for one million American dollars from Mr. Ben Heller in 1973.

Douglas Barrett of British Museum, London pointed out that the genuine image of Nataraja is in the private collection whereas the one in the temple is a fake (Sarkar 1981:56: Barrett 1965 : 32). Meanwhile, the image brought to England for some repairs was seized by the Scotland Yard, on the request of Indian authorities as a stolen property.

After a prolonged Court litigations in England and USA between the Union of India and Mr. Norton, a compromise was reached. Although the title of the image was awarded to India in 1976, the actual restitution , however, could take place only after ten years in 1986 as per the agreement reached.

Terracotta Yakshi, Tamluk: An example of retrieval made through out-of-court settlement is this Yakshi. A find from the excavations (1954-55) from Tamluk, district Midnapore, West Bengal, this terracotta plaque was brought to Delhi in 1961 during the Centenary Celebration of the ASI. It, however, disappeared under mysterious circumstances only to surface in London in 1982 when this plaque was offered for sale to the British Museum, London by Mr. Alastair Scott of Sussex and his associate Mr. A. M. T. Versheyle, London. A Court case was instituted in London for its retrieval. While the case was in progress, an out of court settlement was reached between India and Fine Arts Consultants, London and the Yakshi was returned to India in 1986.

Nataraja, Tiruvilakkudi: The bronze image of Nataraja, was sold in 1979 under a deliberate false declaration by Mr. Bina Khulasi and Albert Amran of Everest Art Gallery, London to Kimbell Art Museum, USA. The image was actually stolen in 1978 from the Isvara temple, Tiruvilakkudi, district Thanjavur, Tamil Nadu. Suspecting the image to be stolen object, the Director of the Museum himself contacted the Indian Authorities at Washington to know its antecedents. The Government of India with the help of Interpol took up the case with the Museum authorities. After prolonged negotiations, the Museum agreed to return the idol when the compromise was reached in 1985 between the Government of India and the Museum. The image come back in 1986 to India.

Stucco heads, Nalanda : An example of both vandalism and illicit traffic (subsequently retrieved) are the sawn heads of the stucco images from Temple 3 at Nalanda, Bihar. Stolen in 1974, one head from London and another found in France from the collection of Krishna Robound have since been retrieved in 1986.

Amin pillars, Amin: The sculptured pillars datable to second century B.C. from the Thakurji temple, on the banks of Suraj-Kund, Amin, Haryana were smuggled out of India in 1967 by replacing the originals with **replicas** which surfaced in London. These pillars have since been returned and are exhibited in the National Museum, New Delhi.

Nataraja, Pathur: Discovered at Pathur, district Thanjavur, Tamil Nadu in 1976, the bronze image of Nataraja surfaced mysteriously in England in 1977. It was seized from the British Museum, London where it was sent for cleaning by the Bumper Development Corporation. Thereafter, a Court case was feild for its retrieval. The title was awarded in favour of India by the London High Court in 1988. But an appeal was again made in the Royal Court of Justice by the Bumper Development Corporation which was subsequently dismissed and the image of Nataraja was restituted back to India in 1991.

REFERENCES

Barrett, Douglas, 1965. *Early Cola Bronzes,* Bombay, Bhulabhai Memorial Institute.

Joshi, M.C. and Ramachandran, K.S., 1980. 'The Problem of Imitations of Antiquities' in Dwivedi, V.P. (ed.), *Museums and Museology: New Horizons* (Essays in Honour of Dr. Grace Morley On Her 80th Birthday),. Agam Kala Prakashan Delhi.

Sarkar, H., 1981. *Museums and Protection of Monuments and Antiquities in India,* Delhi. Sundeep Prakashan.

Sarma, I.K., 1992., Convention on the Means of Prohibiting and Preventing the Illicit Import, Export and Transfer of Ownership of Cultural Property- Country Report: India. Paper Presented at the Regional Workshop, Jamtien, Thailand, 24-28 May, 1992.

UNESCO, 1985. *Conventions and Recommendations of Unesco concerning the protection of the cultural heritage* (Reprinted and Updated), Paris, UNESCO.

Watson, Peter, 1997. *Sotheby's: Inside Story,* London, Bloomsbury. Chapters 'Men from Bombay' and 'Epilogue : The Arrest ' are devoted exclusively of India.

Birth of Civilization: Indian view point

BHAGWAN SINGH*

Childe's hypothesis of Agricultural Revolution and dissemination of agricultural technology throughout the world from the nuclear area of western Asia enjoyed undisputed acceptance for a few decades. Discovery of numerous areas, where agricultural activity started using indigenous sources and local genius, forced the scholars to revise that hypothesis. It was now realized that plant domestication, sedentism and systematic farming were evolutionary in nature rather than revolutionary. Hegemonic role of the Fertile Crescent, thus, suffered a set back. Ameliorating Holocene conditions and oases as early centres no longer remained crucial factors.

Recently, this thesis has also been modified by scholars not only to revive Childe's hypothesis but also to accommodate the biblical lores, although, not exactly bringing Adam and Eve and the Tower of Babel at the centre of discussion[1].

The hypothesis of spontaneous evolution of farming in different areas without any impetus from outside is based, mainly on temporal and spatial distance between the centres. Some of them evolved in a state of ideal isolation, such as the one in the New World. Application of totally different technologies including domestication of different plants is also an important factor. These reasons are strong enough to uphold the hypothesis of spontaneous evolution in favourable conditions. Innovative geniuses with leadership quality could motivate and introduce production technologies independent of any impetus from anywhere.

But at the same time we must not forget that sharing of experiences promises greater and quicker advances, whereas total dependence on local genius has serious limitations. Another factor that deserves serious consideration is that all the groups living in the same vicinity are not motivated alike and all the information passing from one community to the other is not complete information. Transfer of partial information plays the same role in creativity as forgetting in case of acquired knowledge. Many a thing is created just by way of unsuccessful recall of forgotten bits. Again, informations are not always passed directly or synchronically. Even lessons stored in ones own tradition or storage systems are quite often forgotten for centuries and they need a genius to rediscover and use them profitably after many set backs. So not denying the role of local factors it may be conceded that propagation of ideas has played a vital role in popularisation of and improvisations in agricultural technologies.

We must not forget that development of farming "called for scientific understanding of natural phenomena, development of tools and skill, clear idea of the right season for sowing various crops, i.e. elements of astronomy, correct method of storage and preservation of grains from insects, right type of grains for seed, domestication, control, training and use of draft animals, water management, fertilization, tool-kit for weeding out, reaping, thrashing, grinding, pounding and invention of methods of cooking and processing including fabrication of pottery. There should not be, therefore, much to grudge against the modified hypothesis of punctuated evolution

* 136, Maha Rana Pratap Enclave, Delhi.

amounting to a chain of small revolutions. Evolutionary process has neither been smooth nor uniform, otherwise there would be perpetual reproduction but no evolution.

But pronounced bias in favour of preferred theology, mythology and race, in which African Homo Sapiens Sapiens or Modern Man is humbled down to Anatomically Modern Man, and is elevated to Behaviourally Modern Man once it reaches the Biblical area and races straight to Europe to replace Neanderthals, appears to be the result of chronological, biological and geographical compromises. There ought to be sufficient hard data to conclude that African contribution in shaping the Modern Man was limited to the 'hardware', with Levant offering the 'software.'

Moreover, South Asia, as an independent nuclear area, is apparently ignored despite archaeological support in its favour in recent decades, "Large scale cultivation which deserves to be called 'farming' was rather rare development, which came about independently perhaps only in three regions of the world — the nuclear regions of western Asia, eastern Asia, and central Americas."[2] Recent developments in South Asian archaeology are too well known to be summarized here. We may therefore conclude that the entire region from India to Europe is seen, in this scheme, as part of the west Asian nuclear area, which is not an impossibility if, at all, we come across something more clinching than the multilinear evidence suggesting South Asia to be the real nuclear zone in propagation of farming, horticulture and animal husbandry.

India is located in between two nuclear areas. It could have inherited from both — plantation of banana, coconut and sugarcane from South East Asia[3], and wheat and barley from west Asia, if at all. It has its own unique inventory richer than both. It includes domestication of rice and a range of summer crops, pulses and oilseeds. This makes its position all the more complex than ordinarily admitted. If at all it had some link with plant exploiting west Asians and East Asians at the pristine level, it was geographically placed at the centre of an interaction that was far deeper in time and more intricate in nature. If it was itself an independent nuclear zone, which it definitely was, with its own inventory of plants and technical innovations, there is some likelihood that it might have influenced the two areas in their breadth and width and depth while benefiting from their innovations. The problem of agricultural evolution and, in fact, the entire edifice of evolution of civilization, is very complex. It should not be seen in continuity with the nascent stage of evolution of hominids. Much stirring has taken place in-between. Likewise gathering, howsoever improvised, must not be seen as a direct forerunner of productive technology. Even ants and rats and squirrels practice gathering while monkeys do not. There is strong reason to hold that gathering and gathering-techniques have a very long history. So much of the past is lost to us that it is ridiculous to hold too fast to the few specimen that have survived the broomstick of Time. Nautufian sites(15,000 b.p.) have great value for us, but they are not the oldest sites. In Papua-guinea we have evidence of human endeavour in development of productive techniques, going back to 30,000 b.p or still earlier[4].

Propagation of agriculture has definitely been responsible for transfer of languages. At least those who sincerely believe in transfer of language with the spread of agriculture ought to have looked for a nuclear area within the Indo-European 'world'. This could have made the problem simpler for them.

South Asia has its linguistic and cutural air roots spreading on the one hand up to Melanesia and on the other up to the frontiers of Europe. Attempt to make the Fertile Crescent [the]habitat of Indo-European speakers[5] has failed[6]. Attempt[] to establish connection between Finno-Ugrian and Dravidian[7] rest[]s on slender evidence. It calls for better explanation than the one offerred. Splinters fly off from the block rather than otherwise. European origin of Munda on the basis of still smaller number of Austric terms scattered in some languages is simply Eurocentric[8]. It can again be better explained by a journey in the reverse direction and that too not as a mass-migration but as a low-pressure contact of abiding nature. Indo-Aryan, we have been taught to accept, stormed into India with [the] barbaric hordes. They came with their cattle and horses and lo! the war-chariots, across the heights that even salmon could not negotiate. Vedic literature did not support it. Commonsense can not uphold it. Archaeology and ethnology became an object of ridicule for their failure to offer even a single evidence in favour of the Aryan race or invasion of India[9]. To be plain, there is no proof of any en-masse movement of

Aryan, Dravidian or Austric speakers from west to east but there is abundant direct and collateral proof to the contrary.

India has preserved a tenable account of cultural advancements right from gathering and hunting stage. It is preserved in numerous mediums - language, ritual, vesture, sacrificial practice, lores and narratives in numerous texts - Vedas, Brâhmanas, Puânas and texts of other religious schools. Confirmation from multiple sources of any development lends greater weight to the accounts encoded in mythical and allegorical language.

The oldest written record, the Rgveda, which belongs to a very late stage, shows that the people inhabiting India were interacting across linguistic boundaries from an early stage. Sanskrit enjoying superiority over others, had assimilated so much of the other dialects that we can hardly affix a family tag to a large number of terms. Even grammatical features are shared by them. Only bulk of synonyms even for basic terms, such as *jala,* nîra, paya, udaka, ambu, wari, pîtu, sara, apa, osa, sina, etc. for water, which run into hundreds, are a clear reminder as to the number of dialects that could have been spoken flow off from the block rather than otherwise. European origin of Munda on the basis of still smaller number of Austric terms scattered in some languages in South Asia at the hunting-gathering stage. All those dialects could not be genetically explained as members of the three families. Familial identity seems to have developed with merger of these into certain blocks due to geographical proximity, use of the dominant one among them for social institutions, religion, trade, and administration, etc. What we call PIA is Aryan not in racial or linguistic terms, but in cultural terms alone. It is a synthesis of many dialects from which alienation of Dravidian or Austric may be a butchers job, not of a good linguist. A large number of terms deemed to be Indo-Aryan are South Asian but not Aryan alone. It is due to its assimitative compulsions and dissipative obligations that Indo-Aryan emerged as the most powerful of them all and spread over a vast area under their cultural dominance. It is because of the Indo-European obsession that linguists talk of borrowings from Austric and Dravidian into Sanskrit[10]. Terms which could not reach other Indo-European areas but were found in Dravidian or Austric were deemed to be borrowings from these languages. But if we start from India, we may find even Austric terms in Indo-European branches[11]. It is because of the same dynamics that we have a number of identifiable 'Dravidian' terms in European languages.

Merger of numerous dialects into the hegemonic language, is reflected in a high percent of terms which defy familial boundaries on the one hand, and on the other, in variant phonemes such as *g/j/y > gam/jam/yam/gma/jma* with no change in meaning. We have the largest number of phonemes in Sanskrit so as to encompass almost all the sounds available in all the Indian dialects.

The real problem, how the barbarian Aryans gave high-culture terms, civil institutions, civic sense and civil and penal laws to the 'civilized non-Aryans' was never faced. Contribution of the 'civilized non-Aryans' to Aryans, according to the prevailing theory, was limited to a small number of terms related to paltry things mostly onomatopoeic in nature, such as *gurram, kurkura, dardura,* and witchcraft, phallus worship and homicidal *tantra.* Even a passing comparison could bring down the entire edifice of Indo-European and its inroad into non Aryan South Asia.

An interesting point to be noted is that prior to discovery of Harappan civilization, linguists, on the basis of social and linguistic evidence, believed that the Brahui people appear to have migrated from peninsular India[12]. In those days it was also suggested that "Dravidans came from the same region as that of Aryan and almost at the same time"[13]. It was only to deprive the Vedic people of the authorship of Harappan civilization that the tone and timbre changed and the music continues *ad nauseum.*

In clothing we have people claiming Aryan legacy, living in jungles and hills[14], naked or nominally clad. Some of them used mauñjñ or a thick rope of *muñja* as girdle around their loin to cover them, others wore *ajin* or goat/deer skin. We have 'historical' accounts that earlier man moved naked and only later thought of covering his body. By the time we reach Indo-European stage he was wearing linen clothes but even this evidence was distorted in favour of conjectural sewn dress[16].

In sacrificial history there are clear indications of human sacrifice[17]. It was followed by animal sacrifice shifting from the bigger to smaller one. Ultimately animal made of corn flour was symbolically sacrificed as a substitute of fivefold animals[18].

In conjugal history we find accounts of the wild stage when no morality was attached to sexual bahaviour. Women of a group enjoyed complete freedom like birds and beasts[19]. This was followed by a stage when couples lived together with an amount of permissiveness. Finally strong bonds of fidelity was imposed on the female[20], although no such obligation was imposed on man.

Their technique to produce fire by churning is confined to tropical world, but not confined to Aryanised section alone. Marriage in Dhanuk tribe of eastern UP, can not be ceremonised unless the bridegroom produces fire by churning, even if it takes the entire night to churn. This shows not only the antiquity but also the sanctity and cultural depth of sacrificial fire.

We may go on elaborating these developments reflected in Vedic and Puranic history and in some cases surviving in fossilized instituions. These developments throw light on the gradual progress in every sphere of life right from the hunting-gathering stage. They also reflect the ambience in which these developments took place. Indo-European practices and institutions are known to us. They reflect the final point of this history. These developments are pre-Indo-European, systematically preserved only in India. They are crucial in determination of the nature and home of 'Indo-Europeans'.

The collective memory of South Asia goes down to unfathomable depths of time. It has no memory of these people coming from outside. It has, on the contrary, crucial bits to decisively prove that they rose to higher stages of development in the same surrounding in which they composed their immortal poetry handed down to us. The birds that they had intimate association with are cakravâk[24](Anas Casarca) suka[22] (parrot), sârikà (ropanâkâ, that is, *Turdus Salica), sakunta*[24] (crow), *kapota*[25] (dove), *hansa*[26] (swan), *mayûra*[27] (peacock), *syena,* i.e, *garutmân* (eagle, vulture) which are deeply integrated in Indian social aesthetics both high and low. The beasts that they tamed (elephant), domesticated or attempted to tame (lion, monkey, bear, snake) or tamed with little results (antelope) are all culturally and aesthetically part of higher and lower traditions.

Man at his gathering stage collected such ripe fruit that could be dried and kept for longer period. Dry fruit may be a good indicator of the natural habitat of a people. It appears that *pîpala* (Ficus Religiosa), *udumbara* (Ficus Glomerata), *plâksa* (Ficus Infectoria) and *nyagrodha* (Ficus Indica) were the only source of dry fruit to them. That was one of the reasons why these plants enjoyed special status in Indian culture. It is often repeated in the Brahmanas that udumbara is highly envigorating. There was a school namely *paippIâda,* having fancy for *pîpala* fruit[29]. They valued *parna* (Butea Frondosa) perhaps for its leaf which could be stitched to make a plate, so valuable during the prepottery days. Such plates are still in great demand, specially on the occasion of ceremonial feasts. Other plants which enjoyed favour included pine (*pîtadâru, devadaru,* as source of timber), *sisso* and *khadira* as wood for axle and hub of their wheels), bamboo for roofing and birch (*bhûrjapatra* for its bark used as paper). Some of the plants that were found in the countries of their visit were named by them after them in case they had some resemblance with them: pine, birch (< bhûrja), poplar *(<pîpala),* tremulus (adj to poplar< *asvattha,* a case of semantic transfer).

Animal domestication by the Indo-Aryans (by which we mean Indo-Aryan speakers) started with *aja,* goat, and *avi,* sheep[32]. *Avi* - sheep, literally meant 'the protected one'. It appears that they killed the male goat for meat as it produced nothing but avoided killing the male sheep as well as it produced wool and hence this appellation. It leads us back to Mehrgarh IA when cattle, buffalo and ass had not been domesticated.

Gathering-hunting was being practiced not only from ten or twenty thousand years b.p. It was there for hundreds of thousand years. The Asuras stuck to this practice and as it has been repeated time and again, both the Devas and Asuras were indistinct ethnically. Their society was composed of the same composite stock due to a prolonged period of neighbourly contact, intermingling and inter-breeding[33]. Their distinction rested on their ways of life and value systems. Because of this difference, perpetuation of one threatened the very existence of the other. It led to bloody fights for millennia. The tension survives even today when encroachment on tribal wood lands by the civilized section forces them constantly to shrink and withdraw. It creates resentment and greater dislike for civilized sections and slows the pace of change among them.

According to our sources, man had divided the land (hills, valleys, forests and plains) right at the gathering stage[34]. Gathering and hunting was practiced by all and so except territorial transgressions there was little occasion for dispute. Raising plants so long it did not disturb the ecology was encouraged. The tribes that collected rice and other summer grains started plantation of wild rice shoots in order to have better yield over a larger area at a very early stage of plant domestication. Wild rice — tinnî dhâna[35] — is as yet collected from shallow ponds, lakes and low lying areas, and used as non-cereal diet on days of 'fasting'. Rice plantation in waterlogged areas created no problem. It called for simple uprooting of shoots from an area where it grew wild in density and planting it with the help of simplest sticks, even with naked hands. They collected *syâmâka* (*Pancicum Frumentaceum*) as well[36]. We have no definite information regarding other plants, but the two figure in a time depth and technological primacy that it may safely be said that collection and domestication went smoothly with hunting-gathering. For example, course black rice was offered to Nirriti. The husk of rice was pealed off with the help of nail at later stage as well for ritual purposes as a survival of the old practice. This definitely refers to a stage when mortar had not been invented as we find in the Rgveda. It must be pointed out that according to our sources the Devas had come to their 'present' abode not from the west but east[37]. This is also borne out by the grains used in ritual offerings. Except Varuna barly is not offered to the old deities. They are offered some or the other variety of rice, millet, *gavedhuka*, etc. mostly from gathering stage.

The trouble started when they wanted to undertake agriculture on an extensive basis, *i.e.*, to stretch or expand the sacrifice. Now they were under obligation to clear the forests by burning. It had many serious implications. It was unethical to ruin the same trees and plants that had been their source of sustenance. Secondly, there was an amount of uncertainty as to the success of agriculture. Thirdly, it was labour intensive, while gathering was equal to reaping exercise in the entire chain of agricultural operations. Agriculture, according to our sources, was not a choice, but a compulsion. This situation arose after a prolonged spell of aridity when natural resources had exhausted.

In mythical language the earth, during that period of anarchy, concealed all the grains within itself[38]. King Prthu, progeny of Vena (Sun) threatened the earth but it ran in fright in the guise of a cow. Ultimately earth submitted and agreed to release all the corns in the form of milk provided

Prthu arranged for a calf and levelled the uneven earth. Manu had become a calf in this milking exercise.[39] Obviously, this is too simplified a version of a very complex development.

What we know from other accounts, initially, gods themselves started tilling[40]. They cleared the earth of bushes and shrubs with the help of fire. These gods were the first farmers and the users of fire in production technology. They discovered the secret of fire in the course of metallurgy. Thus developed the great divide among the the sons of the soil which rang through the entire history.[41] We may only point out that this contention centred around agriculture and other advances in the course of time. The Asuras refused to advance beyond gathering and hunting. They protested at every step the gradual encroachment of peasantry over their land but were defeated, earlier when they were powerful and far outnumbered the Devas, through the tricks played on them by the Devas, and later because of organised strength of the Devas or the Aryans. It is notable that the institution of state and kingship arose initially to thwart the designs of the hunter-gatherers, Vrtras[42].

The Vedic sources admit that at the out set they were so tormented by the Asura that they had to run from one area to the other.[43] The measures adopted by hunter-gtherers to dislodge the farmers was to plunder their crops when the same were not fully ripe, to lift their animals. Where the Devas were suspected of burning the woodlands[44], they attacked and killed them. The legend that Sîtâ the goddess of furrow was born out of the pitcher filled with the blood of Brâhmans which had been buried under the soil, which rose to annihilate them, tells volumes about the initial sacrifices of the pioneers. The Asuras are normally shown as roaming in forests, *vanargû,* ferocious *ghora* and *ghoracaksu,* disturbing the sacrifices *dhvarasa*[45] eating raw flesh *kravyâda, pisâca,* no social bonds, no culture, who become a threat with the fall of night. The obsessive fear of the Devas, that is

Aryans from the Asuras may be somewhat exaggerated but not totally false. They are also shown enjoying the protection of their haughty chiefs who openly challenge the Aryans and violate them in every conceivable manner. It shows the strength of and the threat posed by the hunters-gatherers. But lower mode of production could hardly withstand the onslaught of the higher one. The were ultimately defeated by Devas not by arms[46] but by gradual burning of the forest land, i.e. *mahâhavi*[47] and through agricultural production, i.e. the *sakamedha*[48], i.e,. Agriculture guaranteed them nourishing diet and freedom from sickness and malnutrition[49]. This distinction between physical suppression and virtual victory is very important.

The solution sought by the Aryans to live and prosper enjoying their peace was to clear larger tract of forest and bushland than they could cultivate. There was a vast tract of buffer land left as pasture so that the wild tribes and animals could not directly attack their crops and homestead. The Aryans used this land for grazing their own animals.They organised on a bigger scale and faced them jointly. Thus, they claim, arose the institution of state and kingship in order to thwart the *Vrtras* with the first solid foundation of farming. This entailed some contractual obligations on the part of the people. It is thus that Manu who produced *Ilâ,* the fertile land, got infatuated with her and violated her virginity. It is thus that Manu become the pioneer farmer, the first king and the first lawgiver at the same time.

A section of Hunter-gatherers that had been displaced from their natural habitat because of the encroachment by the Aryans had to join their work force or *dâsapravarga.* The Aryans, to ensure greater safety and peaceful life, also tried to motivate them to switchover to animal husbandry and farming. This they called extension of sacrifice, *yajña vistâra*[50] *or yajña tanvan*[51] This extension was partly aggressive and partly pursuasive. Even in epics, the princes who defeat the troublesome Asuras do not usurp their territory, but hand it over to the one from among them who has adopted the new value system. Thus started a spate of land reclamation in new areas and introduction of civilized way of life in societies which had remained at hunting-hathering stage.

But in between the initial experiments in agriculture and consolidation of farming as primary source of sustenance, there is a long gap in which numerous trials and errors are reported in the Vedic tradition. It involved initial uncertainties in determining the correct season for sowing[52], which could be solved only after developing elementary astronomy, i.e., minute observation of the cycle of some of the planets and changes in position of the mansions of stars. The hunter-gatherers had not to worry about it. Even simple insights, such as preservation of seed from moths and fleas took its own time. They mixed ash with the grains to preserve the seed.[53] It also involved humbling, controlling and using the animals for traction, which took a long time.[54] It is reported that earlier they yoked cows but it was soon found that they could not bear the stress. Later they evolved technique of castration and control of calves, to humble them to be used as draft animals.

The boldest assertion of this Aryanization program and its salutary results is found in the Rgveda, defining the *ârya-vrata* or the resolve to promote and propagate civilized way of life.[55] This was a continuing campaign, the first of its kind. It continued throughout the period of and area of their dominance with necessary changes according to the level of culture at the time and place.

This plan, as we read from this verse, included:

(i) Propagation of language and philosophy of life including belief system *(brahma).* Presence of Indo-Aryan to the froniers of Asia, in fact, through the entire Indo-European expanse along with mythology, rituals whose purity and lucidity fades the farther we go from the Sarasvati valley in whatever direction is a veritable proof of this claim.

(ii) Animal husbandry which basicaly altered the use of domesticated animals *(gam-asvam).* They were just a source of meat to the herders in other areas. Now animals were domesticated primarily for extraction of milk and other dairy products. Only those animals which did not yield milk (such as *starî/vasâ, vrsa/ûksana, châga,* i.e. a barren or sterile cow, bull, a male goat) were killed for meat. Dependence on milk products reduced the number of animals needed for supporting a family as disproportionately large number of animals were killed in the countries bereft of Aryan impact. This balanced sense of economy introduced a change in man-animal relationship and laid the foundation for use of animals in agricultural and non-agricultural operations. This may partly explain why vegetarianism became such a powerful movement in India alone.[56]

(iii) Farming and understandably, skills and crafts related to farming *(osadhih).*

(iv) Horticulture - gardening, floriculture, planting vegetables and fruit plants and creepers (vanaspatîn)[57].

(v) Search of new lands where earth was plain and farming manageable *(prthivîm).*

(vi) Exploration of mountaneous areas, understandably, for minerals *(parvatân).*

(vi) New sources and courses of water including the sacrificial device for causing rain *(apah).*

They were naturally proud of their being liberally charitable *(sudânavah)* as they have spread civilization across the world as the Sun rising in the sky illuminates the world.

This assertion occurs in Book X, which is supposed to be modern. This is not the only verse to suggest such a venture. There are many more. Take from the same Book X three verses in Griffiths rendering:

"They strode through all the regions with victorious might, establishing the old immeasurable laws....

"In two ways have the sons established in his place the Asura who finds the light; by the third act.

"As fathers they have set their heritage on earth, their offspring as a thread continuously spread out.

"As in a ship through billows, so through regions of air through all toils and troubles.

"Hath Brhaduktha brought his seeds with glory, and placed it here and in the realms beyond us." (*RV*.X.56.5-7)[58].

This rendering is jittery, as Griffith fails to grasp the context following Sayana. They have treated the departure of the son of Brihadukth to the farthest stations where his agents and men are settled as departure to the sphere of the Sun, or heaven. They could not imagine the spread of 'Aryans' in distant countries which in their allegorical language was their paradise, as very explicitly mentioned in Atharvaveda III.15 and discussed by us.[59] They failed to take note of generations of gradual migrations and solid work done by the forefathers of the Vedic folk in those countries. This limitation is understandable. But why did they fail to note that the deity or *devatâ* of funerary hymns is Yama, not *visvedevâs* who mostly include minor deities or deified entities such as mountain, ocean, rivers, forests, winds, *maruts, asvins,* rainclouds, thunderstorms, plants, nights and day, cows, the ordinary men i.e *puñca janás,* whose displeasure or disturbance could make their journey perilous and as such they specially pray that they may remain munificent. In many of the hymns addressed to the *visvedevâs* hints of onward or return journey are very clear[60]. Griffith did not bother to think how any one could take pride in the death of his son, how could he boast of having established his seed or progeny in yonder lands. He hurridly translates *rajas* as region of air, forgetting that the term has been used in unmistakable earthly contexts, *parthivam rajas*[61].

The reason why Brhaduktha is said to have travelled to the inaccessible and distant corners of the world' safely, *pradisas prthivyâs svastibhs atidurgâni visvâs* as if making a journey in a ship through seas around the earth is that he stationed his men *(prajâ)* in substantial numer *(prâsâryant purudh prajâ anu)* at those centres in yonder lands inhabited by other tribes *(paresu)* in fortified or enclosed settlements *(âvaresu adadhus. âvaresu adad dhât).* In our previous publications, we had submitted that the fortified settlements on hills in Kurgan setting might be Indian settlers who made all arrangements to safeguard them from local population whose standard of life was incomparably low and culture distinct. The verses above, specially the fifth of the hymn, refers to their settlement in areas which had not been scaled earlier - *pûrvâ dhâmâni amitâ mimânâ.* The fortified settlements supposed to be Aryan in Dashly Culture may be also explained by 6th and 7th verses. The original Old-Indo-Aryan being in all semblances the oldest among all the branches of Indo-European, we may allow the latter to be synonymous with the OIA and its European branches to have branched off from its terminal centres.

The Iranian[62], Latvian[63], and Sumerian sources concede that civilizing impulse reached there, ready made, from east and in former cases from South Asia. They could not make as deep an impact in Sumeria as we find in case of the other two. Scholars have not been able to identify Sumerians. It would be a mockery to identify them as South Asians. At the best we may talk of a small number visiting that area with elements of an advanced culture and absorbed by the local people who benefited from their contact and whose tradition thankfully remembered this debt.

The Kurgan people represent a complex rather than a people or a culture. But even so, Gimbutas, one of the advocates of Kurgan Culture as the representative PIE culture concedes that agriculture was introduced in that area by a new element coming from the East.[64] It this area which was responsible for spread of agriculture in Europe.[65]

Within a short period of time agriculture is introduced over a large area according to sensibilities of the people and physical conditions, exploiting local resources and skills, in the entire area where Sanskrit was spoken or its locally coloured languages are spoken.

As far *asva* is concerned, according to our source it was not horse at the initial stages, but ass[66]. It was imported from Rann of Kutch through Indus and used for transportation. Only later the Aryans came to know of fine breed of horse which they trained and sold in the world market. There is no dispute regarding introduction of horse through the Indo-Aryans as all the terms regarding horse and wheel at early stages are found to be Indo-Aryan, not even Indo-Iranian. No such credit is given to them for domestication and propagation of the ass. It is likely that ass was also introduced by them earlier than generally believed, i.e. at the initial stages of international trade link. At least Indian tradition emphatically makes such a claim.[67]

Cattle domestication, propagation and deification of cow points to South Asia. We know that due to exacting climate of Iraq, cattle stock deteriorated very shortly despite the fact that grain was added to their feed. Babylonians, therefore, imported fine breed of bulls[68] from northern Iran to improve their cattle breed. But northern Iran and southern Central Asia (Bactria-Margiana Complex) was not known for its cattle wealth. Its favourite animal was camel. A flourishing trade in cattle in India is reported from all available sources. So much so that cattle enjoyed parity with currency. Even though silver, gold, understandably in chips, precious and semi precious stones, copper etc., were freely in use and grain yield was high, anything could be bought in exchange of a cow. The Rigvedic verses refer to cattle being carried through roads in hundreds and thousands to some destinations.[69] Avestan verses refer to cattle having come tired from journey and implore for offering them water and fodder[70] which is not applicable in case of cattle having returned from grazing land. In India the Yadavas or Yadus are specifically mentioned for their fabulous animal wealth.[71] Animal trade route leading from Gujarat to Babylonia *via* northern Iran can be traced without much difficulty. Presence of typical Kutchi bulls on Harappan seals is unmistakable. The same or slightly more hallow attached to cattle is found in Avesta that is found in the Vedic tradition right from the Rgveda. Despite the deification of cow in Rgveda, people ate beef as evident from the appeal to shun killing of cows.[72] Only later complete ban on beef eating could be imposed. In Avesta we find the final stage of complete ban. If we reverse the course taboo>beef eating< taboo can not be explained.

A comparison with west Asian cultural horizon with South Asian scene corroborates the claim of the poets in greater depth. We may cite Shaffer and Lichtenstein on the subject:

"Another factor at Mehrgarh suggesting indigenous development of food production in the pattern of domestic animal utilisation. At the close of the ceramic neolithic, or period II, after ca. 45,000 B.C. domestic cattle accounted for 60% of the animal remains. Although the frequencies of cattle bones in the later chalcolithic and bronze age periods of Mehrgarh never equalled period II varying between 35-40% (Meadow 1991; Jarrige and Meadow 1992:167), they remained much higher than in adjacent Southwest Asian regions (Caloi et al. 1977; Meadow 1986; 1987; Zeder 1991) and, at contemporary and culturally related Indus Valley sites, cattle frequencies ranged as high as 70+% (Possehl and Raval 1989; 172-176). Although similar species were domesticated elsewhere, the pattern in which human actors arranged them in South Asia was distinctive to the region...

"Moreover, available chronologies (Moore 1985) indicate Mehrgarh with comparable southwest Asian phenomena which, combined with the absence of contemporary food producing groups on the Iranian Plateau, argues against diffusion expansion".

"...In comparison with sheep and goats, cattle have larger and less versatile pasturage requirements, cannot range as far away from water, mature and reproduce more slowly and require a greater labour investment. On the other hand these factors are compensated for by a greater quantity of dairy and non-dairy secondary products and by their use for traction(Dahl and Hjort 1976; Russel 1988; Zeder 1991). Given these circumstances, a preference for cattle, after 5000 B.C., undoubtedly influenced other social, economic and political relationships, and suggests that cultural developments in South Asia did not simply parallel those in Southwest Asia, where groups did not have a comparable bias".[73]

In a word South Asian economy was cattle intensive from the fifth millennium B.C. but those who notes incidence of cattle in the Rgveda failed to check the Mature and Early Harappan archaeology. Obsessed as they were with pastoral image they failed to take note that intensive agriculture with cattle as draft animal is attested from the earliest verses of the Rgveda handed down to us.

The misgiving regarding primitive level of farming by the Aryans was complementary to the pastoral fixations. As mentioned earlier, pastoral contexts are almost absent despite rich cattle wealth. Right from Mehrgarh South Asia excelled in food production. Shaffer and Lichtenstein note:

"The numerous and substantial mud brick "granaries" built by the close of Period IIA at Mehrgarh, in the first half of the 5th millennium B.C., suggests a concern, unparalleled in contemporary cultures, for surplus production, irrespective of what was stored in them"[74].

These granaries *(ûrdara)* are specifically mentioned in the Rgveda[75] and prominently present both at Mohenjodaro and Harappa. cartloads of foodgrain was reportedly transported from farmyard to the owner's house which was sufficient to feed thousands[76].

A large number of rivers, lakes and, according to some, even Caspian Sea is named after the river and personal names already known in South Asia.

We, therefore, find that the claim of the Vedic Aryans to be harbingers of horticulture, agriculture and animal husbandry is vindicated beyond reproof. In animal husbandry their effectual contribution was extraction of milk and milk products that provided a source of protein But the stage at which we meet them in the Rgveda was far advanced. Contrary to the general opinion, Rgveda is the document of an urban society, showing only marginal interest in agriculture and animal husbandry although village economy primarily depended on the latter ones. Cattle figure frequently in the Rgveda. Their number in a group is also large, but only in similies does it refer to cowmen and rarely to pasture.[77] In fact, as we find in *RV.*VIII.46.30 there is unmistakable reference to castrated bullocks whose setting and proper use needs no elaboration. In IX.15.4 and IV.2.18 again a pack bullock is chosen for simile. In V.2.4 the poet likens the forest fire to the herd of bullocks moving in the field. In case of cattle given in charity as in *RV.* 1.81.7; VIII.4.20 the setting is urban, because no herder or farmer can give such a large number of cattle to anyone. The bull, *vrsabha,* is an epithet of heaven, *dyausa,* or Lord Indra, who cause rain to fertilize the earth, Fire god, and occasionally of other deities - Soma, Brahmanaspati, Rudra, etc. Hardly ever does it refer to steers, and there too, it is found harnessed in carts or carrying load.

On the basis of close study of the text we have come

to the conclusion that Rgveda is a Harappan document. Its old portion covers the Sârasvat stage of Sarasvati-Indus civilization and the late portion belongs to Indus phase.[78] Aryans were in contact with foreign countries both through land route and sea route during the Sârsvat phase as well but this contact strengthens and acquires a hegemonic role during Indus phase and started shrinking and withdrawing with the ultimate death of Sarasvati. This aspect has not been understood. Scholars appear confused about its implications and, as such, they try to build a case in favour of Aryan advance exactly from the same posts and same areas which clearly bear the Harappan stamp and therefore evinces interchangeability of Harappan and Vedic civilizations. Writes Erdosy:

"As must be evident from the foregoing, we are a long way from fully correlating the linguistic and the archaeological evidence. We, may, however, note the existence of an extensive interaction network linking Central Asia and South Asia from the middle of the 3rd millennium B.C. onwards. It was initiated by the Harappans' demand for mineral resources such as lapis and tin, but maintained even after the end of the Integration Era on the Indus. Along the route of this network circulated not only raw materials, but also a rich repertoire of artefacts frequently associated with the disposal of the dead and rituals which came to be adopted by ethnic groups speaking Indo-Iranian languages. That some of this interaction entailed the movement of peoples has been shown by Hibert and Lamber-Karlovsky in their study of burials; consequently, the last centuries of the 3rd and the first centuries of 2nd millennium B.C. represents the best archaeological dating for the entry of Indo-Aryan languages into the borderland of South Asia."[79]

It is easy to see how the very spread to and withdrawal from the business centres in the borderland and Central Asia is reversed to show the advance of Indo-Aryans towards India. It is because of disturbed perspective of scholars who still think that the Vedic society was pastoral and therefore had nothing to do with the Harappans. Vedic scholarship has suffered a set back both in India and outside. Translations of texts were done at a time when scholars had to grope in the darkness, for there was no material culture to give them a right perspective. This was the reason that most of their renderings are incoherent. The fun of it is that the same people have been shown, some times in the same hymn, as being robbed of their wealth and indulging in raid as well, by translators. For example we may take the first verse of hymn 103 of Book X which Griffith translated as:

"For thee may Indra boldly speed the car that woıks on either side. Favour us, much invoked! in this most glorious fight against the raiders of our wealth".

and the second verse as:

"Loose in the wind the woman's robe was streaming what time she won a car-load worth a thousand,

The charioteer in fight was Mudgalani: the Indra's dart, heaped up the prize of battle".

The reason is that striving to prove the 'Aryans' a war-loving horde, they rendered all the synonyms of profit and gain as booty; all preparations for trade and mining operations as war preparations; all the terms for caravan as army and all conflicts with robbers and thieves as war. They are therefore quite at odd with their own renderings. They try to create an impression that incoherent although is their rendering, they have made their best efforts to create an order out of chaos, adding notes, explanations and comments from Sâyana and/or other interpreters. They might have done their best, but we simply do our worst by following them blindfold. Whatever be their compulsions, in fact, they have created a chaos out of order. Intrinsic analysis of the text is itself sufficient to straighten the twisted cord and a correction of perspective can make more than eighty percent disoriented renderings coherent and consistent. We may cite one example from Sâyana to show how lack of historical perspective makes his rendering absurd. Griffith is equally incomprehensible although not beingsatisfied with Sâyana he takes simple meaning of many a word. The verse in question is:

देवास आयन परशूँरबिभ्रन वना वृश्चन्तो अभि विड्भिरायन् ।

नि सुद्वं दधतो वक्षणासु यत्रा कृपीटमनु तद्दहन्ति ॥

RV. X. 28.8

This verse refers to commercial exploitation of timber in consonance with clearing of a woodland and reclamation of land for agricultural use. It is highly significant as it provides information about the technique of transportation of timber through rivers as well. Sâyana could hardly reconcile to the debasing idea of felling of trees and transportation of timber by gods. He therefore renders *parasûn* (axes) as thunderbolt *(vajrân), vanâ/vanâni* (woodland) as rain-clouds *(vrstilaksanânyudakâni), vrscantah* (cutting, felling) as cleaving the clouds *(meghâñschindantah), sudrvam* (easily floatable) as rain-water *(sobhana dravanam vrstyudakam), krpîtam* (twigs and outgrowths) as water *(nigûdhamudakam),* and *dahanti* (they burn) as they make it dry for flow of water *(udakanirgamanârtham sosayanti),* and we have an incongruous rendering of the verse. The reason is that in each case, except one, *vaksanâsu,* as rivers *(nadîssu),* he ignores the plain meaning of the terms to give a perspective at the cost of consistency.

Griffith renders it as, "The Deities approached, they carried axes; splitting the wood they came with their attendants. They laid good timber in the fire-receivers, and burnt the grass where they found it growing," which is equally inconsistent. He is as confused as *Sâyana* and tries to read it in sacrificial context, twisting the meaning of *vaksanâsu,* rivers, to suit it as 'fire-receiver'. He mellowed the act of cutting to splitting. He did not bother to accommodate `burnt the grass where they found it growing' in this context.

For a correct interpretation plain meaning of the words had to be taken. The verse had to be read in the light of *RV.* X.146.3 in which carriage of timber by bullock-carts *(ut gâva...sakatîriva sarjati)* from forest is referred to, and *RV.* X.155.3, in which unmanned timber floating through the river down-stream, where it had to be harnessed, is referred to. There are numerous verses relating to clearing of earth by burning shrubs and woodlands for farming.[80]

Now we may safely infer that the gods reached forest with their axe wielding workforce for cutting the trees to reclaim the land on a 'big' scale. This operation was conducted in the summer. The trunks of the trees were carried to the dry bed of the river and were properly tied to form a float. With the onset of rain the float was tucked down the swelling river. The branches of the trees and shrubs and grasses growing there were burnt to clear the land. As we know, there was a thriving trade in timber with the gulf countries in olden days.

The operation of clearing shrubs and woodlands figures in numerous verses in the Rgveda and is explained in the *Brâhmanas* as the past act of Devas who made the earth fertile, *ûrjasvatî,* irrigated, *payasvatî,* high-yielding, *susûma* and fit for settled habitation, *susadya.* According to them the same is dutifully followed by men. But due to his personal bias Griffith ignores agricultural aspect and stretches it to fit a war ignoring even Sâyana. where he is definitely more sensible.[81]

Coming to archaeological aspect we find Harappan stations like Manda and Ropar actively engaged in timber trade.

We find that the Aryans do not represent the elite, *i.e.* that section alone which was owner of the land.[82] During the Rigvedic times the elite section was primarily engaged in trade and mining. In social context, at times, it broadly covered the three upper castes.[83] The common man was covered under the term *pañca krstis*[84] and *visa*[85], *praja*[86], and *jana*[87]. Internal relations among the Aryans were not smooth[88]. Apart from the *krstis,* the general working class including the artisans, there were domestic servants or bonded labourers, covered under *dâsa pravarga*[89]. As the proper name *Dâsvesa*[90] suggests, the domestic servants were clad differently. Occasionally Indra punished the *vrtrâs, dâsâs* and *aryâs* perhaps to protect the suffering masses, for otherwise he could not be the good protector in the same verses[91]. In other words we come across a complex society with internal tensions and external threats. The idyllic picture of Aryan society projected under colonial compulsions must change, if we want to understand the text and the society in question.

We do not find the Aryans wandering with animals through grazing grounds. They proceed from a home to a set destination through roads and water courses. In other words we come across traffic and transport in which asses, bullocks, camels, horses, wagons *sakatî* carts, *anas,* chariots, *ratha,* cabs, *sthûrî* and occasionally even load-bearers, *bhârabhrtas* are put to service. They are busy in navigation with boats and floats of all descriptions from stream-worthy to sea-worthy ones — *dronî, taranî, plava, daââritrâ satâritrâ, samudriyâ, trivandhura, trivrta, vataramha, syenpatâ,.*

The text refers to extremely dark roads, *atidhvasan patha*[92], unobscured roads, *adhvasmân patha*[93], open routes, *atûrta patha*[94], underground passage or a passage leading through a tunnel, *antas patha*[95], entry or approach routes, *âpatha*[96], deviant paths, *vipatha*[97], alternate paths, *anupatha*[98], direct or straight paths, *rjupatha*[99], toilsome paths, *vrjina patha*[100], roads leading to a distant place, *prapatha*[101], grand trunk roads *mahaspatha*[102], water-logged roads, *vârna patha*[103], proper *routeâ s,dhistha patha*[104], safe route, right course, *supatha*[105], illuminated roads, *jyotismân patha*[106], comfortable roads, *rajistha patha*[107], dust-free roads, *arenu patha*[108], roads leading to a large number of important stations, *sahasrayâma patha*[109], troublefree and convenient roads, *suga anrksara pantha*[110], tracks leading to the same destination, *sadhrîcînâpathyâ*[111], trunk routes, *pathaspatha*[112], rugged roads, *asama adhvâ*[113], suggestively *daksinâpatha* or road leading to southern countries, *padâdaksinâ*[114], descending tracks, *avayâna*[115], chariot-worthy roads, *niyâna*[116], *vartanî*[117], *vartma*[118] and points from where roads offshoot in all directions *visûcî*[119], etc.

They are not war loving. They prayed that they might not come across the brigands in the course of their journey[120]. Even so they had their encounters with them[121]. Mostly they did succeed. This was possible only when they outnumbered the robbers. They, therefore, moved in caravans. We have frequent references to *srenîs,* caravans[122].

Because of this threat as well as market compulsions, there was an element of urgency in their movements. A large number of terms signifying urgency are attested in the Rgveda, such as perpetual, *ajasra*[123], unobstructed *ajira*[124], quick/fast[125]; *ksipra*[126], *trsvî*[127], *juva*[128], *jîra*[129], *tûya*[130], *prâsu*[131]; *turpharî*[132], *tripala*[133], *maksû*[134], *bhuranâ*[135]; *syenajûta*[136] with the speed of an eagle, proceeding at the speed of sight, *aksnayâvânah*[137], moving by or at the speed of wind, *vâtaramhâ*[138], proceeding at the speed of mind, *manojuva*[139], *dhîjavana*[140], etc.

The distance covered by them in a single trip was very large. Even if we discount the abstract distances mentioned earlier, a hymn narrates the anxiety of the relatives at home whose members had gone on some such mission but had not returned by the expected time while others had come back. They implore, "Let not Rasâ, Anitabhâ, Kubhâ, Krumu, or Sindhu hold you back. Let not the watery Sarayû obstruct your way. May everything be auspicious for us.[141]" Enumeration of the rivers, here, is from west to east, because of the return journey. Obviously, they had travelled as far as Afghanistan, if not beyond. This in not the only hymn of its type. Quite natural that we frequently come across terms like dûre, pâre, parâvatasya pâre, parâvati, parâke, parvatsya prsthe, sânau *adhi*, besides allegorical expressions of *diva, antara, antariksa.*

Once the erroneous notion in these respects are corrected, the entire problem shall become transparent.

How hegemonic Harappan civilization was can hardly be judged unless we look at it with reference of the dominance of its language, Indo-European. But we have submitted our observations on that aspect in our book[142], so we may skip it here. Here we may only emphasize that it was invention of wheel that gave the Aryans absolute control over their contenders[143], not excluding the Assyrians who, because of their tough competition and fight for market control, were dubbed Asuras by the Aryans and the name stuck to them. The Aryan horse[144] trampled the Assyrians and the wheel packed them up.

Conclusion

There is no evidence in our knowledge from any discipline to discount the claims made on the basis of the textual material available to us. All the evidence from the length and breadth of Harappan contact area which delimits the Indo-Aryan linguistic zone in and outside South Asia which appear discordant in any other scheme of things and puzzle the specialists match with the rare perfection of torn bits of single hole once we approach the problem from this angle. Even puzzles of the Indo-European 'world', which, includes Indo-Aryan influence zone via secondary centres as well, dissolve like salt in water.

There is clear evidence from Mehrgarh itself that some sort of interaction with Central Asia had started right from the inception of Neolithic period in South Asia. We may therefore have some justification to claim that sedentism, farming and proto-urban developments along the approach roads got some inspiration at every stage from South Asia.

Mehrgarh is a submontane station and despite its long life, its position, habitational pattern, a few unique finds - ivory, pipal motif, storage bins - point to the mainland. The missing link responsible for the chain extending on the one hand to the sea (sea shells) and on the other to central Asia (Turquoise) was in Sarasvati valley for nò other area satisfies all the conditions. Our source vindicates it.

Mature Harappan sites, such as Mohenjodaro, start as Mature with all the characteristic features including urban planning and foundation with a construction of high mudbrick platforms whose scale and proportion upsets us by its magnitude. There is no other area promising such developments and high investment. Those who migrated to Indus sites had obviously suffered the ruination's of heavy floods and had found the old home perilous as well as uneconomical.

NOTES AND REFERENCES

1. Sherratt, A. 1997 Climatic cycles and behavioural revolution : the emergence of modern humans and the beginning of farming, *Antiquity* 71:271-87.

2. Ibid

3. "...The evidence of botanists that many important garden plants are of New Guinea origin, e.g. sugarcane, pansanuts, breadfruit, probably one of the bananas, perhaps coconut, possiblly the swmp taro and many tree crops, strengthen these hint (Reinhardt, 1985, p.91)." Josephine M. Flood, Australia and New Guinea in the period of Homo Sapiens sapiens, *History of Humanity*, Vol 1, 1992, 276-289

4. Flood, J. 1996 Culture in early aboriginal Australia, *Cambridge Archaeological Journal*, Vol. 6, No. 1, April 1996, 3-36.

5. Renfrew, C. 1987 *Archaeology and Language.* (London)

6. Mallory, J.P. 1989 *In Search of the Indo-Europeans.* London.

7. Annamalai, 1968 *Collected Papers . . Dravidian Linguistics.*

8. Dyen, Insidore 1970 Background 'Noise' or 'Evidence' in comparative linguistics: the case of the Austronesian-Indo-European hypothesis. In George Cardona, Henry M.Hoeningswald and Alfred Senn, eds., *Indo-European and Indo-Europeans.*, Philadelphia: 431-440.

9. Kennedy, K.A.R. 1995 Have the Aryans been identified in the prehistoric records of South Asia? Biological anthropology and concepts of ancient races. In George Erdosy, *The Indo-Aryans of Ancient South Asia,* Berlin, New York, 12-66.

10. Linguistic position in India is so complex that terms like godhûma can be better derived from a general term for *kot*, *water, *food, Hindi(H) *kodo*, a coarse summer grain closer to syâmâka, H. goda-fig, Skt. *gud*, to enjoy, Tamil (T) kodi, Kannad(K) *godi*, Toda kodja, Skt. godhûma, Persian *gandum*, wheat.

Likewise pana, pani, is traced back to Munda in which 20 cowries= 1/4 pana, 80 cowries = one pana. *Bengali pan/pon* -one anna = 4 piece= 80 *cowries*. S.K.Chatterji takimg a hint from Trikandasesa III.3.206 in which Skt. pana has the same value as pân in Santali, i.e. 80 coweries, suggests that the term and the value might have Mundari origin (*Chatterji, S.K. Introduction to P.C. Bagchi and S.K.Chatterji, op.cit*). We are not as accommodative as Dr. Chatterji is. The data appears to be contrived. The term Pani has been associated with Parnians, the tribes suggested to be inhabiting northern Afghanistan (Hillebrandt, *The Vedic Mythology*, II, 1981. New Delhi, 159). If we want to decide the direction of the flow of linguistic impulse it is easy to see it trekking from south-east to north-west: *ko*> *kodo*> *kodi*> *goda*> guda> *godhûma*> *gandum: pân/pon* >*pana*>*Pani*>*Parnians*.

We may add to it mythological currents: *ahi*>*azi*, *Vritra*/vrtrâni> *vrtraghna*/ *vrtrahan* > Iranian *Verethraghna; Dasa*> *Dahae; Deva*> *Daevas (for semantic shift, see B. Singh, 1995, 82)*; *Asuras* >Ahura >*Assur*>*Assyrians.*

11. It may be pointed out that a scholar working on Pre-Aryan and pre-Dravidian elements in Sanskrit, came to the conclusion that the terms having 'ing' and 'ang' as a particle are Austric. He concluded that *linga, lângûla, lângala,* Kalinga, Trilinga, etc., are Austric.(Przyluski, in Bagchi, P.C., and S.K.Chatterji, *op.cit.*} But looking at the *ing* and *ang* as one of the strongest components in English we may reconsider the issue.

12. "It is equally possible that they (the Brahuis) have come to their present locality in a comparatively recent epoch (cf. Denys Bray, *Census of India*, 1911, Vol. IV, Baluchistan, p. 168 sq.) as a result of the movement of the same kind and perhaps due to the same causes which have brought the Oraons and the Malers of Dekhan to Chota-Nagpur or the nomad tribes of Dekhan studied by Prof. Sten Konow in Vol. XI of the *Linguistic Survey* to all over Northern India (the first of the two groups speak Dravidian language and Prof. Konow is inclined to attribute a Dravidian origin to the second also J. As. 1923, I,p. 135). The Brahuis of to-day are not sedentary, they go out of their country for temporary immigration and for forays and even for true migrations ...Dravidian Brahui is connected with Kanara, Kurukh, and Malto (the last two are spoken by Oraon and Maler mentioned above." Bloch, J. Sanskrit and Dravidian. In Bagchi and Chatterji, *op.cit.*

13. *Ibid*, 42.

14. *Vâyupurâna* 20.8

15. *Satapatha Brahmana* III.1.2.13.17

16. "In the warmer climates of Iran and India, the old Indo-European dress became considerably modified. The sewn coat or tunic as well as breeches fell in disuse among the Aryans in India". (Chatterji, S.K. 1968, *Balts and Aryans in their Indo-European Background,* Simla, 98). It is interesting that Chatterji has not brought Spartan dress which was exactly like the Indian one into this discussion. Cf. Schrader, Otto 1972 [1890] Prehistoric Antiquities of the Aryan peoples. Tr, Frank Byron Jevons. Delhi, 336. While one is discussing survivals in Indian tradition, an eye on the time depth must always be kept open. We have many survivals reaching back to the last Ice Age.

17. "At first, namely, the gods offered up a man as the victim. When he was offered up, the sacrificial essence went out of him. It entered into the horse. They offered up the horse....They offered up the ox....They offered up the sheep....They offered up the goat. When it was offered up, the sacrificial essence went out of it. It entered into this earth. They searched for it, by digging. They found it (in the shape of) those two (substances), the rice and barley...When it (the rice cake) still consists of rice-meal, it is the hair. When he pours water on it, it becomes skin. When he mixes it, it becomes flesh. ...When it is baked, it becomes bone. ... And when he is about to take it off (the fire) and sprinkles it with butter, he changes it into marrow. This is the completeness which they call 'the fivefold animal sacrifice.' The fact that man was offered up in sacrifice is borne out by the Sunah Sepa episode also, which is accounted in the Rgveda (I.24.12; 13; V.2.7) and the epics (Râmâyana I.61 and 62). In one of the tribes in Orisa, human victim (*mariya*) was sacrificed to ferilize the earth till the past century.

18. RV. X.9; I.24.12; V.2.7; S.B. I.3.2.1; 2.3.6-7.

अनावृता किल पुरा स्त्रियः आसन् वरानने ।
कामचारविहारिणयः स्वतन्त्राश्चारुलोचने ॥
तासां व्युच्चरमाणानां कौमारात्सुभगे पतीन् ।
नाधर्मोऽभूद्वरारोहे स हि धर्मः पुराभवत् ॥
तं चैत धर्म पौराणं तिर्सम्योनिगताः पूजाः ।
अद्याप्यनुविधीयन्ते कामद्वेषविवर्जिताः ।
पुराणदृकृटोधर्मोऽयं पूज्यते च महर्षिभिः ॥ *Mahâbhârat*, I.113.4-6

20. ऋतावृतौ राजपुत्रि स्त्रिया भर्ता यतव्रते ।
नातिवर्तव्य इत्येवं धर्म धर्मविदो विदुः ।
शेषेष्वन्येषु कालेषु स्वातन्त्र्यं स्त्री किलार्हति ।
धर्ममेतं जनाः सन्तः पुराणं परिचक्षते । *ibid*, 25, 26.

21. *RV.* II.39.2. The couple birds figure regularly inVedic literature, epics, folklores and written poems.

22. *RV.* I.50.12

24. *ibid.*

25. *RV.* II.42; 43.

26. *RV.* I.30.4; X.165.1-4.

27. *RV.* I.65.5;124.9; 163.10; .III.8.9; 53.10; IV.40.9; IX.32.3

RV. I.191.14; III.45.1; VIII.1.25.

28. I.118.4; 4; 140.9; 154.46; IV.6.10; : VIII.20.10; X.149.3.

29. S.B. V.2.1.23, etc.

30. The term *pippala* literally means nourishing food as evident from *RV.* VII.101.5. In verses like अश्वत्थे वो निषदनं पर्णे वो वसतिस्कृता ।... *RV.* X.97.5, fig tree is said to be the home and Parna tree to be the mansion of cultivable plants which again suggests that the fruit of these plants was used in the season and off the season for sustenance. The same is inferred from *RV.* I.135.8 and *RV.* VI.47.24 as well.

31. Singh, B. 1987 *Harappa Sabhyta aur Vaidic Sâhitya;* 2 Vols, New Delhi; 1995 *The Vedic Harappans,* New Delhi; 1997. *Parivahan keâdima carana meñ gadhe aur ghode, in Bharat taba se aba taka, Delhi.*

32. Singh, B. 1995, *The Vedic Harappans,* 115-16;

33. देवाश्च वाऽअसुराश्च । उभये प्राचापत्या... *Satapatha Brahmana* V.1.1.1. पदेवाश्च वा असुराश्च प्रजापतेर्द्वया: पुत्रा: आसन् । *Tandya Brahmana XVIII.1.2.*

34. "The gods and the Asuras, both of them sprang from Prajapati, were contending for superiority. Then the Gods were worsted, and the Asuras thought :'To us alone assuredly belongs this world!' They thereupon said, 'Well let us divide this world between us; and having divided it, let us subsist thereon!' They accordingly set about dividing it with ox-hides from west to east. *Satapatha Brahmana* I.2.5.1-2 SBES Vol XII, 59.

35. एतद्वै देवानां परमान्नं यन्नीवारा: । *Tattiriya Brahmana* I.3.6.8; See also *S.B.* V.1.4.14; 3.3.5-5

36. Syâmâkas among plants doubtless are most manifestly Soma's own. *S.B.* V.3.3.4

37. From the east, indeed,the gods came westwards to the men..." *S.B.* II.6.1.11.

38. अयरश्रके नृपश्रेष्ठ धरित्रया सकलौषधी: ।
ग्रस्तास्तत: क्षयं यान्ति प्रजा: सर्वा प्रजेश्वर । *Visnu Purâna* I.3.67.

39. V.P. 78-88.

40. Even in the Rgveda VII.101.5 cultivated plants are said to be protected by gods, सुपिप्पला ओषधीर्दिवागोपा: ।

41. Singh. B. 1987, II 52-108

42. *RV*, X,124.8

43. *S.B.* III6.1.27;

44. *S.B. III.6.3.12*

45. *See also* S.B. VII.4.137.

46. *S.B. I.5.4.6*

47. *S.B.II.5.4.1;6.1.1;2.1*

48. *S.B.* II.6.4.1

49. *S.B.* V.2.4.2-3

50. आपथयो विपथयो अन्तस्पथा अनुपथा: । एतेभिर्मह्यां नामभि यज्ञ विस्तार ओहते । V.52.2.

51. यज्ञं तन्वाना उषिजो न मन्म । *R.V.* VII. 102; तं त्वामज्मेषु वाजिनं नत्वाना अग्ने अध्वरम् । VIII. 43.20; यानि स्थानान्यसृजन्त धीरा यज्ञं तन्वानास्तपसाभ्यपश्यम् । VIII.59.6(*khila* 11).

52. ...for even while the foremost (of the Asuras, i.e. Devas) were still ploughing and sowing, those behind them (the Asuras) were already engaged in reaping and thrashing: indeed even without tilling the plants ripened forthwith for them. *Satapatha Brahmana* 1.6.1.3. The episode runs from 1-8. SBES XII. 155-157. Emphsized words are ours.

53. *S.B.* VI.7.4.14; 8.2.1

54. In the Rgveda castrated, *vadhri* such as castrated horse *vadhryasva,* castrated bull *vadhrivrsa* and castrated (coward) ones *vadhris,* of imperfect speech, *vadhrivaâca,* occur quite frequently.

55. ब्रह्म गामश्वं जनयन्त ओषभी: वनस्पतीन पृथिवी पर्वतौं: अप: ।
सूर्य दिवि रोहयन्त: सुदानव आर्या वता विसृजन्तो अधि क्षमि ॥ *RV.* X.65.11

56. It was neither Pârsvanâtha, Mahavîra, Buddha who introduced non-violence. It was already there in the Vedic value system. Jarrige, J.F. (1994 The Indus Civilization and the civilization of ancient India. "South Asian conference, Madison, 5th Nov.

1994b "Recent Discoveries at Nausharo, a third millennium site of Baluchistan, Pakistan." The World Archaeological Congress-3, Dec. 4-11. Delhi), very sensibly traces its roots right from Mehrgarh down to Mughal period. Lord Mahavîra and Buddha simply changed the emphasis and there too not very prudently. The Vedic approach was utilitarian, theirs was spiritualistic.

57. Man has been plucking fruit and flowers and tubers from gathering days but selective plantation and nursing of plants is a very late phenomenon. Even maintenance of vineyards and apple orchards coincides with the buoyant phase of Aryanization.

58. सहोभिर्विश्वं परिचक्रमू रज: पूर्वाधामान्यमिता मिमाना: ।
तनूषु विश्वा भुवना नि येमिरे प्रासारयन्त् पुरुष प्रजा अनु ॥
द्विधा सूनवोऽसुरं स्वर्विदं आस्थापयन्त तृतीयेण कर्मणा ॥
आवरेष्वदधुस्त्न्तुमात्तम् ॥

नावा न क्षोद: प्रदिश: पृथिव्या: स्वस्तिभिरति दुर्गाणि विश्वा ।
स्वां प्रजां बृहदुक्थो महित्वा ऽऽवरेष्वदधादा परेषु ॥ *RV.*X56.5-7

59. Singh. B. 1995, 262-63.

60. आ नो भद्रा क्रतव: यन्तु विश्वत: अदब्धासो अपरीतास उदभिद: ।
अग्निजिह्वा मनव: सूरचक्षस: विश्वे नो देवा अवसा गमन्निहा । *RVI89.7*
ऋजुनीती नो परुणो मित्रो नयतु विद्वान् । अर्यमा देवै: सजोषा: । *RV.I90I*
ते अस्मभ्यं शर्म यंसन्नमृता मर्तेभ्य: । बाधमाना अपद्विष: । *RV.I90.3*

61. मधु नक्तमुषषो मधुमत पार्थिवं रज: । मधु द्यौरस्तु न: पिता । *RV.I.90.7*

62. It is Yama - Djamasîd who taught "fabrication of weapons, saddles, briddles, other tools and implements, spinning and weaving of silk, linnen and cotton, the whole national economy, quarrying and masoning of stones, making chalk and cement, architecture, hydraulics wheels and mills, bridge building, mining, perfumery, pharmaceutics, medicine, ship-building, and pearl fisher." Hertzfeld, 1997, 330 As evident, recording of this civilizing role of the First Person, is somewhat modern and so it adds many additions. But looking at the range of his contributions, it may not be difficult to guess the land within the Indo-European world from where he might have gone. Hertzfeld thinks that it is in tune with the other accounts of the First One, but such is not the case. They have limited role to play, as in case of Adam or Manu. Manu for instance introduces agriculture, kingship and the law book. The three are linked togehter. Protection of farm and cattle from the Vrtra or the surrounding gahterers and hunters necessitated organised body entirely devoted to security aspect and institutions and codes of conduct. Manu does not go beyond this expected configuration.

The fact that the Vedic sages, the Atharvans roamed freely sermonising the public there and were later not permitted to do so is very cogently preserved in Iranian legendry history:

A further echo of the anti-Magian feelings may be heard in Yasna IX.24(75): Haoma overthrew Keresâni, who rose up to seize royalty, and he said: "No longer shall the Âthravans go through the lands and tach at their will."...The struggle of Haoma against is an old Indo-Eduropean myth, Keresâni being the same as the Vedic Krsânu, who wants to keep away the Soma from the hands of men. His name becomes in the Avesta the name of anti-Magian king (it may be Darius, the usurper (?), and ten centuries later it was turned into an appellation of the Christian Kaisars of Rûm (Kalasyâk; Tarasyâka)

Apparently, two schools of Aryan missionaries are referred here. The Atharvans who populariesed the Fire cult followed by the school practicing Soma cult. The latter prevailed for some time and were subdued again by the Fire worshippers. The difference is represented by *Âhitâgnis* and *Somâdas* and the boastful claim of the Soma cultists that ordinary people can not perform Soma sacrifice - न सोमो अप्रता पपे । Only later the two were reconciled as hinted by Darmestater, "Probably on account of bitter animosities prevailing betwwen their more southern neighbours and themselves, and the use of Soma by the Indians as a stimulant before battle, the Iranians of the Gathic period had become lukewarm in their H[a]oma worship. But that it should have revived as we see in this Yast, after having nearly or quite disappeared, is mot interesting and remarkable," SBES,XXXI, 231.

A very clear reference to this aspect occurs in RV. which in Griffiths rendering reads as, "Agni, those firends of thine have turned them from thee: gracious of old, they have become ungracious. They have deceived themselves by their own speeches, uttering wicked words against the righteous. He who pays sacrifice to thee with homage, O Agni, keeps the red Steers Law eternal Wide is his dwelling. May the noble spring of Nahusa who wandered forth come hether." V.12.5 and 6.

It appears that the area under their influence was throbbing with their activities and contact with home country was so live that every new strain of thought had its impact abroad.

63. Chatterji, S.K. 1968, 23-24; Singh, B. 1987, II 137-41; 1995, 64-65.

64. Gimbutas Marija 1970 Proto-Into-European culture: the Kurgan culture during the fifth, fourth and third millennia B.C. In George Cardona et al. eds., Indo European and Indo-Europeans.

Philadephia: 166-197.

65. Gimbutas, M. 1977 The First Wave of Eurasian Steppe Pastoralists into Copper Age Europe. Journal of Indo-European Studies. 5, 4: 277-337.

66. The order of pack animals appears to be the same as was followed in the animal procession at the sacrifies -- goat, ass, horse, *Satapatha Brahamana* VI.4.4.12. For detailed discusion see Singh 1995, chap III and 1996 *Parivahana ke âdima carana meñ gadhe aur ghode, in Bharat Tab se aba taka, 90-112.*

67. *RV.* I.116.2; *Aitareya Brâhmana.* IV.9; *Kausîtaki Brâhmana.* XVIII. 1;

68. Frankfort, Henri 1954 *Birth of Civilization in the Near East.* London.

69. Singh, B. 1975, Op.cit, 274.

70. *ibid*

71. उत वामस्य वसुनश्चिकेतति यो अस्ति याद्वः पशुः । *RV.* 8.1.31

72. *RV.* VIII.101.15

73. Jim G. Shaffer and Diane A. Lichtenstein, 1995, 1995 "The concepts of 'cultural tadition' and 'Palaeoethnicity' in South Asian archaeology, in Erdosy, The Indo-Aryans of Ancient South Asia, 127-154

74. Ibid.

75. RV.II.14.11

76. अस्मे धेहि श्रवो बृहत द्युम्नं सहससातमम । इन्द्र ता रथिनीरिषः । 1.9.8

Grant us high fame, O Indra, Grant riches bestowing thousands, those. Fair fruits of earth borne home in wains. सहसयातमम-अतिशयेन सहससंख्यादानोपेतम । ताः - ब्रीहियवादि रूपेण प्रसिद्धाः । रथिनीः बहुरथोपेताः । इषः अन्नाः । सायण । RV1.9.8.

77. We checked 28 entries of *yûtha,* herd. Not a single one refers to a herd in reality.

वृषा यूथेव वंसगः कृष्टीरियर्त्योजसा । *RV* 1.58.5
मदे मदे हि नो ददिर्यूथा गवामृजूकृतः । *RV.*1.81.7
क्व स्वित सूते नहि यूथे अन्तः । *RV.* I.164.17
यदन्यासु वृषभो रोरवीत सो अन्यस्मिन यूथे दधाति रेतः । *RV.* III.55.17
आ यूथेव क्षुमति पश्वो अख्यत् । *RV.*IV.2.18
श्रवश्चाच्छ पशुमच्च यूथम् । *RV.*IV.38.5
क्षेत्रादपश्यं सनुतश्चरन्तं सुमद यूथ् न पुरु शोभमानम । *RV*V.2.4
यूथेव पश्वो व्युनोति गोपा । *RV.*V.31.1
अभि न इला यूथस्य माता । *RV.*V.41.19
यूथेव पश्वः पशुपा दमूना । *RV.*VI.19.3
यूथेवाप्सु समीजमान ऊती । *RV.*VI.29.5
अजा यूथेव पुरक्षिरस्तम् । *RV.*VI.49.12
सं यो यूथेव जनिमानि चष्टे । *RV.*VII.60.3
षष्ठिं सहसानु निर्मजामजे निर्यूथानि गवामृषि । VIII.4.20
अधि या बृहतो दिवो३ अभि यूथेव पश्यति । *RV* VIII.25.7
गावो न यूथं अभियन्ति बध्य उप मा यन्तु बधयः । *RV.*V. III.61.8
अश्वानां इन्न यूथं । *RV.*VIII.56.4
त्वं पुरू सहसाणि शतानि च यूथा दानाय मंहसे । *RV.*V. III 61.8
एष शृंगाणि दोधुवच्छिशीते यूथ्यो वृषा । नृम्णा दधान ओजसा । *RV.*IX.15.4
उक्षेव यूथा परियन्नरावीत् । *RV.*IX.71.9
वृषेव यूथा परिकोशमर्षसि । *RV.*IX.76.5; IX.96.20
अत्यो न यूथे वृषयुः कनिक्रदत् । RV*IX.77.5*
यूथे न निःष्ठा वृषभो वि तिष्ठसे । *RV.*IX.77.5
माता यन्मन्तुर्यूथस्य पूर्व्या । *RV.*X.32.4
वृषभो न तिग्मशृंगं अन्तर्यूथेषु रोरुवत् । *RV.*X.86-15

78. Singh, B. 1987 Op.cit., I, 64.

79. Erdosy, G. 1995 Language, material culture and ethnicity: Theoretical perspectives. In George Erdosy ed. *The Indo-Aryans of Ancient South Asia : Language, Material Culture and Ethnicity,* Berlin, New York, 1-31.

80. स यो व्यवस्थादभि दक्षमुर्वी पशुर्नैति स्वयुरगोपाः ।
अग्निः शोचिष्मा अतसान्युष्णन् कृष्णव्यथिरस्वदयन्न भूम । II.4.7

Around consuming the broad earth, he wanders, free roaming like an ox without a herdsman/

Agni refulgent, burning up the bushes, with blackened lines, as though the earth he seasoned. II.4.7. (अग्नि) अप्नस्वतीषूर्वरास्विष्टनिः । in fertile cultivated fields adorable, in desert spots adorable...I.127.6; Agni with sharpened jaws chews up and eats trees.I.143.5.

81. गवे चकर्थोर्वरासु युध्यन् । *RV.*V.33.4 (Indra) active warrior in the fields for cattle. सायण-गवे-वृष्टयुदकार्थं । उर्वरासु - सस्योपेताषु भूमिषु निमित्तभूतासु ।

82. अहं भूमिं अददं आर्याय । *RV.*4.26.2

83. तिसः पूजा आर्या ज्योतिरग्राः ब। *RV.*7.33.7.

84. You (Indra) subdued the dasas and provided *krstis* to the âryâs. *RV.* VI.18.3

85. *RV.* X.28.8

85. *RV.* VIII.35.10-12

86. *RV.* VI.11.4.

87. *RV.* II.12.8

88. *RV.* I.92.8

89. *RV.* II13.8

90. *RV.* VI.60.6; VII.83.1; X.69.6.

91. *RV.* VIII.55.5

92. *RV.*VIII.55.5

93. ...अध्वस्मभिः पथिभिः भाजद्दृकृटयः । *RV.* II.34.5. What is important is the use of plural *pathibhih* which is indicative of a very long journey. The other important word is *bhrâjadrstayah* which shows the extraordinary vigilance on the part of the caretakers against possible attack by robbers. The same is reflected in choice of a route which is not obscured by vegetation or any other object on both the sides.

94. *RV.* V.42.1

95. *RV.* V.52.10

96. *RV.* V.52.10

97. *RV.* V.52.10

98. *RV.* V.52.10

99. *RV.* I.41.5

100. *RV.* VI.46.13

101. *RV.* I.166.9

102. *RV.* II.24.7

103. *RV.* II.4.6

104. *RV.* VII.64.3

105. *RV.* I.25.12

106. *RV.* X.53.6

107. *RV.* VIII.101.10

108. *RV.* VI.62.6

109. *RV.* IX.106.5

110. *RV.* I.41.4

111. *RV.* III.55.15

112. *RV.* VI.49.8

113. *RV.* VI.46.13

114. *RV.* X.61.8

115. *RV.* I.185.8

116. *RV.* X.142.5

117. *RV.* I.53.8

118. *RV.* I.85.3

119. *RV.* III.55.15

120. *RV.* I.42.3

121. *RV.* I.53.8

122. *RV.* I.126. 4; 163.10; III.8.1; IV.38.6; V.59.7; X.142.5

123. *RV.* II.35.8

124. *RV.* III.9.8

125. *RV.* ,*âus* II.38.3

126. *RV.* IV.8.8

127. *RV.* IV.IV.1

128. *RV.* I.134.1

129. *RV.* III.3.6

130. *RV.* III.53.16;

131. *RV.* I.40.1

132. *RV* X.106.6

133. *RV.* IX.97.8

134. *RV.* VI.66.5

135. *RV.* VII.67.8

136. *RV.* IX.89.2

137. *RV.* VIII.7.53

138. *RV.* I.181.2

139. *RV.* 181.2

140. *RV.* IX.97.49

141. RV. V.53.9

142. See Singh, B. 1995 *The Vedic Harappans* for detailed discussion on every aspect of the material culture and textual confirmation.

143. "The gods drove around on wheels (cars), and the Asuras stayed at home." Eggling, *Satapatha Brahmana* VI.8.1.1. It is repeated in so many ways that the Aśvins conquerred the world with their wagon driven by asses. *RV.* I.116.2.

144. *Aitareya Brahmana* V.1.

NOTES AND NEWS

Geographic Information System (GIS) For Archaeology

Information science is one of the key factors responsible for modernising the ways to look at data, especially in data-intensive disciplines. In such disciplines the volume of field and analytical information is enormous as well as spatially diversed. It is true of archaeology as well, which has witnessed changes in handling of its vast data-dependent analytical procedures, in the last decade. This is because of introduction of a number of applied techniques, borrowed from various disciplines such as statistics (quantitative methods), space science (remote sensing), microcomputer-based image processing programmes etc. Especially after increasing use of microcomputers for data processing, a number of new tools have become handy to deal with geography-oriented databases for drawing archaeological inferences. Geographic Information System (GIS) is one of these multi-disciplinary applied tools adopted from information science as well as geography. The purpose of this article is to provide an introduction to the GIS and highlight its potential for archaeological applications as also to explain: (a) what is GIS, (b) what are its various components, and (c) different types of GIS applications in archaeological research.

Background

First operational GIS was developed in Canada in the mid-1970s (Tomlinson *et al.* 1976). However, it remained restricted primarily to engineering and defense resource–management in the U.S. and U.K. for about a decade. It was during the late 1980s that potentials of GIS were being recognized in archaeology (Marble 1990).

The GIS originated from the developmet of the Computer Aided Mapping (CAM) during the 1970s. CAM system is useful for quality map production and is fast. GIS is a computer-aided spatial data handling system, and is particulary designed for collection, capture, storage, retrieval, analysis and presentation of spatial data (Clarke 1986). Although, GIS incorporates certain capabilities of the CAM, such as computerised data-bases and statistical packages, it is significantly different in its structure and purpose (Cowen 1988) in that it has the added strength to generate new information on the data held within it due to simulation or model building.

Gradually the demand for computer storage of spatial information grew. Also a need was felt to develop computing systems that could allow easy retrieval of data for the production of theme maps. These changes were responsible for the development of the GIS.

GIS is a package of technology, which is based upon developments in cartography, computer graphics, computer aided design (CAD), photogrammetry, geodesy, remote sensing and other related fields. As a result, GIS is being rapidly adopted by various disciplines that require detailed analysis of space. The spatial nature of data in archaeology has thus necessitated application of GIS.

Components of GIS

As a system GIS involves essentially various components (Fig. 1 redrawn after Madry 1990):

1. inputs in the form of maps, images, drawings,

satellite pictures, aerial photog: ps and tabular information;

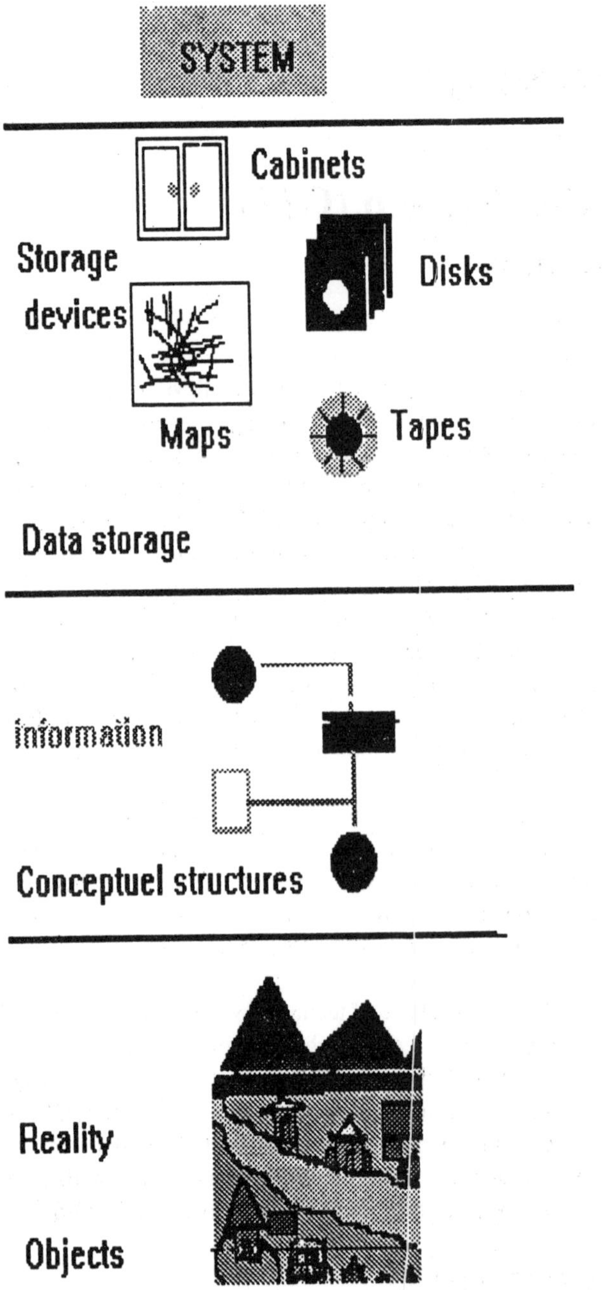

Fig. 1 Components of GIS

2. an information-base composed of spatial as well as non-sptial database;

3. an information management system which is the core of the GIS with a Data Base Management System (DBMS); and

4. outputs in the form of maps, database summaries in tabular formats and so on.

For working of these components a specific software and a set of computer hardware is necessary.

Hardware for GIS

GIS, like every other computer-based system, requires a series of devices for data input, central processing, data storage and its output in desired format (Fig. 1) Except the input devices, general computer devices can be used for the GIS.

The central processing unit (CPU), brain of every computing system, controls data management as well as the procedure of their input, output and storage. Storage devices such as diskettes, disks and tapes are magnetic based. However, these can be replaced by optical storage devices. Output devices include common monitors, printers and plotters.

Principal data input devices are the keyboard, the digitiser and data obtained from other sources such as satellite sensor used in remote sensing. Digitisers can be used to convert a printed map into digital data. Digitising devices are of two types– scanners and co-ordinate digitisers. Remote sensing data is available in digital format on floppy disk which can be used directly to feed information to a GIS package (Deo and Joglekar 1996).

GIS Software

A vast number of GIS softwares are available, suitable for different kinds of computer systems and work environments (Parker 1989). GIS packages useful for archaeology are Arc-Info, Idrisi, GRASS and ERDAS (Table 1). All GIS software packages have four basic modules:

(i) Core Module which provides basic facilities for the data acquisition.

(ii) Ring Module or data processing module that

facilitates complex analytical operations

(iii) Peripheral Module useful for data transfer and conversion

(iv) Image Processing Module for digital image processing.

Table 1: Types PCs-DOS based GIS software useful in archaeology

Package	Data Structure	Compatibility
Arc/Info	Vector	Info, ORACAL
ERDAS	Raster	Infor
GRASS	Vector, Raster	not available
IDRISI	Raster	LOTUS, QUATRO
IMAGE	Vector	LOTUS, dBase
MAPINFO	Vector	dBase

VB-GIS 3-D GIS has been developed specially for exploration, analysis, hypothesis testing and statistics in spatial or distributional archaeology (Reynoso 1994).

Working of GIS

GIS, an integrated system covers various aspects of data preparation, data management, information processing or data analysis. GIS requires to store data-both image and numerical/descriptional in such a way that one can do necessary queries on both these types of information formats simultaneously. There are two basic ways in which images (visuals) can be stored: Vector-based and Raster-based storage

VECTOR-BASED STORAGE: The spatial patterns are constructed using the vector quantities such as line, circles and polygons (Fig. 2). However, in archaeological research, often certain features are difficult to visualise only as regular vector formats. Typically the question of vector image becomes important in defining the site boundaries, limits of artefacts scatters and so on.

RASTER BASED STORAGE: The data is considered in the form of a grid of x, y cells and the values are stored as

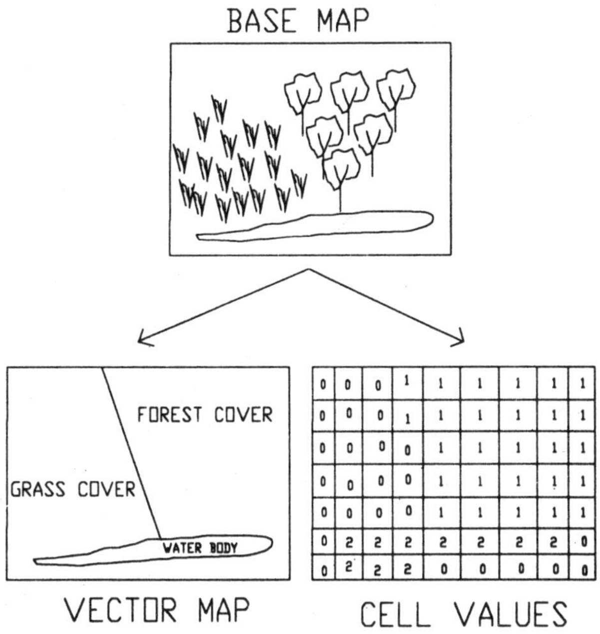

Fig. 2 Vector and Raster Data types in GIS

'z', thus making it a x, y, z system similar to that a Cartesian system of point co-ordinates. This data structure is easy to handle mathematically, but also requires a large space in terms of computer memory and storage media (Savage 1990). Even powerful computers with advanced memory operations cannot cope with handling multiples of matrices of high degree such as 800x800. Several GIS softwares overcome the above mentioned difficulties by converting the data to the Raster format from the Vector format and *viceversa* when a specific operation is to be performed.

GIS Applications in Archaeology

In archaeology, a complex structure of information needs to be handled while doing interpretations and/or drawing inferences about past cultures and their role *vis-a-vis* interaction to their geographic locales. The ability of

GIS to simultaneously handle large amount of information makes it a powerful analytical tool in archaeology which involves intergration of facts about cultural characteristics and environmental parameters. Manual processing of such a voluminous body of information is possible, but it it is slow and troublesome; consequently limits its scope. For example, visual analysis of simple distributions of sites across various landscapes can be done even without a computer or GIS. However, by using GIS, archaeological spatial information in relation to landforms could be viewed at several levels, e.g. study of distributions of different culture entities at a macro level, settlement pattern studies at regional level and spatial pattern analysis of objects/artefacts within a site at the intra-site level (Fig.3).

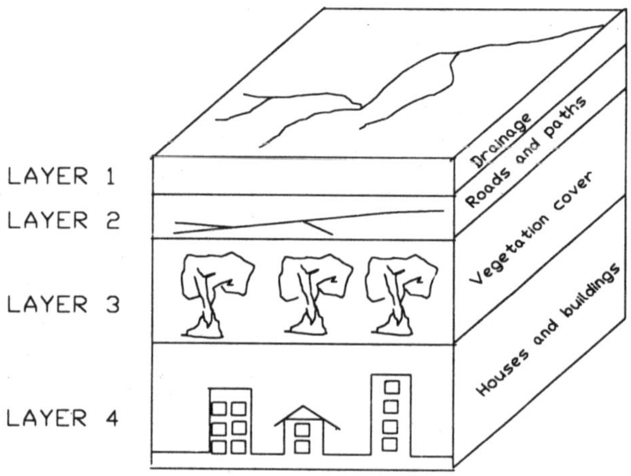

Fig. 3 Concept of layers of information in GIS

Archaeological Resource Management (ARM)

Management of archaeological and/or historical culture resources is vital because in recent times a large number of such cultural heritage sites are being destroyed or disturbed for a variety of reasons (Paddayya 1996, Mohan 1996, Balaji *et al.* 1996).

Management of such heritage sites or monuments of archaeological/historical importance is virtually unrealisable without using a computing device since it involves handling of an immense information spread over a wide geographic area, e.g. Indian subcontinent. GIS is a new methodological tool that can help administrators to manage the heritage sites in a better manner. GIS can be used for ARM in two ways–firstly by using GIS as a data management and presentation tool-kit and secondly as a research device for development of newer and better ways of mapping and evaluating archaeological/historical locations.

Table:2 Comparision of vector and raster based GIS models

Raster Data Model	Vector Data Model
easy and simple model	problems in digitizing the maps
data updation is easy	data updation is difficult
area-distance calculation is error-prone	area-distance calulation is error-free
superimposition is easier	superimposition is error-prone
less accuracy in point-line data	accuracy in point-line data
unnatural forms of maps/boundaries	natural forms of maps/boundaries
low resolution small features ignored	high resolution with minute details
operations are slow	operations are faster
requires more space on a PC	requires less space on a PC
easy to implement	easy to implement

GIS and Spatial Analysis in Archaeology

GIS has the potential for undersanding of the spatial patterns of archaeological remains as well as effects of naturtal/site forming factors. All achaeological sites have a matrix of lanscapes on which the ancient habitations grow and perish. To investigate the outcome of complex interplay of various natural and human agents at an archaeological site, a correct picture of the spatial relationships of all such agents is necessary. In such a situation that demands thousands of computing and logical steps, GIS is an ideal tool. For example, the concept of 'cultural landscape' provides a clear link between the cultural remains of human occupation in a specific environmental setting. In pre-industrial age the human occupation has been always constrained by their immediate physical surroundings. A flourishing culture can continue to survive or can perish in course of time if it does not adapt to its changing environment. Obviously, a large number of causative factors operate at every stage during occupational history at an archaeological site. GIS provides a means by which large amounts of cultural and geographical data can be synthesised to draw inferences at any desired stage of site formation modelling.

Archaeologists have had used a variety of techniques to analyse and interpret spatial patterning in archaeological record even before emergence of GIS. In general, they use map-based or statistically-oriented approaches to look at archaeological records. GIS assists in the spatial analysis by permitting greater flexibility to be exercised in structuring the raw data as well as it enabls both map-based and quantitatively oriented approaches to be more complementary to each other (Harris and Lock 1990).

To correlate cultural data with those of the with environmet, traditionally archaeologists have measured geographical variables such as slope, elevation, dissection, distance to water, drainage morphology etc. Such measurements are made either directly by field-observations or using the printed topographic maps.

Data obtained from maps, no doubt represent a level of abstraction which due to genealizations is not same as the field reality (Fig. 1). The regional analyses in GIS are based on computer programmes. Such data represent a second level of abstraction because there is further generalization of the map data. For instance, to work on an elevation theme in a GIS setting-usually referred to as a digital elevation model (DEM), contour lines printed on the maps are required to be electronically digitized and then feed them to the GIS core programme that handles such information. The programme then uses one of the several interpolative methods in a systematic manner to estimate an elevation between the contour lines. Further, the slopes, local reliefs, drainage locations and other information relevant to archaeology can then be derived from the digital elevation model (DEM). In GIS an elevation model represents nothing but a picture of the locally relevant landform. This model is based on analysis of the interrelations among the stored elevation values for which various algorithms are applied (Kvamme 1990).

Accuracy of the elevation model, therefore, is an important concern as it controls not only the quality of over all landform representation, but also the nature of all secondary information derived from it. Such environmental matrix approach has been utilised by archaeologists for a long time, but the logical steps and calculations are done manually. Naturally, GIS allows for more rapid update, storage and modelling capabilities, and a better accuracy than would be possible with manual cartographic methods. Fast access to data allows one to use GIS to take a multi-scaler, multi-disciplinary approach to landscape interpretation. It can be applied to examine interrelationship among various physical and cultural features at a particular time and space as well as to understand how such these interrelationships can change over time. GIS can also be useful for site location analysis, site pattern prediction and site patten reconstruction (Wansleeben 1988).

Concluding Remarks

In general it is possible to recognise various GIS application areas suitable for archaeological studies: (i) three dimentional viewing, (ii) GIS-based simulations, (iii) palaeo-environmental modelling, and (iv) heritage management and evaluation of status of the sites of archaeological/cultural value.

GIS can be used to deal with question related to past and present envrionmental setting of the archaeological habitations at the site or the regional scale. It is an ideal tool to investigate archaeological settlement patterns in relation to various geographic parameters that affect human settlement in a given area/region.

Since GIS provides fast creation, storage, management, retrieval and display of geographically linked information it can serve as a powerful decision making tool. It can be used to plan a field-research strategy and also help a constant update/evaluation of the research goals.

The GIS software applications in Indian archaeology could be of enormous consequences. In Indian context, GIS seems to have an unlimited potential because the amount of data in Indian archaeological, historical field is really colossal. An archaeological information system (AIS) would be a natural extention of the logic of GIS. Development of such a system for Indian archaeological and historical sites would positively augment archaeological research and help highlight one of its main themes–understanding complex past human and envrionmental relations.

Acknowledgements

The first author wishes to acknowledge lecture notes of Dr. V.S. Kale, University of Pune, during the Workshop on GIS, organised by MIT, Pune in 1995. The second author wishes to acknowledge the training received from Dr. Luca Bondioli on GIS theory and applications during his stay at IsMEO, Rome in 1993 under Italian Government Scholarship.

REFERENCES

Balaji, K., Suresh L.S., Raghavswamy V. and Gautam N.C. 1996. 'The Use of Remote Sensing in Monitoring Changes in and around Archaeological Monuments - a Case Study from Hyderabad, Andhra Pradesh.' *Man and Environment* XXI (2) : 63-70.

Clarke K.C. 1986, 'Advances in Geographic Information Systems.' *Computers, Environment and Urban Systems* 10: 175-184.

Cowen, D.J. 1988. 'GIS vs. CAD vs. DBMS: What are the differences?'. *Photogrammetric Engineering and Remote Sensing*, 54(11): 1551-1556.

Deo, S.G. and P.P. Joglekar 1996. 'Satellite Remote Sensing for Archaeology.' *Man and Environment* XXI (2): 59-62.,

Harris T.M. and G.R. Joglekar 1996. 'The Diffusion of a New Technology: a Perspective on the Adoptation of Geographic Information Systems within U.K. Archaeology, in K.M.S. Allen, S.W. Green and E.B.W. Zubrow (eds.) *Interpreting Space: GIS in Archaeology* 32-53. London: Taylor and Francis.

Kvamme K.L. 1990. 'GIS Algorithms and their Effect on Regional Archaeological Analysis in Allen K.M.S. Green, S.W. and Zubrow, E.B.W. (eds.), 112-125. London: Taylor and Francis.

Madry, S.L.H. 1990. The Realities of Hardware in K.M.S. Allen, S.W. Green and E.B.W. Zubrow (eds.), *Interpreting Space: GIS in Archaeology.* 173-183. London: Taylor and Francis.

Marble, D.F. 1990. The Potential Methodological Impact of Geographic Information Systems on Social Sciences, in K.M.S. Allen, S.W. Green and E.B.W. Zubrow (eds.), *Interpreting Space: GIS in Archaeology.* 9-21. London: Taylor and Francis.

Mohan, Vijneshu. 1996. 'The Destruction of Archaeological Sites Under the Impact of rapid Development in Haryana: an Area of High Archaeological Potential.' *Man and Environment*, XXI (2): 71-74.

Paddayya, K. 1996. 'Modern Impacts on Archaeological Sites in India: a Case Study from the Shorapur Doab, Karnataka.' *Man and Environment* XXI (2): 75-88.

Parker, H.D. 1989. 'GIS Software 1989: a Survey and Commentary.' *Photogrammetric Engineering and Remote Sensing.* 55: 1589-1591.

Reynoso, Carlos 1994. 'VB-GIS 3D-A Development Report on a GIS Model for Archaeology,' *Archaeological Computing Newsletter.* 38: 3-7.

Savage, S.H. 1990. 'GIS in Archaeological Research, in K.M.S. Allen, S.W. Green and E.B.W. Zubrow (eds.), *Interpreting Space: GIS in Archaeology.* 23-38. London: Taylor and Francis.

Tomlinson, R.F., D.F. Marble and H.W. Calkins 1976. *Computer Handling of Geographic Data.* Paris: UNESCO Press.

Wansleeben, M. 1988. 'Application of Geographical Information Systems in Archaeological Research in S.P.Q. Rahtz (ed.),. *Computer and Quantitative Methods in Archaeology.* 435-451, Oxford: British Archaeological Reports.

Deccan College , Pune

SUSHAMA G. DEO AND P.P. JOGLEKAR

Report on the Faunal Remains from Kelshi, District Ratnagiri, Maharashtra

This report is based on bones and marine shells collected from the site of Kelshi on the coast of Ratnagiri District. The site has been identified as of historical period based on study of cultural materials comprising pottery, bones, etc. as well as on fluorine-phosphate anaylsis (A. A. Kshirsagar personal communication).

Bones

The bones were identified using a comprehensive collection of modern animal and human skeletons available at the Deccan College, Pune. The collection is very small comprising only 11 bones of which 3 were human (Pl. 1). However, a descriptive list of bones (Table 1) reveals that even such a small assemblage represents domestic cattle *Bos indicus*– buffalo– *Bubalus bubalis* (Pl. 2), spotted deer/*chital* - *Axis axis* (Pl. 3), marine turtle and two marine fish species, possibly one of shark (Pl 3). Total weight of the animal bones was 0.365 kg. Most of the fragments were white in colour and exhibiting erosion due to tidal waves. The metatarsal bone of buffalo showed presence of barnacles attached over the distal anterior surface, indicating that this bone had settled on the shore for a prolonged period of time and has been exposed to recurring wave action.

Bone measurements add significant information to archaeological data since they can be used to estimate the size of the animals at archaelogical sites (Joglekar 1991). At Kelshi, one cattle astragalus (No. KEL 9) reveals the presence of an individual, 98.10 cm tall at the withers (height estimated using factor given by Zalkin 1970).

Molluscan Shells

A total of 55 shells were examined at the Archaeozoological laboratory, Deccan College, Pune. The shells were washed, cleaned, sorted and then recorded. Identification was done with the help of the modern reference shell collection at the Archaeo-zoological laboratory, and by referring to Wye (1991) and Abbott and Dance (1991).

All the shells were examined for features like charring, breakage patterns, perforations, use-wear and other taphonomic details. Dimensional details were recorded of each measurable shell following the Muckle's method (Muckle 1985).

From a total of 55 shells, 5 speices have been identified (Table 2). All are marine bivalves and gastropods are altogether absent. In general, shell preservation is good and a majority of the shells are complete. Of the five species, one belonging to the genus *Paphia* could not be identified further due to close similarities with *Papia gallus.* Hence, it is referred to as *Paphia* sp. (Pl. 4).

Meretrix meretrix: A total of 8 specimens are present (one is broken). These shells are thick, ovate in shape and the outer surface is glossy. They have an average length of 39.31mm and breadth 33.82mm (Table 3). These are found in estuaries and creeks and are fished regularly on the Konkan coast today (Nayar and Mahadevan 1974). It is interesting to note that although the length and breadth varied considerably; the breadth/length index showed a highly homogeneous sample of this species.

Shells belonging to the Genus *Paphia* include ovate, bivalves whose exterior is glossy and covered with concentric ribs. At present, these shells are regularly fished on the Konkan and Karwar coasts (Nayar and Mahadevan 1974). At Kelshi, two species belonging to this Genus

Table 1 : List of Identified Bones at Kelshi (Measuremens in mm)

Sr. No.	Description	Weight (g)
KEL 1	Complete mandible of *Bos indicus* Age more than 36 months Length of p4 : 16.60 Width of p4 : 10.50 Length of m1 : 21.30 Widht of m1 : 10.55 Length of m2 : 24.25 Widht of m2 : 10.94 Lenth of m3 : 30.50 Width of m3 : 10.50	205
KEL 2	Left second metatarsal of human	6
KEL 3	Completely rolled femur fragment of *Bos indicus/Bubalus bubalis*	26
KEL 4	Marine fish vertebra possibly of shark Dorso-ventral diameter : 32.01 Lateral diameter : 32.80	10
KEL 5	Complete human rib of left side	10
KEL 6	Marine fish vertebra with a half perforation, edges are polished possibly a half-finished pendant Dorso-ventral diameter : 22.40 Lateral diameter : 22.87	6
KEL 7	Antler fragment of *Axis axis*, this is shed antler	28
KEL 8	Human femur, distal epiphysis is fused	80
KEL 9	Complete right astragalus of *Bos indicus* 40 Lateral Length : 56.86 Medial length : 53.61 Maximum distal width : 36.08 Maximum lateral thickness : 29.20 Maximum medial thickness : 30.57	
KEL 10	Femur, proximal end of large marine turtle 6	
KEL 11	Distal end of right side metacarpal of 44 *Bubalus bubalis* Maximum distal width : 63.18 Thickness (lateral) – trochlea : 25.68 Thickness (medial) – trochlea: 35.92	

have been identified.

Table 2: List of Molluscan species identified at Kelshi

Speices	Family.	Class	Type
Meretrix meretrix	Veneridae	Bivalvia	Marine
Paphia gallus	,,	,,	,,
Paphia sp.	,,	,,	,,
Placuna placenta	Anomiidae	,,	,,
Crossostrea cucculate	Ostreidae	,,	,,

Table 3: Measurements of *Meretrix meretrix* shells

No.	Length mm	Breadth mm	Side
1	48.49	41.43	right
2.	46.43	38.93	left
3.	39.68	34.06	left
4.	40.69	34.78	left
5.	42.43	37.49	right
6.	28.83	25.45	left
7.	29.27	24.61	left
	-	-	left

Range 48.49–28.33 41.43-24.61

Mean 39.31 33.82

Breadth/Length Index: 0.859± 0.018 (C.V. 2.095%)

Paphia gallus: It is more ovate and compressed. The umbo is more curved and prominent. The posterior shell–margin abruptly slopes downwards. Ten shells of this species are present at Kelshi. These have an average length and breadth of 25.90 and 17.47 mm respectively (Table 4). The breadth/length index showed that these shells varied in size, perhaps according to their age, yet the variation is as small as 4.348%.

Table 4: Measurements of *Paphia gallus* shells

No.	Length mm	Bredth mm	Side
8.	31.26	22.30	right
9.	33.99	24.12	left
10.	26.75	20.78	right
11.	29.15	21.39	left
12.	30.21	22.44	right
13.	29.99	22.21	right
14.	27.25	19.91	left
15.	29.71	20.57	left
16.	26.72	19.05	right
17.	22.90	17.46	right
-	-	-	left

Range 31.26–22.90 24.12-17.46

Mean 25.90 17.47

Breadth/Length Index: 0.736± 0.032 (C. V. 4.348%)

Paphia sp.: This species is dominant in the entire shell assemblage and is represented by 27 shells (2 non-measurable). Since it closely resembles *Paphia gallus* it is referred to as *Paphia* sp. The shell valve of this species is fairly elongated lengthwise as compared to *Paphia gallus.* The umbo is insignificant and less curved. The shell is shallow and the shell– margin on the posterior side curves gradually. Its average length and breadth is 28.53 mm and 18.12 mm respectively (Table 5). The magnitude of variation in the breadth/length index is as small as 2.571% although the length and breadth varied considerably.

Table: 5 Measurements of *Paphia* sp. shells

No.	Length mm	Breadth mm	Side
18.	35.80	23.81	right
19.	–	26.48	right
20.	30.73	22.20	left
21.	31.11	21.47	right
22.	35.40	23.13	right

No.	Length mm	Breadth mm	Side
23.	34.43	24.39	right
24.	29.60	21.03	right
25.	33.05	21.53	right
26.	29.56	21.36	right
27.	29.27	20.12	right
28	–	22.94	left
29.	20.16	20.14	left
30.	–	16.19	left
31.	24.88	16.51	left
32.	25.22	15.41	left
33.	–	18.60	left
34.	–	21.56	left
35.	28.18	17.79	left
36.	24.66	17.12	right
37.	24.21	17.19	right
38.	24.31	16.67	left
39	17.95	12.74	left
40.	–	20.96	left
41.	–	18.87	right
42.	26.08	–	right
Range	35.80-17.95	26.48-16.19	
Mean	28.53	18.12	

Breadth/Length Index: 0.700 ± 0.081 (C.V. 2.571%)

Crassostrea cucculata: Eight fragments of this species are present at Keslhi which have an approximate size range of 31.43 mm length and breadth 29.11mm. This oyster species occurs as clusters on rocks and mangroves in the inter-tidal and mud-flat areas. These are smaller in size as compared to the other oyster species and are common on the west coast.

The shell valves are hard and pear-shaped. The right valve is flat while left one is deep. The margins of both valves have well developed angular folds sculpted with laminae (Rao 1987). These are collected as food along the Gujarat and Maharashtra coasts (Rao 1987).

Placuna placenta: These are commonly referred to as the windowpane oyster. These shells are found in the muddy flats along the Mumbai coast, Gulf of Kachch etc. (Rao 1974). These are thin, transparent, flat, circular shells. This species is represented by only one fragment in the collection at Kelshi.

Conclusions

The faunal collection made at Kelshi is very small, yet it is significant to know about the animals associated in the historical period especially of coastal historical sites. Such information may be useful in future to understand features of historical sites from faunal point of view.

Shells from archaeological sites can yield a great deal of information on past subsistence, palaeoenvironment, chronology etc. Thus they are often used as suitable tools in interpreting the past. At Kelshi however, due to the small size of the sample it is very difficult to determine the degree of shell-use at the site. The possibility of these shells used as adornment or utility objects is ruled out because the shells do not have any traces of modification or shell-working.

One probable use of shells at Kelshi could have been for food purposes. The site being coastal in nature, which might have enabled the inhabitants to procure shell- fish from the nearby estuarine and creek area. Some of the shells like *Meretrix, Paphia* and *Crossostrea* form an edible component of the diet of the people in this region even today. At Kelshi, molluscan species were collected in smaller size range as compared to the modern fishery size. These could have been consumed along with other food items. However, in order to know more about the role of marine resources in the cultural history of the site, more detailed studies of this nature are essential.

Acknowledgements

We wish to acknowledge Dr. S. N. Karlekar who discovered the site, and Prof. S. N. Rajaguru for guidance. We also thank Mr. Deodhar and Ms. Manjiri Thuse for their help during the fieldwork at the site.

REFERENCES

Abbott, R. T. and Dance S. P. 1991. *Compendium of Seashells.* London: Charles Letts.

Joglekar, P. P. 1991. A Biometric Approach to the Faunal Remains of Western India with special reference to Koathe and Walki. Ph.D. Thesis, Pune: University of Poona.

Mahadevan, S. and Nayar K. N. 1987. Ecology of Oyster Beds, *Central Marine fisheries Bulletin* 38: 7-16.

Muckle R. J. 1985. Archaeological consideration of Bivalve Shell Tapahonomy. M. A. Thesis. Dept. of Archaeology Simon Fraser University, Barnby, Vancouver, British Columbia.

Nayar, K. N. and Mahadevan S. 1974. Edible Bivalves: Clams and others in *The commercial molluscs of India.* Central Marine Fisheries Research Institute - 25 41-53. Cochin. CMFRI.

Rao, K. S. 1974. Edible bivalves: Mussels and Oysters in *The commercial molluscs of India.* Central Marine Fisheries Research Institute 25: 4-39. Cochin. CMFRI.

Rao, K. S. 1987. Taxonomy of Indian Oysters, *Central Marine Fisheries Bulletin* 38: 1-6.

Wye, K.R. 1991. *The Illustrated Encyclopaedia of Shells.* London: Headline Book Publishing.

Zalkin V.I. 1970. *Drevniejsije domsnije zivotnije vastocnoj Europy*, Moskva.

Deccan College, Pune 411 006

P.P. Joglekar
Arati Deshpande-Mukerjee
Sharmila Joshi

A Little Known Buddhist Relic Stupa in the Santhal Parganas

Of the various transformational processes in the recent past that have caused the destruction of fragile archaeological relics and sites, the 'contribution' made by the Indian Railways has been particularly notorious. The details of the trail of the damage that resulted from this development–activity are many, involving systematic brick robbing of the city of Harappa to the cleaving of Mathura's ancient ramparts. It is, however, with a more humble site in the Santhal Parganas of Bihar that this brief note is principally concerned. In itself, the destruction of a mound for 'development' purposes is commonplace (for some recent examples, see Mohan 1996. 2:71-74 and Paddayya 1996:2.75-78) but here, what was obliterated was, possibly still is, unique for that area. It is this that makes the little known instance of the *stupa* mound of *Sambodhi/Samadhi* and the story of its destruction and 'burial' in a government file of the Home Department in 1905, presently in the National Archives of India in New Delhi, important and worth recounting.

The Stupa mound at Bagiawari and its significance

Sambodhi or *Samadhi* as it was known in 1855 stood at the foot of hills called Budda Thoon dari near a village known as Bagiawari, close to Sakrigali in the Santhal Parganas (De la Croix 1905). It stood in front of the bungalow occupied by E.B. de la Croix, an Inspector of works in the East Indian Railway during its construction and, from the note written by his son (De la Croix 1905), it seems that the mound was composed of "heaped up coloured stones". For some unspecified reason, de la Croix decided to remove the mound and in the process, "underneath at ground level a smooth platform was discovered made up of only three bricks, each brick measuring 2 1/2′ x 1 1/2′ x 1/2′ and under this the Relics were found deposited in a stone chest of the following design. On the four sides there was a figure engraved representing a man dressed in flowing robes but there was no inscription of any kind on the Chest" (De la Croix 1905).

This was evidently a *saririka stupa* and as in the case of other similar ones, considerable care had been taken to encase the bone relics in a series of caskets. These were composed of, the note continued:

> "A large dome of Red Marble circling a large Marble casket.
>
> A smaller, fitting in it and
>
> A small crystal casket fitting therein containing pieces of bones.
>
> On the outside of the dome was:
>
> A large marble casket containing a small marble casket in which there were pieces of bones, and along with the small casket there were two Agate beads, three pink stones bored, two yellow stones bored, one white stone and a crystal phial with stopper, One of the yellow stones... dots punched, and the white stone...9 dots" (de la Croix 1903).

Possibly, the 'bored stones' with 'punched dots' were etched beads, a common variety of stone beads in historical India (Dikshit 1949).

Some more details are available in a report from A. Fuhrer, then the Curator of the Provincial Museum at Lucknow. Apparently, on 28th August 1885, at the request of Alfred Lyall, Lieutenant Governor of the United Provinces of Agra and Oudh, the Museum Committee asked Fuhrer to examine the Bagiawari relics. Fuhrer (1885) believed the find to be an important one and noted:

"From the fragrant smell still attached to the relic box I conclude that the dome and the relic caskets before the deposition had been sprinkled with scented powder, apparently with a mixture of aloe powder 'Agaruchurna' and Sandal powder 'Chandana churana' which the Buddhist Pali books frequently mention as thrown on Buddha by the gods".

The absence of inscribed objects precluded the possibility of identifying whose bones were interred or the date of the relics. He, however, specifically mentioned that the red marble dome that encircled the casket was "a perfect imitation in the miniature of the famous 'Sanchi tope". Presumably, he meant a semi-circular-shaped dome, flattened on the top and capped with three superimposed umbrellas. Because of this similarity, he believed that the Bagiawari *stupa* could not be older than 1st century A.D. The basis of Fuhrer's dating is evidently incorrect– the enlarged version of the great *stupa* or Stupa I at Sanchi, its stone encasing and elaboration belong mainly to the 2nd and 1st centuries B.C.

At the same time, it is not easy to suggest, from the records of the file or Fuhrer's report, a precise date for the *Sambodhi* mound. That the mound was known as *Sambodhi* is interesting and evokes an early association; this being the ancient name of Bodh Gaya. We also know of several relic-bearing *stupas* dating to the late centuries B.C. (Mitra 1971 and 1989) but in this case, the representation of a figure, specially if it was that of the Buddha, on all four sides of the stone casket would mean that it cannot be earlier than the 1st century A.D. The large size of bricks would also fit in with the above mentioned date. Of course, in the absence of sufficient detail, one cannot preclude the possibility of its having been constructed later since during the Gupta period, the building of *stupas* continued (Agrawala 1977:81-84), although, with some exceptions (cf. Devnimori; Mehta and Chowdhary 1966), generally these later *stupas* were not relic bearing. Debala Mitra has opined that this was due to the dearth of body relics and consequently, "texts of the *Pratitya-samutpada sutra,* tablets with the Buddhist creed and images of the Buddha were enshrined within the *stupas* during that period" (Mitra 1971:16).

It is not the precise date, however, but the geographical location of this find that makes it so significant. Bagiawari was apparently close to Sakrigali, a well known town on the strip between the Rajmahal hills and the Ganga. Incidentally, on the map of the Taljhari C.D. Block of villages of the former Santhal Parganas district (Lal 1988:61) and at a distance of less than 5 km from Sakrigali, there are two villages, both called Chhota Bhagiamari, fairly close to each other - the one (No. 4) which is towards the south must be nearer to the hills but is not connected by rail, while the one towards the north (No.6) does have a railway station. In any case, keeping in mind their physical proximity to the Rajmahal hills, Sakrigali and East Indian Railway line in whose construction de La Croix was involved, there is little doubt that Bhagiamari is 'Bagiawari' whether the one nearer the hills the other of the Taljhari Block connected by rail can only determined through a field study.

Having ascertained its location, it can be said with same degree of confidence that whether the *Sambodhi stupa* is dated to the 1st century A.D. or to a later period, this was a unique and singular site in the context of the Santhal Parganas. The Buddha is known to have spent his life almost exclusively in the middle Ganga valley and several places that are associated with incidents in his life there are marked by relic-bearing *stupas.* However, the distribution of such sites in Bihar till date has not extended east to include that narrow strip of land flanked by the Ganga and the Rajmahal hills. In fact, as a survey of the entries in *The Antiquarian Remains of Bihar* (Patil 1963) reveals, there are no Buddhist antiquities or structural remains in the Santhal Parganas at all. Apparently, the earliest available evidence in the form of historical antiquities is a sculpted doorway moulding, probably part of a temple, from Sakrigali, dated to the 8th century A.D. (Asher 1980: 97) and this has also been reiterated in Chakrabarti's recent field survey of South Bihar (Chakrabarti *et al.* 1995:131). The discovery of this information about a *stupa* at Bagiawari, thus is significant in two ways: First, it provides a new dimension to the historical past of the Santhal Parganas and secondly, it allows us to archaeologically visualize, for the first time, the Ganga valley strip to the east of Antichak as being within the ambit of the historical circuit of *stupas* and related Buddhist establishments.

It may also throw some light on the antiquity of communications in this zone. Sakrigali was an important point of transit between Bihar and Bengal since it is around here that, on the one hand, the Ganga turns sharply southwards while on the other hand, a narrow defile through the Rajmahal hills provides a land route connecting the two areas. D. R. Patil's (1963 : 508) notes in this regard are worth quoting:

> "The hills here terminate on a high rocky knoll with the river on one side and with a very narrow road, hardly 9 to 12 feet wide, in between cut through the rock and hemmed in on either side by impenetrable jungle. The road or pass is the famous Sakrigalli pass which in historical times was known as the gateway of Bengal......"

Incidentally, Francis Buchanan in 1811 had noticed fortifications "extending from the river to the hills near its eastern side, and consisting of two ramparts of earth with a very wide ditch between" (Oldham 1930 : 98). These were apparently medieval. However, in the light of what has been stated above, the possibility of Sakrigali being a more ancient point of access needs to be considered.

From Bagiawari to the Home Department

But, how did these scattered scraps of information on the Bagiawari *stupa* enter the Public Branch of the Home Department, where they have remained effectively buried ? No information is available from 1855, when the relics were exhumed, till 1885. One presumes that they remained packed up and locked away with de la Croix. We do know, however, that during this time the circular stone coffer in which the relic caskets were kept has been given away (or sold)? and was said to be somewhere in Agra. In 1885, the relics were examined and authenticated by the Provincial Museum of Lucknow probably because de la Croix or his family wished to sell them for a reasonable sum. This is evident from the last noting made by Fuhrer (1885): "the relic caskets, and especially the bones will be very valuable to any Buddhist community of Ceylon, Burma, Siam or China, and will undoubtedly realize good price."

A formal advertisement for sale, however, appeared much later, towards the end of 1899. There is no information on the range of offers that were received but the British Museum in London certainly offered £ 100 sterling for the relics. However, "the price offered not being tempting the sale was not effected" (Pramanaik 1905).

The Bagiawari material again came up for sale around the turn of the present century, also the point when details on it, which form the basis of the present note, entered the Government of India records. This is because the sale offer was made in a letter to the Secretary of the Victoria Memorial Fund. Following the death of Victoria, a memorial to the "Queen-Empress of India" has been planned by the Viceroy, Lord Curzon (1899-1905). The Victoria Memorial in Calcutta was finally completed only in 1921 but several proposals for honouring the late queen's memory and a great deal of correspondence in connection with those proposals was exchanged from 1901 itself. Among them for instance, was the suggestion of Anagarika Dharmapala, Secretary of the Maha Bodhi Society (1901) to "perpetuate the gracious memory of the saintly Queen by erecting two permanent Lights to burn day and night at the holy spot- Buddha gaya - the Central Shrine of the 475 millions of Buddhists, and also have a Marble Altar under the Sacred Bodhi tree"!

The offer of the Buddhist relics from Bagiwari, however, was made later, around 1905. In a letter to the Secretary of the Victoria Memorial Fund, which came from the Mission School Street, Secundrabad (in the present Andhra Pradesh) and was written by N. C. Pramanaik, who claimed to be a close friend of the son of de la Croix, it offered these relics for a suitable price in case the government wished to collect "rare things for the Victoria Memorial in Calcutta" (Pramanaik 1905). It also enclosed a note by the son of de la Croix and a copy of Fuhrer's report.

The relics were not wanted for the Victoria Memorial but the Home Department forwarded the file to John Marshall, Director General of Archaeology in India, in case he wished to acquire them for one of the Indian Museums. It is a pity that Marshall did not recognize the significance of these finds. His handwritten note states (Marshall 1905):

> "The best market for the sale of these relics would probably be in Japan. I would not myself give more than £ 15 for them for any Indian Museum".

Pramanaik's offer was thus refused and in the Part B Proceedings of 'Home Department - Public', the only available details on a *stupa* in the Santhal Parganas were filed and effectively lost. Because these details have been unearthed, we now know a few things about the Bagiawari *stupa*. But what about the relics themselves? About the whereabouts of the crystal and marble caskets, the beads and bones - and so many other artefacts of this kind that have disappeared without leaving a trace - we still know nothing.

REFERENCES

Agrawala, V. S. 1977. *Gupta Art.* Varanasi: Prithivi Prakashan.

Asher, F.M. *The Art of Eastern India.* Minneapolis: The University of Minnesota Press.

Chakrabarti, D. K., Prasad, A. K., Jha, S. K., Anand , K and Chattopadhyay, R. K. 1995. Preliminary Observations on the Distribution of Archaeological Sites in the South Bihar Plains, *South Asian Studies* 11:129-47

De la Croix, 1905. Notes on the find of a Buddhist relic in Proceedings Nos: 341-42 of Home Department - Public - Part B (May).

Dharmapala, A. 1901. Letter to the Private Secretary to His Excellency the Viceroy (7th February) in Proceedings Nos: 466/69 of Home Department - Public - Part B (February).

Dikshit, M.G. 1949. *Etched Beads in India.* Deccan College Monograph Series:4. Poona: Deccan College Post Graduate and Research Institute.

Fuhrer, A. 1885. Report... to the Secretary Provincial Museum, Lucknow (22nd September) in Proceedings Nos: 341-42 of Home Department Public - Part B (May).

Lal, B.B 1988. *Santhal Pargana District* Series - 4 Bihar District Census Handbook, Part XIII-A, Village & Town Directory. Census of India 1981.

Marshall, J. 1905. Note to Home Department in Proceedings Nos: 341:-42 of Home Department -Public-Part B (May).

Mitra, D. 1971. *Buddhist Monuments.* Calcutta: Sahitya Samsad. 1989. Relics and Relic Caskets in A. Ghosh (ed.) *An Encyclopaedia of Indian Archaeology,* Volume II, 270-275. New Delhi: Munshiram Manoharlal Publishers Pvt. Ltd.

Mehta, R. N. and Chowdhary, S. N. 1966. *Excavation at Devnimori.* Baroda: Faculty of Arts, M. S. University of Baroda.

Mohan, V. 1996. The destruction of archaeological sites under the impact of rapid development in Haryana: an area of high archaeological pontential, *Man and Environment* XXI, 2:71-74.

Oldham, C.E.A. (ed.) 1930. *Journal of Francis Buchanan kept during the survey of the district of Bhagalpur in 1810-1811.* Patna: Superintendent, Government Printing, Bihar and Orissa.

Paddayya, K. 1996. Modern Impacts on Archaeological Sites in India: a Case Study from the Shorapur Doab, Karnataka, *Man and Environment* XXI, 2: 75-88.

Patil, D. R. 1963. *The Antiquarian Remains of Bihar.* Patna: Kashi Prasad Jayaswal Research Institute.

Pramanaik, N.C. 1905. Letter to the Secretary to the Victoria Memorial fund, Calcutta (20th March) in Proceedings Nos: 341-42 of Home Department-Public-PartB (May).

Department of History,
University of Delhi, South Campus.
New Delhi

NAYANJOT LAHIRI

Langudi : An Early Historical Buddhist Site in Coastal Orissa

During the early historical period South Asia saw the reemergence of cities, polities and the growth of Buddhism throughout the subcontinent (Heitzman 1984; Kosambi 1989; Sarao 1990; Ray 1994; Chakrabarti 1995; Morrison 1995). Lasting transformation took place all over the subcontinent; the major Buddhist reformation and research was confined to the Gangetic valley and the Deccan, regions which have always been viewed as the core areas of Buddhism (Dehejia 1972; Ray 1986). However, Orissa, which has yielded a large number of Buddhist sites with impressive art and architecture (Kittoe 1838; Beglar 1874-75; Mitra 1880; Gangulee 1912; Chanda 1930; Mahapatra 1936; Sahu 1958; Panigrahi 1961; Mitra 1981-83; Tripathy 1955a; Chualey 1996; Prusty, Mohanty and Mishra 1996; Mohanty, Mishra and Basa 1997), has been relegated to the secondary centre of Buddhist development and has not received adequate attention.

The present paper seeks to highlight Orissa's role in the development of early Buddhism on the basis of archaeological findings already reported and mainly from Langudi, a unique rock-out Buddhist site.

Both literary (Sahu 1985) and archaeological findings (Chauley 1996) suggest that early Buddhism was widely prevalent in the pre-Mauryan period. Recent excavations at Lalitagiri have revealed a large *stupa* containing gold, silver and stone relic caskets kept one inside another; relics probably are those of lord Buddha or of his close disciple, Sariputta. The finding of relic caskets of this kind is unique in the entire eastern India.

In South Asia, during the Mauryan periods a network of well established internal trade routes allowed rapid inter-regional commerce and ideas. Within a short period, new political concepts in the form of Mauryan imperialism and administration were introduced. New religious faiths and institutions like Buddhism and Jainism, with profound impact on language, art and architecture, literature and the economy came into being . The extension of the trade networks, both domestic and overseas, had far–reaching economic implications and was accompanied by the introduction of currency (Sharma 1983; Begley 1986; Kosambi 1989; Lahiri 1992).

This gained momentum in the post-Mauryan era (*cicra* 200 B.C.–A.D. 300) and is marked by far–reaching changes in the socio–economic fabric of the subcontinent. Buddhism witnessed a tremendous growth with the evolution of *stupas.* (Schopen 1987). *The stupas* and their railings were embellished with artistic and decorative panels as revealed in the reliefs of Amaravati, Ajanta, Barhut, Bedsa, Bhubaneswar, Bhaja, Bodhgaya, Karla, Pitalkhora and Sanchi. These early centres spread over a wide geographical area reflect the development of urbanism, growth of communication and the increased mobility of people. Along with the *stupas*, the numerous symbols such as the lion, elephant, tree, serpent, horse and lotus medallion etc. which represent Buddha in the early Hinayana sect, merit our attention . The monuments were constructed mainly through active patrons of Buddhism and donation by the merchants and traders.

Orissa comprising vast delatic plains, long coast line with rich mineral and forest resources, also come in the firmanment of this development during the post-Mauryan period. Both internal and overseas trade routes linked various urban centres and port-cities of South and South-east Asia. Buddhism played a significant role in coordinating the entire system.

Though a number of early historical Buddhist sites were reported from Orissa, particularly from the coastal region, there was no evidence of rock-cut sites except the spectacular Jaina relics at Khandagiri and Udayagiri near Bhubaneswar till now. However, at Langudi, a series of rock-cut *stupas* with lotus medallion and flying vidyadharas were noticed for the first time not only in Orissa but in the entire Eastern India (Prusty and Mohanty 1995: 325-327).

The Site

Langudi (20° 41' N. and 86° 11' E.) is a low hill running north-south, located in the delataic plain of Salipur village under Mirjapur Gram Panchayat in the newly formed Jajpur District (Fig. 1). The hill is mostly devoid of vegetation. Khondalite is the main geological formation of the area. The river Kelua, a tributary of the Brahmani, flows in the north-east and east at a distance of two kilometres . Another small nullah flows in the west and south of the hillock.

Intensive exploration carried out in and around the hill has revelaed a series of rock-out *stupas* of the early historical period together with a number of early medieval Buddhist shrines. This includes Dhyani Buddhas in variegated postures, Bodhisattva Avalokitesvara and other feminine divinities like Tara and Prajnaparamita, and the dilapidated remains of an imposing brick central *stupa* as well as large, brick quadrangular monasteries indicating that it was a large centre of Buddhism, of Hinayana, and Mahayana Vajrayana sects .

Remains

The northern spur of the hillock is covered with 34 rock-cut *stupas* of various sizes, exquisitely carved in low relief recalling those of the Amaravati school. The most outstanding is the gigantic central rock-out *stupa* with fine workmanship . It represents the traditional *stupa* architectural norms comprising a circular drum, the cylinderical dome as well as a rectangular *harmika* with an elongated monolithic cylindrical shaft surmounted by a crescent moon like *chhatravali.* The topmost extreme left and right terminal edges with two kneeling vidyadharas of Udayagiri–Khandagiri prototype, offer floral tribute and deep obeisance to the *stupa.*

The rock-cut tradition began in the early historical period and continued in the succeeding early medieval period also . The southern spur of the hillock contains a galaxy of Buddhist rock-cut sculptures, beautifully carved in relief in extensive panels. In the first part of this panel, the seated Dhyani Buddha Amitabha in *samadhi mudra* and seated Tara in *varada mudra* are carved with particular attention to minute details.

The Buddha in *samadhimudra,* resplendent with all sorts of auspicious marks characteristic of *"Mahapurusha Chakravartin"* is elegantly poised on a *visvapadma* in *vajraparayankasana* pose. The serene-looking, contemplative and compassionate Buddha, whose pacific face, benign-smiling rhythm and thrilling yogic ecstacy reveals the intense meditative posture of his two hands, resting one upon the other on his lap. Stylistically and iconographically this rock-cut image of Buddha can tentatively be attributed to the 7th-8th centuries A.D.

Homogeneously designed, draped and decked in all sorts of gorgeous garments and celestial ornaments, the two-armed, round–faced, serene looking and mild-smiling benign Buddhist tantric goddess Tara is elegantly seated on a *Visvapadma* in *ardhaparayankasana* attitude. She has bisected bun-shaped coiffure. Tara, has her right hand in the *varada* pose and a fully blossomed *uptala* in her corresponding damaged left hand with the an elongated stem emerging between her thumb and the index finger respectively.

The rock-cut feminine Mahayana Buddhist goddess Prajnaparamita, is a beautifully shown on the extrême end of the rock-cut panel. The smiling, compassionate goddess of transcendental wisdom either held a red lotus or was depicted in the *varada* pose.

The crescent-moon-like rock-cut panel of the seated Dhyani Buddha is at the centre of rock-cut monolithic *stupa* having a circular drum, an elongated dome as well as a damaged rectangular *harmika* reminiscent of those of the identical structural khondolite *stupa* hoards discovered at Lalitagiri (Donaldson 1985; Mohapatra 1986).

Besides rock-cut *stupa* and images, the hillock also reveals a strong tradition of relief figures. The presence of a two-armed, round– faced image of Padmapani Bodhisattva in graceful thrice-bent posture is one of the finest Buddhist images of early medieval Orissa. In this image the left hand carries a fully blossomed *utplala* with its elongated stem emerging from between the thumb and index fingers. In addition to this image is a smiling Buddha on a *visvapadma* of double-eight radiant petals in *vajraparayankasana.* The image represents the sacred wheel marks *(Dharmachakras)* on the right palm and the soles.

The images at Langudi show the artist's mastery over form and skill in depicting figures in every position–front, back and side. The poses of the figures are easy and natural; their movement vivacious and elastic. The composition is fairly coherent and effective, matured depth, displaying a considerable plasticity of form and naturalism of modelling. Slender figures of men and women are marked by a suavity of outline.

Other noteworthy features of this hillock comprise a plain monolithic khondalite rectangular pillar base erected on the stone paved verandah and courtyard of a brick quadrangular monastery (*sangharama*) lying buried along with numerous burnt-bricks and brick-bats all over an extensive mound of 50 by 50 metres. Ruins of a small *stupa* which is circular in appearance located over a flat surface at the north-eastern limit of the hill, associated with khondalite pillars, earth and laterite blocks resembles those of khondalite pillar fragments from the excavated monastic complexes at Lalitagiri, Ratnagiri and Udayagiri (Mitra 1981-83).

Langudi hill with its early historical and early medieval Buddhist remains is situated in close proximity of the ancient city of Radhanagar, which has been tentatively identified with Dantapura, the capital of ancient Kalinga, a prosperous trade and mercantile centre of eastern India during the early historical period (Prusty, Mohanty and Mishra 1996:123--127). Langudi's location, neither too far from a community of a prosperous laity capable of supporting the *samgha* nor too close to the urban centre of Radhanāgar which could have caused distraction, was an ideal place for meditation and scholarly pursuits of the resident monks and nuns, exemplifying the complementary interrelationships of the lay and the monastic communities in early Buddhism.

Postscript

Recent excavation at Langudi hill by the Orissa Institute of Maritime and South East Asian Studies (OIMESEAS) has confirmed the identity of Langudi Hill with Pushpagiri Mahavihara and equated with that of Huen-Tsang's pu-sie-po-ki-li. Huen-Tsang visited Udra (the present Orissa) during A.D. 639 and mentioned the name of Peu-so-po-ki-li Buddhist monastery in his book, where he had said that a supernatural light was emanating from top of hill. He has also said five monasteries were found near Peu-so-po-ki-li. The excavation in this hill has revealed a fragmented stone Brahmi inscription, Sunga terracotta, 43 rock-cut panels of miniature *stupas,* neolithic tools etc. According to Prof. K.S. Behera, the Director of OIMSEAS and Mr. Debraj Pradhan, incharge of the excavation of this site, the images discovered from the area were similar to those found in Borobodor in Indonesia, one of the biggest Buddhist sites in the world. The Brahmi inscription has been studied by Prof. B. N. Mukherjee of Calcutta University who has confirmed after deciphering the inscription that the controversy over the identification of Pushpagiri Mahavihara had been solved. The inscription points out that as Pushpa Sabhar Giraya (load of flowers over a hill) dating back to the 1st century A. D.

Acknowledgements

We are extremely grateful to Thomas Lawton and Balaram Tripathy for reviewing the manuscript and suggesting many changes. We have incorported many of their ideas in the present article.

REFERENCES

Basa, K.K. (in press) Archaeological Heritage. In O. K. Mishra. (ed.) Comprehensive History and Culture of Orissa.

Beglar, J. D. 1874-76. *Report of Tours in South Eastern Provinces in 1874-75 A.D. and 1875-76,* Archaeological Survey of India, Varanasi: Reprint Indological Book House. Vol. XIII, pp. 95-98.

Begley, V. 1986. From Iron Age to Early History in South Indian Archaeology. in J. Jacobson (ed.) *Studies in Archaeology of India and Pakistan* New Delhi: American Institute of Indian Studies, pp. 297-321

Chakrabarti, D.K. 1995. Buddhist Sites Across South Asia as Influenced by Political and Economic Forces, *World Archaeology,* 27 (2) pp. 185-201.

Chanda, R.P. 1930. *Exploration in Orissa* Calcutta: Memoir of Archaeological Survey of India.

Chauley, G.C. 1996. Excavated Remains at Lalitagiri-A Buddhist site in Orissa in C. Margabandhu and K.S. Ramachandran *et al* (eds) *Spectrum of Indian Culture,* Delhi: Agam Kala Prakashan, pp. 216-220.

Dehejia, V. 1972. *Early Buddhist Rock Temples: A Chronological Study.* London: Thames and Hudson.

Donaldson, T.F. 1985. *Hindu Temple Art of Orissa.* Vol. I, Leiden: Brill.

Gangulee, M.M. 1912. *Orissa and Her Remains.* Calcutta: Thacker Spink and co.

Heitjman, J. 1984. Early Buddhism, Trade and Empire in K.A.R Kennedy and G.I. Possehl (eds) *Studies in the Archaeology and Paleoanthropology of South Asia.* New Delhi: Oxford University Press, pp. 121-38.

Kittoe, M.1838. A Journey in Orissa. *Journal of Asiatic Society of Bengal.* 7, pp. 679-685 and 1060-1063.

Kosambi, D.D. 1989. *The Culture and Civilization of Ancient India in Historical Outline.* New Delhi: Vikas.

Lahiri, N. 1992. *The Archaeology of Indian Trade Routes up to c. 200 B.C.* Delhi: Oxford University Press.

Mahapatra, K.N. 1936. Some Interesting Remains in Bhubaneswar. *Vaitarani.* 10 (3 and 4), pp. 52-59.

Mitra, D. 1981-83. *Ratnagiri (1958-61),* 2 vols. Delhi: Archaeological Survey of India.

Mitra, R.L. 1880. *Antiquities of Orissa.* Calcutta: Govt. of India.

Mohanty, Mishra P. J., and Basa. K.K. 1997. An Archaeological Investigation into Ptolemy's *Paloura. AH-SAN* 5:14.15.

Mohapatra, R.P. 1986. *Archaeology in Orissa,* Vol. II. Delhi: B.R. Publications.

Morrison, K.D. 1995. Trade, urbanism and agricultural expansion: Buddhist monastic institutions and the state in the Early Historic Western Deccan. *World Archaeology.* 27 (2) pp. 203-221.

Panigrahi, K.C. 1961. *Archaeological Remains at Bhubaneswar.* Calcutta: Orient and Longman.

Prusty, H.C. and Mohanty, P. 1995. Langudi: A Unique Rock-cut Buddhist Site in Orissa. *Bulletin of Deccan college Post-graduate and Reseach Institute.* 53 pp. 325-327.

Prusty, H.C. Mohanty, P., Mishra, J. 1996. Dantapura, The Capital of Ancient Kalinga: A Reappriasal. *Puratattva.* 26, pp. 123-127.

Ray, H.P. 1986. *Monastery and Guild: Commerce Under the Satavahanas.* Delhi: Oxford University Press.

Sahu, N.K. 1958. *Buddhism in Orissa.* Cuttack: Utkal University.

Sarao, K.T.S. 1990. *Urban centres and Urbanization as Reflected in the Pali Vinaya and Sutta Pitakas.* Delhi: Vidyanidi Oriental.

Schoper, G. 1987. Burial "Ad sanctos" and th Physical Presence of the Buddha in Early Buddhism, A Study in the Archaeology of Religions. *Religion.* 17, pp. 193-225.

Sharma, R.S. 1983. *Perspectives in Social and Economic History of Early India.* New Delhi: Cosmos.

Tripathy, B. 1995. Archaeological Sites in Boudh District, *Orissa, District Souvenir.* 1, pp. 8-16.

Decean College,
Pune

HARISH PRUSTY
PRADEEP MOHANTY
JITU MISHRA

Vajrasattva : Varieties and Worship

Vajrasattva, the Buddha of Supreme Intelligence, is a widely revered deity of the Buddhist pantheon. Yet his position here is difficult to establish. Various Buddhist schools and scholars look upon him differently. The Svabhavika sect identifies him with Svabhava, the Adi Buddha (Getty 1928: 5). He is also designated as the sixth Dhyani Buddha (Saraswati 1977: 5.) of the pantheon who presides over the mind, and as such is an embodiment collectively of the five *skandhas* over which the five Dhyani Buddhas are said to preside. In Nepal, he is regarded as the priest of five Dhyani Buddhas (Bhattacharya 1958: 74). Certain Lamaistic sects consider him to be an active form of Vajradhara (Getty 1928: 4). He is looked upon as an emanation of the Dhyani Buddha Akshobhya (Getty, 1928: 5). However, his white complexion and the position of Vairochana on the crown of a few Vajrasattva images indicate that Variochana was regarded as his spiritual sire (Mitra 1978: 63).

Several forms of Vajrasattva are known in Indian art and recorded in Tantrik works as well. The earliest reference to Vajrasattva is found in *Guhyasamaja Tantra,* but not as a Dhyani Buddha (Bhattacharya 1967: 103). He is described as two-armed, bearing an axe and a club. This form, however, is not known so far. Vajrasattva is the central deity of *Satachakravarti mandala* and holds *vajra* and *vajra-ghanta* in his hands (Bhattacharya 1972: 79). The *Advayavajrasamgraha* describes a two-armed and one-faced form of Vajrasattva. He holds in his two hands the *vajra* and *vajra-marked ghanta* (Shastri 1927: 4). The *Vajradaka Tantra* mentions a form of Vajrasattva with four faces, four arms and three eyes. He is in the act of dancing the *tandava* on a corpse. He holds the thunderbolt, sword, bell and human skull in his hands (Bhattacharya 1974: 18). Getty refers to Japanese forms of Vajrasattva with four and six arms (Getty 1928: 8). In the four-armed form, the original arms hold *vajra* and bell while two of the accessory arms always brandish the bow and arrow. In the six-armed variety, the symbols held by the fifth and sixth may vary.

Images of Vajrasattva have been reported in a fairly large number from various sites in Bihar, Bengal, Orissa and Kashmir where the worship of Vajrasattva seems to have been more popular. Most of the images portray Vajrasattva as two-armed. He is elaborately crowned and bejewelled like a Bodhisattva, seated on a lotus in *ardha-paryankasana* or *lalitasana* and carry a *vajra* in his right hand against the chest and a *vajra*-marked *ghanta* in the left hand resting against the left thigh. Besides the two-armed form, other forms of Vajrasattva how so ever rare are also knows in Indian art :–

(i) Vajrasattva with his consort,

(ii) Four-armed Vajrasattva, and

(iii) The *Yab-Yum* form.

Nalanda, the famous seat of Vajrayana Buddhism has yielded a variety of beautiful Vajrasattva images. A stele showing five figures, embellished with crown and ornaments, seated within a separate aureole is unique. The central figure portrays a two-armed Vajrasattva holding a *vajra* against chest and a bell resting against thigh. Four female figures within separate aureoles appear on four corners. The deity on the upper right corner holds a garland while the other one on the upper left carries a musical instrument. The deity in lower right corner has her hands on her thigh holding something in both hands which is too indistinct to be identified and the other one on the lower left corner, slightly bent towards left, has both her hands joined together in an attitude of clapping. These female figures could possibly be the representation of the four dancing goddesses known as Lasya, Nritya, Malya and Gita (Pl. III.3. Saraswati; 1977: fig. 161). Another image of Vajrasattva, probably from Nalanda, with four dancing goddesses, but in different style is also known (Pal 1978: fig. 52). The stele portrays Vajrasattva as the main deity and the four dancing goddesses are shown on the four cornes of the stele. Several other images of Vajrasattva with two arms are also known from Nalanda (Saraswati 1977: figs, 156, 157 & 159).

Ratnagiri in Orissa is another famous Buddhist site from where several images of Vajrasattva have been reported. Besides a few stele (Mitra 1981: Pl. CLXXII-C, CCXL-A, CCCLV-C), nine images are portrayed in the niches of monolithic votive *stupas* (Mitra 1981: Pl. LXV-C&D, LXVI-A, B&C, XC-A, CCXLVII, CCXXVII-Stupa 43, CCLXIX-C) and drum slabs (Mitra 1981, Pl. LII-C). All these images show him with two arms, seated in *Vajraparyankasana* or *paryankasana,* holding *vajra* and *ghanta* and adorned with crown and ornaments.

The famous bronze hoard from Achutrajpur contains some exquisite Vajrasattva images with two arms, seated on a high lotus throne and embellished with various ornaments and crown (Mitra 1978: fig. 54, 55, 56, 57 & 58). The crown, sometimes, bears the effigy of five Dhyani Buddhas (Mitra 1978: 63-64, fig. 54).

The Vajrasattva images from Kashmir region present a remarkable variety in form, of which, some are rare types in Indian art. The two known four-armed images of Vajrasattva are from Kashmir. The one, cast in copper, shows him seated in *ardhaparyankasana* against a flaming aureole on a lotus throne supported by two lions and human figure. He carries a *vajra,* arrow, bow and bell in his four hands and wears a *dhoti,* chased ornaments and a crown bearing effigies of seated Dhyani Buddhas. The eyes and *urna* are inlaid with silver (Schroeder 1981: fig. 28C). The image can be dated to around 10-11th cent. A.D. Another image of this type from Kashmir has been acquired by the National Museum, New Delhi in 1994 This form is identical to the Japanese form of four-armed Vajrasattva referred by Getty (Getty 1928: 8).

The image of Vajrasattva with his spiritual consort Vajrasattvatmika from Kashmir is also rare and unique. This shows Vajrasttva seated in *ardhaparyankasana* on a lotus throne supported by three elephants. The goddess sits on the left thigh and her legs are encircled by those of Vajrasattva. Both wear rich ornaments and crown and hold similar attributes in their hands, i.e., *vajra* and *ghanta.* The damaged crown of Vajrasattva bears the effigy of five Dhyani Buddhas (Pl. III. 4 and Pal 1978: fig. 29).

In yet another rare and interesting representation, cast in brass, from Kashmir, Vajrasattva has been shown seated in *lalitasana* on a lotus supported by a rock-like structure which seems to represent Mount Sumeru, the abode of Vajrasattva. He wears various ornaments and a crown with the figure of the five Dhyani Buddhas.

Besides these, several other images of Vajrasattva are also known from Kashmir (Schroeder 1981: Fig. 20B & 28D), Sarnath (Huntington 1985: 460, Fig. 13), Salempur (Saraswati 1977: fig. 158), Sukhbaspur (Bhattasali, 1972: 24) and other places which are remarkable from iconographic point of view.

Vajrasattva is also depicted in *Yab-Yum* form but, generally kept secret (Bhattacharya 1958: 75). In this form he is closely associated with his Sakti and is particularly popular in Nepal and Tibet region. He is shown in both peaceful and wrathful aspects and is invoked for the atonement of sins (Bartholomew 1965: 68).

The above types portray Vajrasattva as principal deity in the composition. But in a few cases he also appears on the crown, pedestals and stele of other Buddhist deities. The *Chunda sadhana* mentions presence of Vajrasattva on the crown of deities (Bhattacharya, 1968: 272). In a rare depiction from Tibet, he has been portrayed on the streaming hair of Mahakala (Rhie and Thurman 1991: 293, fig. 110). In another case he is represented on the pedestal of Ashtamahabhya Tara from Sompara (Saraswati 1977: fig. 103). One of the pedestals of Buddha image (Mitra 1981: PL. CLXV) and a stele of Akshobhya (Mitra 1981, PL. CCCXXIII-A) from Ratnagiri also portray the image of Vajrasattva.

From the numerous representations, multiplicity of forms and the varying interpretations, it is apparent that Vajrasattva occupied unique position in Buddhist pantheon and by looking at the number of images found, it can easily be said that the worship of Vajrasattva in India was more popular than those of the five Dhyani Buddhas and Vajradhara, the Adi Buddha. The finds also reveal that the worship of Vajrasattva came into prominence during the Vajrayana phase and was confined, more or less, to eastern India and Kashmir, the region which contributed significantly to the evolution of Vajrayana school and art.

REFERENCES

Bhattacharya, B. 1958. *The Indian Buddhist Iconography.* Calcutta: 74-75.

______________, (ed.). 1967. *Guhyasamaja Tantra,* Gaikwad's Oriental Series No. 53. Baroda : 103.

______________, (ed.). 1972. *Nispannayogavali of Abhayakargupta.* Gaikwad's Oriental Series No. 109. Baroda : 79.

Bhattacharya, D.C. 1974. *Tantric Buddhist Iconographic Sources.* New Delhi: 18.

Bhattasali, N.K. 1972. *Iconography of Buddhist and Brahmanical Sculptures in the Dacca Museum* Delhi: Pl. III.a, 24.

Bartholomew, R. (ed.) 1965. *Tibet House Museum.* New Delhi : 68.

Getty, A.. 1928. *The Gods of Northern Buddhism.* Oxford: 4, 5 and 8.

Huntington, S.L. 1985. *Art of Ancient India.* New Delhi: 460, fig. 13.

Mitra, D. 1978. *Bronzes from Achutrajpur.* New Delhi: 63, fig. 54, 55, 56, 57, 58.

______________, 1981. *Ratnagiri,* Vol. I, New Delhi.

Nath, J. 1996. "Vajrasattva", *Puratattva.* No. 26: 129-130.

Pal, P. 1975. *Bronzes of Kashmir.* New Delhi: 162.

______________, 1978. *The Sensuous Immortals:* Los Angeles, fig. 52.

Rhie, M.M. and Thurman, R.A.F. 1991. *The Sacred Art of Tibet:* London., 293, fig. 110.

Saraswati, S.K. 1977. *Tantrayana Art–An Album.* Calcutta, fig. 156, 157, 158, 159, 161.

Schoroeder, U.V. 1981. *Indo-Tibetan Bronzes.* Hong Kong: 153, fig. 28C, 28D, 20B.

Shastri, H (ed.). 1927. *Advayavajrasamgraha.* Gaikwad's Oriental Series No. SL. Baroda: 4.

National Museum, Janpath,
New Delhi

JITENDRA NATH

A Unique Panchakuta Temple at Sirval, Gulbarga District, Karnataka

Sirval is a small village 13 km north-east of Shahapur town in Gulbarga District of Karnataka State, and is located about 2 km away from the south bank of the river Bhima. Sannati, the famous Buddhist site is situated on the north bank (Sundara 1987, Fig.1). Sirval has attracted the attention of scholars, especially art historians on account of the several Rashtrakuta structural temples found in and around the village and have been documented by Soundara Rajan (1986) and Nagaraja Rao (1994). A few Kalyana Chalukya temples are also found here (Hardy 1995; Dhaky 1996). An interesting *panchakuta* temple, locally known as the Siddalingesvaragudi, is in the north-western corner of the village, on the right bank of the Sirval nala. Although this temple has been noticed by several scholars, its plan was not carefully studied. This paper brings to light the unique features of this structure.

Panchakuta (pachaytana) temples, consisting of five *garbhagrihas* in one complex, are well known from the earliest times. The Deogarh Vishnu temple of the Gupta period represents the earliest *panchakuta* temple in India (Percy Brown, 1970). On plan the main *garbhagriha* is at the centre and the rest of the sanctums are at corners of the plinth.

In Karnataka, *panchakuta* temples were built during the Ganga, Kalyana Chalukya and Hoysala times. The Panchalingeswara temple of the Gangas at Somanatha, the Hoysala *panchakuta* at Govindanahalli (Settar 1992:201) and a *Panchakuta* temple at Huli of the Chalukyas of Kalyana (Dhaky 1996: 209) are some noteworthy examples. These temples have a uniform plan, five *garbhagrihas* in a row, with a common *antarala* and a *sabhamandapa.*

The Plan

The *panchakuta* temple at Sirval, however, has a distinctive plan in the form of a 'cross'. There are four *garbhagrihas* at the four cardinal points and a fifth one, the main *garbhagriha* in the centre. The central *garbhagriha* opens on all four sides, and in each direction it has *antarala, ardhamandapa, sabhamandapa* leading to adjoining *garbhagriha* in all the four directions. The *prakara* wall encloses the temple on all sides with an entrance gate on the north wall. (Fig.2)

The garbhagriha

The central *garbhagriha* is square on plan with an elevated floor. The four doors have elaborate four *sakas* with : (1) square and star-shaped flowers, (2) scrolls and creepers, (3) pilasters, and (4) lions standing on their hind legs. At the base of the *sakas, dvarapalas* stand in *tribhanga,* bearing Saivite attributes such as *damaru, trisula, sarpa, gada* and *abhayamudra.* The projected *lalata* blocks have prominent *kapotas* which are highly ornate and carved into hanging buds.

Above the *kapotas* are five miniature *nagara* turrets in a row, and four *yalis* stand on their hind legs between these turrets.

Above the central *garbhagriha* is a *sikhara* or the superstructure. The *sikhara* is of the *Dravida* order containing three *talas,* each with *salas* and *kutas*. The original *sikhara* was in a dilapidated condition but it has now been renovated.

Antaralas

The *antaralas* around central *garbhagriha* are rectangular and each is provided with a door . These doors also have elaborate *sakas,* similar to the *sakas* of central *garbhagriha.* The lintel blocks contain Ganesa and Gajalakshmi figures. Some of the *antaralas* have deep recesses in their walls. The doors are decorated and are similar to the doors of the *garbhagriha.*

Ardhamandapas

The *ardhamandapas* adjoining the *antaralas* are rectangular with two massive rectangular pillars in the front supporting a horizontal beam, which divides the *ardhamandapa* from the *sabahamandapa.* The ceilings of the *ardhamandapas* have lotus relief decorations in a square block. The northern and southern *ardhamandapas* have *devakoshtas* on either side walls.

Sabhamandapas

The square *sabhamanadapas* and the associated *ardhamandapas* connect the central *garbhagriha* with the four cardinal *garbhagrihas.* The entrances on either side are marked by *mukhamandapas* with balustrades which provide access to the main *garbhagriha* from the four *kutas.* The western and eastern *sabhamandapas* are covered by walls, whereas the northern and sourthern ones are *kakshasana* type. The four pillars within each of these *sabhamandapa* are elaborately carved and set on a raised platform. The ceilings are either domical or square slabs with a lotus relief in the middle.

Mukhamandapas

The *mukhamandapas* on either side mark the entrances. These *mukhamandapas* have two short pillars in the front, set on raised *kakshasana* and pilasters at the back supporting the roof and the projected sloping eave. The short pillars in the front have round shafts and circular abacus. The doorways are similar to those of the central one but two *nidhi* figures carved at the bottom of the door jambs. The *mukhamandapa* of the eastern *sabhamandapa* is enclosed by walls, while the southern *mukhamandapa* is now modified into a two-storyed structure and has an arched opening which functions as the principal entrance to the central *garbhagriha* (Fig.3). The pillars of the these two *sabhamandapa* are similar and have a moulded base shaft having square with convex base scroll crobels. Four niches *(devakoshtas),* flanked by pilasters, with miniature *nagara* turrets on the top, are found on the interior walls of *sabhamandapas* . The ceilings are rotated square blocks with a lotus figure in the centre.

The northern and southern *sabhamndapas* are of the *kakshasana* type with two entrances on either side marked by *yalis* in the balustrade. The four central pillars, made of dolerite rock are set on a raised floor. They are well polished and consist of a moulded base, shaft which is divided into upper and lower square shafts, disc capital and a square abacus. The upper and lower shafts contain several sculptures of Amruatamanthana, Kiratarjuniya Siva, Hanuman and Vali fighting scene, Ganesa, Yoganarayana, Venugopala, Suryanarayana, Sarasvati, Kartikeya, Hari, Vishnu, Bhairava, Rati-Manmatha and Kali. The central ceilings of these two *sabhamandapas* are domical in shape, consisting of seven tiers decorated with cusps, geometrical designs and flowers and hanging bud in the centre; the dwarf columns are simple and set on *kakshasana* supporting round abacus.

The cardinal garbhagrihas

The four cardinal *garbhagrihas* have an *antarala,* each leading to the *sabhamadapa* and to the central shrine. The doorways of the *antaralas* are framed with pilasters and imitation of *jalavatayana* without perforation on either sides. The pilasters contain two standing female attendants at the base. Above the door is the *makaratorana* in which Siva is depicted in *tandava* pose flanked by Brahma on his right and Vishnu on his left. The rectangular *antaralas* have plain walls and the sqaure ceilings have lotus relief decoration. The *antaralas* and the *garbhagrihas* are divided by a wall and have an entrance which leads to the *garbhagriha.* The doorways of the *garbhagriha* are simple and consist of two *sakas* with *dvarapalas* at the base.

Sikhara

The *sikhara* or superstructure rises only above the central *garbhagriha.* It is a *Dravida sikhara,* consisting of three *talas.* Each *tala* is adorned with *salas* and *kutas.*

The original *sikhara* was till recently, in a dilapidated condition but it has been renovated now. Many figures of Saiva saints are carved on the lower *tala* and brightly painted.

Gateway

An impressive gateway is on the northern wall of the enclosure. It is rectangular on plan and faces north. The doorframe is simple and plain, the *lalata* block has a Gajalakshmi figure. The passage is flanked by raised platforms on either side with three bays each. The pillars are simple with two square shafts intervened by an octagonal part. They support the angular brackets and the beams across. The roof is made of horizontally arranged rectangular granite blocks. Perhaps, it is one of the earliest examples of Chalukyas of Kalyana temple-gateway.

Date

Two inscriptions belonging to the Chalukyas of Kalyana and Silahara family of Tardawadi (Bijapur District) are found here. The earliest inscription is on the pillar of the eastern *sabhamandapa* dated to A. D. 1138 issued by Somesvara II, the famous king of Kalyana Chalukyas. It mentions that king Somesvara II donated a land for renovation and daily offerings to the temple at Sirval. Another inscription which is issued by the Yadava subordinate Singanarasa of Silahara dynasty of Tardawadi, a north-eastern administrative division of *Sagara*-300. This inscription is dated to A.D. 1189 and refers to a grant of land to the temple for daily rituals and the proformance of *angabhoga* and *rangabhoga* to the god (Shivananda 1992: 66). However, the founding date of the temple is not clear from these two inscriptions. On stylistic grounds the temple can be assigned to the Later (Kalyana) Chalukya period.

Discussion

The importance of this temple lies in its unique plan. The layout of the *garbhagrihas,* four on cardinal points and one at the centre, suggests that the temple represents the five aspects of Siva i.e. *Sadasiva* or *Mahadeva: Sadasiva* has five faces representing *Tatapurusa, Agora, Vamadeva, Sadyojata* and *Isana.* The *Vishnudarmottara Purana* says that *Sadyojata,* which faces west, is of pearl-like colour of the moon and represents earth (Prithvi); that of *Vamadeva,* facing north, has red colour and represents water (*apa*); that of *Agora* which facing south is dark-blue and represents fire (*agni*); and that *Tatapurusha* facing east has golden yellow colour and represents sky *(akasa).* These are also individually known as *Mahadeva* (eastern), *Bhairava* (southern), *Adivaktra* (western), *Umavaktra* (northern) and *Sadasiva,* the fifth face on the top also known as *Isana* (Sharma 1976: 3). The *garbhagriha* that is positioned at the centre may represent *Isana* or *Akasa,* while the other four *lingas* enshrined in cardinal sanctums may represent the other four aspects of Siva as mentioned above.

Acknowledgements

The author is grateful to Indian Council of Historical Research. New Delhi for financial support. I thank Prof. K. Paddayya for his guidance and comments on the first draft. I also wish to thank Drs Gauri Lad, R. K. Mohanty, Ravi Korisettar for their valuable suggestions. My sincere thanks are to Dr. Selvakumar, Mr. K. Bilal, Ms. Suchi Dayal and Mr. Ashok Chincholi for their help and assistance both in the field and in preparation of this article.

REFERENCES

Bose, N. K. 1932. *Canons of Orissan Architecture:* Calcutta.

Cousens , Henry. 1926. *The Chalukyan Architecture of the Kanarese District* . Archaeological Survey of India, vol. 42. New Imperial Series: Delhi.

Dehejia, V. 1979. *Early Stone Temples of Orissa.:* New Delhi.

Deva, Kirshna 1995. *Temples of India.* 2 volums: New Delhi.

Dhaky, M.A. 1977. *The Indian Temple Forms in Karnataka Inscriptions and Architecture.:* New Delhi.

____________1996. Calukyas of Kalyana: Phase I Transitional in Dhaky M. A. (ed) *Encyclopedia of Indian Temple*

Architecture South India, Upper Dravidadesa, Later Phase.: New Delhi.

Gopal, B.R. 1981. *The Chalukyas of Kalyan and Kalchuris.*: Dharwad.

Krishnan, K. G. 1964. Traipursa-Trikuta Cults in Karnataka. *The Quarterly Journal of the Mythic Society.* 55. 2. 53-56.

Kramrisch, Stella. 1976. *The Hindu Temple.* 2 vols : Delhi

Lorenzon, David N. 1972. *The Kapalikas and Kalamukhas–Two Lost Saivite Sects.*: Berkely

Michell, George. 1977. *The Hindu Temple., An Introduction to its Meaning and Forms* : Chicago.

Patil, C. S. 1992. *Temples of Raichur and Bellary Districts. A. D. 1000 to 1325:* Mysore.

________ 1996. Art and Architecture of Rashtrakutas, in Ramesh, K. V. *et al* (ed)*'Gauravam', Recent Researches in Indology* (Prof. B. K. Gururaja Rao Felicitation volume) : New Delhi.

Percy Brown 1970. *Indian Architecture, Hindu, Buddhist and Jaina:* Delhi.

Rajasekara, S. 1985. *Karnataka Architecture:* Dharwad

________ 1991. *Rashtrakuta Art in Karnataka:* Dharwad.

Rao, T.A. Gopinatha. 1914. *Elements of Hindu Iconography.*: Delhi.

Rao, Rama M. 1967. Some Temples of Medieval Deccan, a paper presented in Seminar on Indian Architecture, November 17-24 at The American Academy of Benaras.

Sarma, I. K. 1982. *The Development of Early Saiva Art and Archiecture* : Delhi.

Sharma, B. Nath. 1976. *Icnography of Sadasiva* : New Delhi.

Settar, S. 1992. *The Hoysala Temples* : Bangalore.

Soundara Rajan. 1986. Rashtrakutas of Malkhed, Upper Variation, Phase II in Meister, W. M. & Dhaky. M. A. (ed.) *Encyclopadia of Indian Temple Architecture. South India, Upper Dravidadesa, Early Phase.* Vol. 2 : Oxford

Sundara, A. 1987. Excavations at Sannati. *Puratatva,* 17.

Deccan College,
Pune

S. K. Aruni

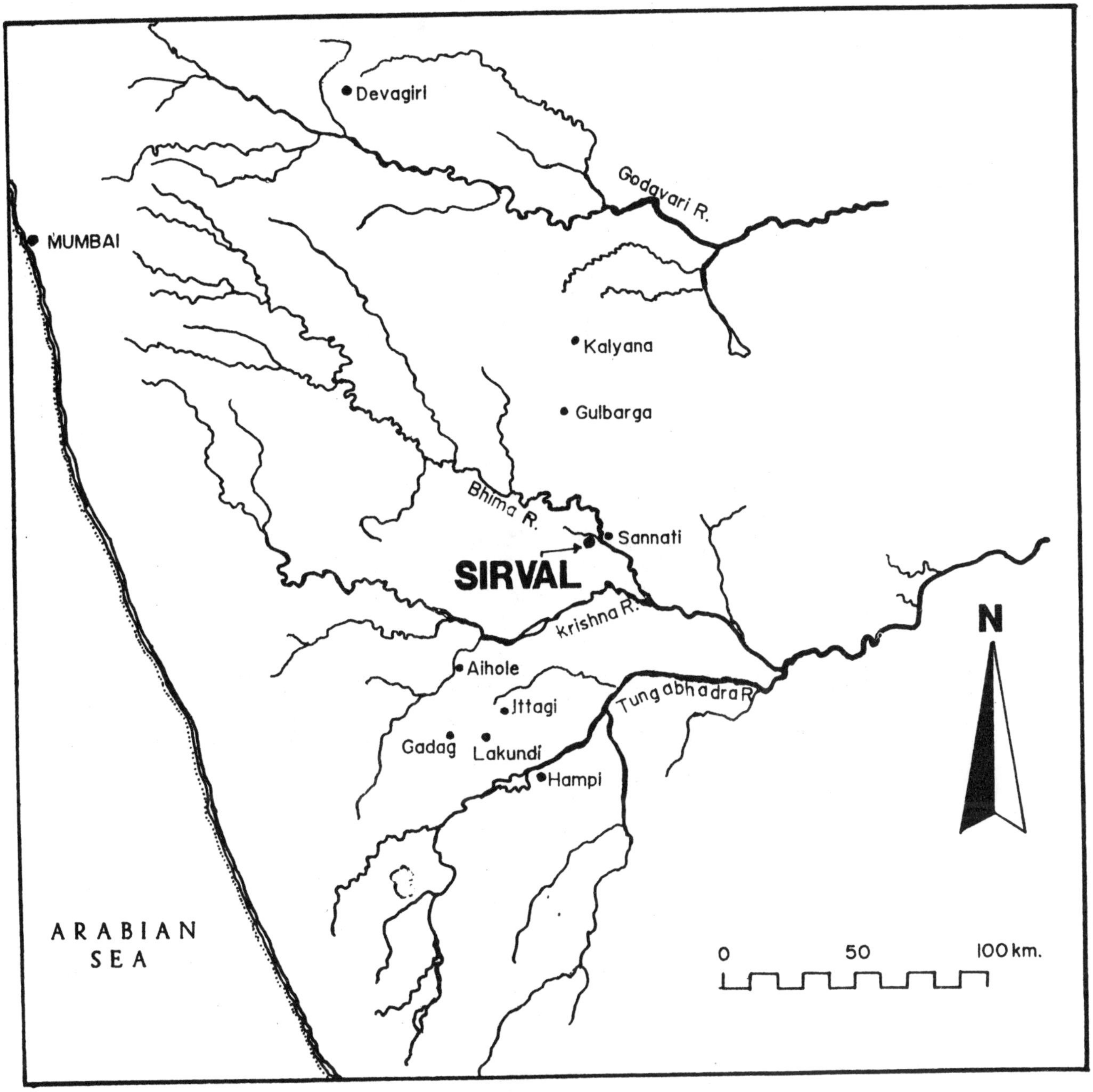

Fig. 1 Map showing the important Kalyana Chalukyan temple sites in the Western Deccan, India.

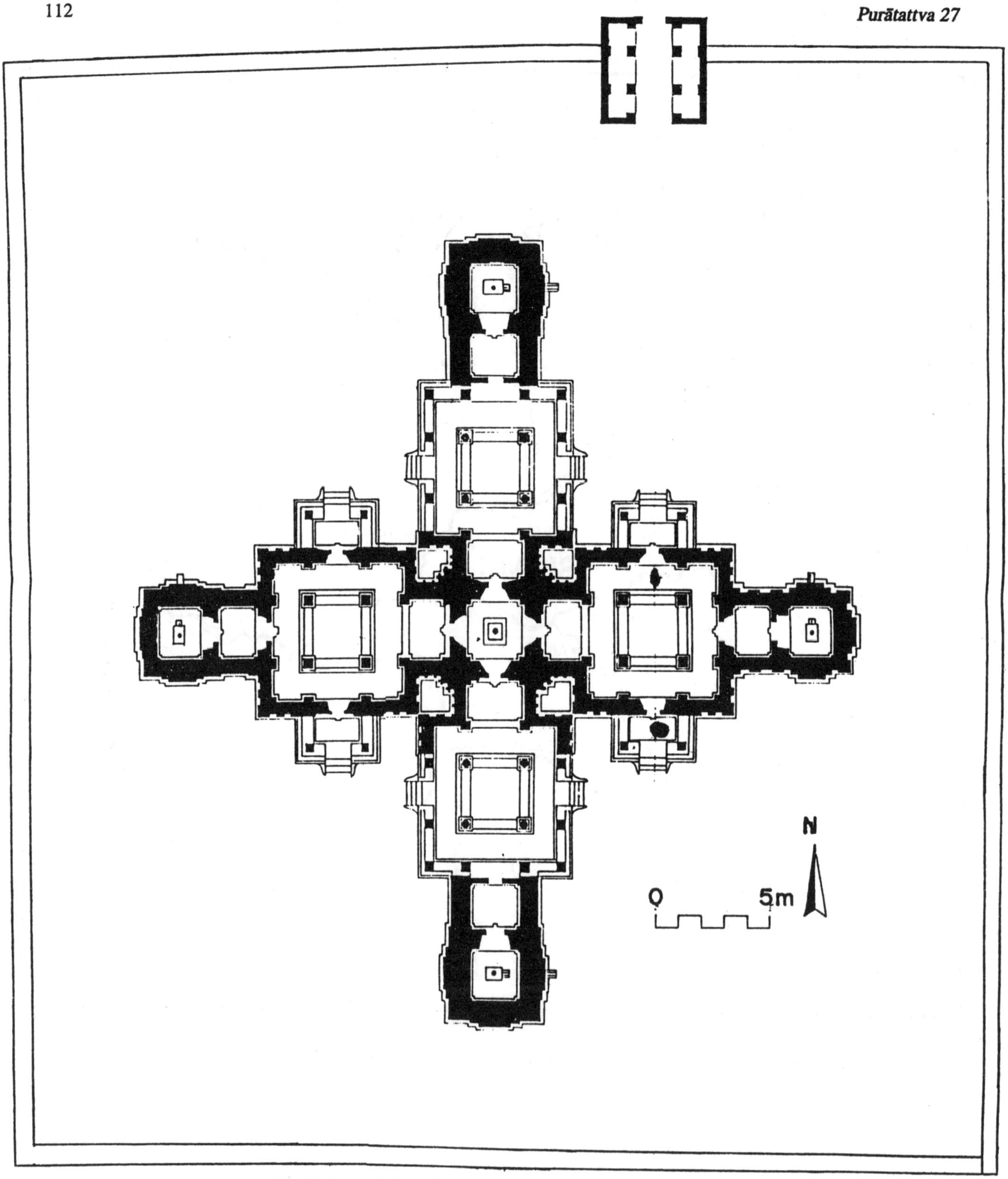

Fig. 2 Ground plan of Pancakuta temple, Sirval, Karnataka.

Colour of the Sea : An aspect of Ancient Indian Navigation

Ancient navigators, besides using available instruments for navigation and for sighting land employed extensively sighting birds as also the colour of the sea. Sighting birds were one of the aids by which direction towards land could be ascertained.

Here we shall confine ourselves to the colour of the sea and how it came in handy to the ancient navigators. Before going into the navigational aspects of the colour of the sea let us try and understand how water of the sea and ocean gets its colour and different hues.

Sea water as we all know reduces the intensity of sunlight selectively according to its wavelength. Attenuation is minimum for blue and maximum for red and infra-red and is caused by absorption and scattering of light in all directions. The blue-wavelength being less absorbed is more scattered as a result clear water looks blue and that is what the colour of the sea is. Till now what we consider to be different colours of the sea and ocean is actually areas of discoloured water which are almost always biological in origin and this varies with the seasons and therefore, are usually omitted on modern charts. Another reason for discoloured water is the difference in the penetration of light in clear water and muddy coastal areas. The *Mariner's handbook* published by the British Admiralty has a subsection dealing with colour (1978:88-89).

The normal colour of the sea in the open ocean in middle and low latitudes is an intense blue or ultramarine. The following modifications in its appearance occur elsewhere:

(a) In all coastal regions and open seas in higher latitude, where minute floating animal and vegetal life of the sea called plankton are abundant the blue colour of the sea undergoes change into shades of bluish green and green. This results from a soluble yellow pigment given off by the plant-constituents of the plankton;

(b) When plankton is very dense, the colour of the organisms themselves may discolour the sea, giving it a more or less intense brown or red. The Red Sea, Gulf of California, the regions of Peru current, South African waters and the Malabar coast of India are particularly liable to this phenomenon seasonally;

(c) Planktons are sometimes killed more or less suddenly by changes in the temperature of sea producing dirty or gray-brown discolouration or 'stinking water'. This occurs on an unusually extensive scale at times. In the Peruvian coast this phenomenon is called *Aguaje.;*

(d) Larger masses of animate matter such as fish spawn or floating kelp may produce other kinds of temporary discolouration;

(e) Mud brought down by the river produces discolouration, which in case of bigger river may be carried far into the sea by wind or dust storms and volcanic dust may fall over the sea area. In all such cases the water is more or less muddy in appearnace. Submarine earthquake may also produce mud or sand discolouration in relatively shallow waters. Oil has sometimes been seen to gush up. The sea may also be extensively covered with floating pumice stone after a volcanic eruption; and

(f) The play of Sun and cloud over the sea may often produce an illusion of discoloured patches far into the sea.

There is a very interesting reference in *Vishnudharmottara Purana* (Jatabatmela 1963:137-143), where iconography of divine beings are described. Here Varuna, the lord of the ocean is described as of the colour of glossy lapis lazuli *(vaidurya)* because that is the colour of the waters. His garment is said to be white because the water is white in colour. *Markandeya Purana* which gives *lakshana* for Varuna explains the natural and unnatural colour of water. It explains that *vaidurya* (lapis lazuli) like colour of the water is *athya* (unnatural) because that is due to the colour of the sky reflected in waters due Sun's rays. Its natural form is the one seen; in a cataract which resembles the ray of the moon. Agarwal (1961:311), draws our attention to an important reference on the colour of the sea in *Matsya Purana.* It is said that the ocean changes its colour; sometime it is dark and in other places clear. This is the same as the description in the *Divyavadana, Supriyavadana (Maha–Samudre–Udakasyavarna–Samsthana* :iii.)

Thus a scientific theory explained in the *Mariners Handbook* which I had just quoted is put in such a simple manner as can be understood by anybody.

Coming back to colour, the waves breaking over coral reefs or rocks cause frothing which gives a white colour to that part of the sea.

Bioluminescence is another factor which gives white look to a part of the sea. Bioluminescence of the sea formerly termed as phosphorescence can occur anywhere in the world but it is more frequent in the warmer tropical seas. In the Arabian sea it is maximum in the month of August and the phenomenon is recognized as 'milky sea' which gives a constant white glow. This is due to a 'variety of organisms, from microscopic marine life to many forms of deep-sea fish, and the peculiarity of the light is that it is generated very efficiently with negligible waste of energy as heat' (Handbook:89). Its production is attributed to biochemical reaction which though apparently automatic in the lower forms of life are under nervous hormonal control in higher forms.

These facts tell us that colours of the sea is a phenomenon of a particular region albeit seasonally. In other words it is possible to identify a region by the colour of its water. Now whether the ancient marines had developed this science or had a highly developed perception of sea in marking the various area of the ocean by its colour at different times of the year is debatable. However, we do know from our ancient literature this was a field which had been explored.

Here the *Suparaka Jataka* (Fausball: 1963: 137-143) is worth mentioning. *Jatakas* are stories of Buddha's previous lives. The story of Suparaka, a Bodhisattva, a master navigator, could not only read the stars to orient himself but also take cognizance of the colour of the sea and thus helps a group of merchants on a voyage. In the course of the voyage the ships sail through different parts of the sea, Suparaka could ascertain his position by the colour of the water of the region. Thus he could identify an area as Khuramalin (wearing hoof garland), by looking at a particular fish found abundantly there. An area little further ahead as Dadhimalin (wearing garland of coagulated milk), because of its colour which had a lustre of silver, looking bright with the mass of white foam on its waves giving an illusion of sea being draped in fine white linen. After crossing that part of the ocean the ship reaches Agnimalin (wearing garland of fire), since in this part waves were tinged with the splendour of gold; the next part of the ocean is identified as Kusamalin (wearing garland of *kusa* grass), as the stretch of the sea resembled a grove of ripe *kusa* grass and its water illuminated with the lustre of topazes and sapphires. The ship sailed on and reached a stretch which had greenish colour and resembled a meadow and Suparaka identifies it as Nalamalin (wearing garland of reeds), and tells them that the end of the world is near which he identifies as 'maremouth', a place from where no one returns, a mouth like enterance to death. Then the story goes that Bodhisattva Suparaka by the power of Act of truth changed the current and wind to opposite direction and made the vessel go back. Suparaka knew Nalamalin and other seas to be full of precious stones and told the merchants to draw from the bottom sand and stones, as much as the ship can hold and in one night from the mare's mouth they reached Barukachha.

The remarkable thing about the story is Suparaka's excellent navigation at sea. He was never at a loss at sea and could always orient himself by its colour. A few attempts have been made to identify the route followed by them. K.P. Jaiswal identifies Dadhi sea as the Red sea:'Both names having their origin in the appearance of the water of the sea thickened by the peculiar matter which floats in it'. Khuramalin as Persian Gulf on the basis of Khur, a Babylonian god mentioned in the time of Hammurabi (1800 B.C.). There are two basic problems in accepting Jaiswal's theory. First, navigator Suparaka identifies Dadhi sea as a place which is giving out a constant white glow and has a lustre of silver; Jaiswal fails to explain the "Peculiar Matter" which he talks about. Second, Suparaka's identification of Khuramalin is based on fishes which resemble horses and the association of Babylonian god is not understood.

Puroshattam Singh (Singh 1988: 120-122) identified Khuramalin as the Persian Gulf and Agnimalin as the Red Sea but he also fails to state on what basis does he identify them. Then Sarvamangla (Sarvamangla 1988: 57-58) tried to approach the subject in more logical manner and her tentative conclusion was that "the ship might have lost its way in the western coast beyond the Sopara area". She gives two reasons for this, firstly, the western coast beyond Sopara area has sand submerged vegetation and coral reefs; secondly, the sediment samples collected in the Gujarat sea reveals precious and semi-precious stones like sapphires, garnet, beryl, etc.

Let us take Suparaka's voyage step by step. He starts from a port bearing his name. This has been more or less identified with Sopara near Mumbai. As the ship reaches the first sea Khuramalin, Suparaka says it to be far from coast. It might have been possible as the description of the fish given resembles the sea-horses which are only found in deep sea. The second is sea Dadhimalin or milk ocean which had a lustre of silver and gave out a white glow probably due to bioluminiscence of the sea and as mentioned this phenomenon occurs most frequently in the Arabian sea. Therefore, the area which Suparaka identifies as Dadhimalin most probably might have been in the Arabian sea. In the third phase the ship reaches a sea by the name of Agnimalin which was red-brown in colour, the colour could have been due to dense plankton which gives brown or red colour to the sea. This kind of discolouration has been recorded near Malabar coast. In the fourth and fifth phases found the ship in Kusamalin and Nalamain. The name and colour suggests somewhere near the coast where minute floating animals and plankton are in greater abundance. But from the description it is very difficult to identify these parts; possibly the ship was along the Gujarat coast. The last phase of the journey takes the ship to Mare-mouth or Entrance of Death where sea is making tremendous noise. Shipwrecks are very frequent in these parts. Considering this fact, the name Entrance to death is very apt. As mentioned in the *Jataka,* it was one night's journey from Barukachha or Broach in Gujarat aided by winds and currents; and as currents and winds can take a ship of reasonable size to a speed of 6 to 10 knots we can tentatively say the ship was around 200 to 250 miles south or north of Broach.

How authentic is this story ? Being a keen observer he might have noticed these changes in his voyages. It is nearly impossible to identify different seas merely by the colour as these changes are seasonal. So Suparaka must have corroborated his previous observation with stars as it has been mentioned in the story that he was also an astronomer too.

Coming back to navigation a question that comes naturally to mind—Does colour of the sea really help in navigation ? The search for the answer took me to the Naval Officers, especially hydrographers (Chakravorty 1997). They all agreed that changes in colour tell them the approximate distance from the shore, the outflow of the water and to a certain extent the position of coral reefs. But it is not in any way an infalliable guide in modern navigation especially in the mouth of river.

In this connection the hydrographer related a very interesting incident which happened to him while conducting a survey. Hydro-vessel INS Investigator was sent to survey near the approach of Dharma, Lat. 20° 47′ North and Long. 86° 75′ East, a river in Orissa. Most of the boats sent from the vessel to take soundings got grounded. The colour of the sea by which the approximate depth of the sea can be ascertained went haywire here. Muddy patch near the coast where river meets sea indicate shallow depth, but here depth was nearly 9 to 10 m (Chakravorty 1997).

Generally, with the increase of the distance from the shore the depth becomes more and water less muddy. Surprisingly, here the boats got grounded and finally they had to take help from local fisherman to find the channels. After an investigation they found out that cause of depth near the shore was due to river current cutting into the bottom and with the passage of time the depth increased. The shallow patches at the distance was due to sand and mud deposit brought by the river.

Therefore, it can be said that colour helps us to tell approximate depth, distance from the shore and to a certain extent position i.e. if the destination is known. For instance, when a vessel heading towards Andaman approaches intense blue colour the navigator can say that they have neared their destination as the water around the Andaman is of that colour. The water in the Caribbean Sea is turquoise blue which is much darker than in the Atlantic Ocean and one of the recognizable features of that area, which is even identified from air.

Dr. Arunachalam (Arunachalam 1996) has mentioned a very interesting reference from a *pothi* of a Gujarati seaman of the century. 'When sun is overhead, observe the reflection of the solar spectrum of the polished surface of an alloy plate, well scrubbed with sea water. If whitish, vessel is 20 *zams* offshore, if greenish it is 30 *zams* offshore and if reddish in appearance the boat is far out at sea". There is a heavy sediment discharge along the Kutch coast and may be the Gujarati navigator by this method was trying to measure the transparency and colour of the sea water for finding the distance from the shore. Here a parallel can be drawn with Sechhi Disk observation carried out by modern hydrographers and oceanographers by which clarity and color of the sea is assessed. This is done by a disk of 30 cm in diameter painted matt white and supported on a 3 legged sling and weighted. To take an observation the disk should be lowered into the water on a marked line and various depths are recorded under the heading deep blue, blue, greenish blue, bluish green, green, yellowish green, dirty green, brownish green and brown.

At the end, we may add that the colour of the sea was an aspect in navigation which an ancient navigator had explored, may be for the want of better aids. Lets us admit that there is one field which has not been looked into and that is the oral tradition which is still preserved among traditional sailing communities, the practice of observing the colour of sea while sailing. To understand the colour of the sea from their perception might add a whole new dimension to our study. This aspect is being investigated by the author along the Western Coast of India.

REFERENCES

Agarwal, V.S. 1961. *Matsya Purana.*

Arunachalam B. 1996. Traditional Sea and Sky wisdom of Indian seamen and their Practical wisdom in Hamanshu Prabha Ray, and Jean Francois Salles (ed). *Tradition and Archaeology–Early Maritime Contacts in the Indian Ocean.* New Delhi.

Fausball V. (ed), 1963. The *Jatakamala,* IV. No. 463.: London. (reprint).

1997, Personal Communication by Lt. Cdr. R.S. Chakravorty. Hydrographer, Indian Navy.

Sri Pantha. 1997. Dariyay Draghimar Sandhane. *Des.* (Bengali), 64. 6 Calcutta.

1978. *The Mariner's Handbook,* (Fifth Edition).

Prince of Wale's Museum,
Mumbai

SUMITA CHAKRAVORTY

BOOK REVIEWS

Prakash Sinha, *Model for Land use in Late Acheulian Tradition Prayag Pustak Sadan, Allahabad,* 1991, pp. i-xvi + 224, Plates 36. Price: Not given.

Prehistoric archaeology in India, like in the West, has undergone a sea-change from the days of V.D. Krishnaswami in the 1950s; from simple geological formations, cultural stratigraphy and tool-typology we have come to what is popularly called 'Environmental Archaeology' of Prof. F.E.Zeuner and others. The concepts of the so-called 'New Archaeology' with emphasis on the determination of functionality of work-spaces under the impact of Binford and Binford, reconstruction of biosphere during the prehistoric periods etc. are being gainfully used by some bright and young Indian prehistorians among whom Prakash Sinha is indeed one. His present work is the product of painstaking labour he has put in the field-work conducted in Distt. Satna, Madhya Pradesh. He has evolved several significant approaches through new methodologies at the Institute of Archaeology, London.

This book has been divided into: 1. Introduction, 2. Methodology and Terminology, 3. Environment, 4. Field-work, 5. Alluvial stratigraphy of the Upper Tons Valley, 6. Analyses and 7. Discussion.

The second chapter is crucial since as against the chaos created by preferential collections of tools by individual researches at one and same site, leading to different conclusions, the author has proposed models of methodologies which can be gainfully used in field-work and tool collection to reduce subjectivity in interpretation based on unplanned collections. Here he has quoted various methods evolved by different field-workers in Asia, Africa and Europe, each with some merit in it but not without pitfalls.

The chapter on field-work is very useful for workers. The chapter on analysis is really illuminating since it takes into not only Site Analysis but also Assemblage analysis, Comparative analysis and Analysis of the findings. The use of simple calculations and sometimes statistics in analysis is the basic to all the four. A number of charts and histograms illustrate the assumptions of the scholar.

It is a very useful work for the field-workers in India.

S.P. Gupta

M.K. Dhavalikar, M.R. Raval and Y.M Chitalwala, *Kuntasi –A Harappan Emporium on west coast,* Deccan College Post-Gradute Research Institute, Pune, 1996. pp. i t– xii + 383, Rs. 1000/-.

The Harappan or Indus-Saraswati site of Kuntasi, District Rajkot, Taluk Malaya locally known as "Bibi-no-Timbo", was discovered by the late P.P. Pandya of the former Saurashtra State Department of Archaeology. In 1972 Shri Y.M., Chitalwala of Gujarat Deptt. of Archaeology at Rajkot reassessed its importance. The exavation at the site was, however, carried out jointly by the Deccan College, Pune and the State Department of Archaeology, Gujarat for three consecutive field seasons, from 1987 to 1990. Kuntasi is of considerable interest not merely because it is an impressive mound (220 m × 150 m) with a deposit of 7 m thickness, but also because of the evidence that has helped the excavators in 'reformulating issues connected with the socio-economic organisation of the Harappans, the expansion of the Harappan Culture in Gujarat, the nature of interaction between the autochthonous people and the migrating people, the causes of the decline of the Harappan Civilization as well as the Late Harappan Culture-complex.'

The report is divided into fourteen sections. The first three sections are introductory. The fourth section summarises the details of the cultural sequence and main features of each cultural phase, including the sectional cuttings and chronology. The fifth to seventh sections deal with the documentation of architectural, ceramic and antiquarian remains unearthed at Kuntasi. Sections eight to thirteen contain the results of the scientific analysis of plant remains, pollen analysis, faunal remains, shell remains, X-ray Diffraction analysis of pottery and beads and, habitational analysis. Section fourteen is the concluding part. The sum-up of the results of the excavation is in the light of the Indus-Saraswati Civilization as a whole with the help of several line-drawings, maps and other illustrations.

The two-fold cultural sequence of Kuntasi—Period-I Harappan (*ca* 2400-1900 B.C.) Period-II Late Harappan (*ca* 1900-1700 B.C.) and ^{14}C dates obtained are significant since it shows that by the middle of the third millennium B.C. the Indus-Saraswati Civilization had been fully established in Gujarat.

It is a very valuable contribution to the studies of the Indus-Saraswati Civilization since it supports in many ways the cultural sequence and importance of several coastal sites Gujarat such as Dholavira and Lothal. Kuntasi was indeed a very important site and its defence agaisnt enemies of sorts was essential. But the problem of 'defence walls' *vis-a-vis* 'attack by enemies' still remain unsettled in the context of th Indus-Saraswati Civilization as a whole. The authors have raised a few other theoretical issues which are more controversial. In any case, though the site was comparatively very small and the antiquarian remains limited, yet as a trading port-town its importance cannot be underestimated.

S.P. Gupta
Ashwani Asthana

Urmila Sant, *Terracotta art of Rajasthan from Pre–Harappan and Harappan times.* Aryan Books International, 4378/4B, Pooja Apartments 4, Ansari Road, Darya Ganj: New Delhi 1997. Pages 263, Plates 65, Hard bound. Price: Rs. 1150.

India is a land of living traditions. The Potter's craft, practised for both utilitarian and artistic output in the world is the most ancient and rich. India is no exception to this norm.Terra cottas-both human and animal forms, either hand-modelled or turned out in moulds or combination of this two techniques are well known.

The book under review enlightens us on the evolutionary trends of the terracotta art and technique in the state of Rajasthan from the Mesolithic times to the Gupta period .

The author has taken much trouble to relate her study of terracotta art objects with socio-economic *milieu* of Rajasthan. The significance of this book lies in that the author has endeavoured to compare the terracottas of Rajasthan with those from other areas focussing her attention on the least known specimens such as votive objects, ornaments, tools etc.

The book is a welcome addition to the study of terracotta art.

Brij K. Chauhan

Shivaji K. Panikkar, *Saptamatrika –Worship and Sculptures,* D.K. Printworld (P) Ltd. New Delhi; 1996 pp. 300, Plates 196, Price Rs. 1500/-/

The evolution of the cult of the Mother goddess in India has always been a fascinating study fortually hundreds of scholars of all shades and opinions. There are numerous sources of our knowledge, both archaeological and literary. For the study of origin, functions and relationships of the cult of Mother worship in ancient India we need to be perfect in our study of Indian literature; art and archaeology alone would not do.. Early terracotta figurines of the Neolithic-Chalcolithic periods and sculptures and murals of the historical period bear witness to the popularity of this cult. Shivaji K. Panikkar examines the iconological growth and development of the cult of Mother goddess in the Gangetic plains as well as Central and Western India from the fourth century to the ninth century A.D. While doing so, he questions the accepted norms of art history by presenting the study with in the theoretical framework of dialectical materialism. However, in defining and interpreting the meanings and forms of Devi, literary and archaeological sources need a much more careful examination. Besides, the *Devimahatmya* and other classical Sanskrit works, a large corpus of literature, including the *Agamas, Yamalas, Arnavas* and *Tantras* deal with the ritualistic and philosophical development of the Saptamatrika tradition which have been hardly mentioned in this monograph. The author has shown this limitation of his towards the highly technical works composed in early urban centres of south India, like Kanchipuram. The important treatises that evolved in north-east India could have been included as source-material for the present study but unfortunately the author has missed it.

Instead of documenting the original sources for an in-depth study of the month cult, the author has incorporated theories of class conflict, feudalism and Brahmana-Kshatriya power nexus etc. Discussions on socio-economic changes that influenced the Saptamatrika tradition the author have depended on D.P. Chattopadhyaya's theorizations on Indian materialism. Chattopadhyaya's conceptualisations were essentially moulded by George Thompson's study of ancient Greek Society and Robert Briffault's anthropological treatise, 'The Mothers'. The author has not explained their relevance in the Indian archaeological and cultural context: hence the work is somewhat lop sided.

A map showing the Saptamatrika cult-centres in India would have been much helpful to understand the spread of Mother goddess cult. The icons on the basis of region and chronology could have been classified and presented in a tabular form with illustrations.

It is a well illustrated book and, therefore, may be consulted by all those who are interested in the study of mother goddess cult with special reference to Saptamatrikas or Seven Mothers.

B.S. Harishankar

Channabasappa S Patil, *Panchatantra in Karnataka Sculpture,* Directorate of Archaeology and Museums, Mysore, 1995, Plates 85, pp. 71 Price : Rs. 75.

Panchatantra is attributed to one Vishnusarman, who took up the challenge of 'educating' three worse than an 'Athenian blockhead' –sons of the king within a period of six months. It is more than a *nitisastra;* it guides one how to survive in the world. It is divided into five sections *mitralabha, mitrabheda* etc. The book is meant "for the harmonious development of the powers of man, a life in which security, prosperity and resolute action, friendship, and good learning are so combined as to produce joy". The stories are witty, educative and most of the 'actors are animals'.

The stories of Panchatantra have become so popular and universal that this "book has made an unparalleled triumphal progress from its native land over all the civilised parts of the globe and which for more than fifteen hundred years has delighted young and old, educated and uneducated, rich and poor, high and low, and still delights them. Even the greatest obstacles– whether of language or customs or religion– have not been able to check the triumphal progress'. Haertel avers that "no book except the Bible has enjoyed such an extensive circulation". There are about two hundred versions of *Panchtantra* in more than fifty languages including, Persian, Arabic, Greek, Latin, Italian, Spanish. Polish Czech, Hungarian etc.

Panchatantra stories are depicted in sculptural panels in many temples all over India particularly in south India. We find them in the temple of the Chalukyas, Rashtrakutas, Gangas, Cholas, Hoysalas and others.

There are two traditions of this work: one by Vishnusarman and the other by Vasubhaga. From these two, more versions sprang up. One such was composed in Kannada by Durgasimha in A.D. 1031. The present book by Dr. Patil deals with the sculptural panels which have been executed on the basis of Durgasimha's Kannada version. The author has compiled, photographed and described these stories after an extensive field-work. He has identified twenty-six stories from out of one hundred panels. The panels portraying the stories are dealt with in the chronological order of the dynasties that ruled over Karnataka from the Chalukyas through Rashtrakutas, Gangas, Chalukyas of Kalyani, Hoysalas etc. These are found in the temples of Pattadakkal, Aihole, Alampur, Kittur, Begur, Narasamangala, Kolaramm temple Beilagave, Belur, Halebid etc. Some panels are found on pillars (Kadur) and in a well in Sirvel. Description is vivid.

Dr. Patil has also identified the text on which the

sculptures are based—Durgasimha's, *Tantropakhyana,* Vishnusarama's etc. Besides three Appendices –Sculptures based on the versions of the texts, Monument-wise list and Story-wise sculptures are given.

This scholoarly work by Dr Patil, deserving all praise, is otherwise marred by the poor, almost clumsy reproductions of photographs.

K. S. Ramachandran

Channabasappa S. Patil, 1992. *Temples of Raichur and Bellary Districts, Karnataka 1000-1325 A.D.,* Directorate of Archaeology and Museums, Mysore, xxiv + 273, 356 Plates and 33 line drawings.

For sheer variety, sculptural wealth and architectural eminence the temples of Karnataka are poems in stone. The student of temple architecture would perhaps never find a region where he can study and contemplate on the development of temple art and architecture, right from the rock-cut caves to the imposing structural abode of gods, from the times of the Chalukyas of Badami, the Rashtrakutas till the flowering of the Hoysala temples, outstanding among which are those in Halebid and Belur. Besides we have representative models of the feudatory chiefs like the Nayaks of Ikkeri etc.

In the early twentieth century Henry Cousens and Alexander Rea were the pioneers in the study of the temples of the Kanarese country. The former, surveyed and published a bulky tome *"Chalukyan Architecture of the Kanarese Countries".* To him the term 'Chalukyan' was not exclusive but encompassed the myriad dynasties that held sway over Karnataka. The merit of the book is that for the first time we have a book with copious illustrations– plans, elevations, drawings of sculpture and architectural member like pillars, door-jambs and lintels, etc., and lithographs. However, the Mysore Archaeological Survey silently carried on its own programme and invariably its Annual Reports carried a chapter "Study of Ancient Monuments" where systematic study, though brief, of temples were carried and results published along with plans sections, elevation etc. This tradition furthered by Narasimhachar, M.H. Krishna and others is still being carried on by his successors in the Mysore Archaeological Department. One such book is under review.

The book is limited in time and space and yet it presents the results of an intensive and exhaustive field investigation and study of seventy-six temples in two districts-Bellary and Raichur; forty-two in the former and thirty-four in the latter.

The book is in nine chapters wherein Patil discusses the role of temples as a socio-religious organization (Ch. II); construction, restoration, architects, sculptors, engravers etc. (Ch. III). However, the most important ones are the chapters analysing architectural features with plans, elevation, sections etc. (Ch. VI); sculptural art (Ch. VII) and the discussion on the development of temple architecture and the dates of the temples themselves (Ch. VIII).

The results of his investigation and epigraphical data prove that the temples were the hub of socio-economic activities of the place/region besides being a religious centre. These temples were built by people in all walks of life—army chiefs, ministers, high officials, mercantile guilds, common-folk besides kings, queens and the royality– for their merit. An important point is that Dr. Patil has been able to identify from the epigraphs the text that was followed in the building of the temple. The inscriptions also give the name of the architects well-versed in *vastusastras* as also of the sculptors. The author's study also revealed that there were two *–vesara* and *Kalinga–* types of temples.

An exhaustive bibliography, glossary of technical terms, an index besides plates and figures enhance the value of the work.

Such regional studies of groups of temples are a desideratum and should be encouraged. It is heartening to see that the author following the footsteps of his predessors has not only improved upon but also excelled them.

K.S. Ramachandran

B.K. Chauhan and K.K. Sharma, *The Indian Economy Through the Ages,* J.P. Publishing House, Delhi, 1997, pp. 264, Price Rs. 300/-.

The book divided into four chapters deals with economic life of ancient, medieval and colonial periods. The first chapter deals with ancient agricultural implements, water structures viz. canals, wells, reservoirs, tanks, different varieties of land, cattle rearing, fields, forests, deserts, climate and various industries concerning leather, textile, pottery, metal, ornaments, besides taxation.

Subsequently *silpa*-texts prescribed the rules for layout of towns, temples, cities and forts. In some cases the guilds of artisans were also responsible for this. During medieval period market –both economy permanent and seasonal– played a key role. The opening and closing days of markets were also fixed depending on days and festivals of different sects.

During Mughal period the big markets were designated as *'mahalas'* for the purpose of tax collection. This arrangement was done with a view to infuse transparency. In the last chapter focuses on economy since independence, green revolution, industrial development, issues concerned with inflation, reforms, industry and trade, direct and indirect taxes etc. The work based on archaeological and literary data is also appended with an useful bibliography of primary and secondary sources and an index. As a whole this reasonably priced book would be useful to every library and readers interested in different facets of Indian economy from the earliest times.

P.K. Trivedi

A Report on Agra Monuments and Mathura Refinery– A Regional Environmental Plan for Controlling Pollution

This project was originally submitted by the Indian Archaeological Society as 'Agra Mnuments and Mathura Refinery - A Regional Environmental Plan for Controlling Pollution' to the Indian Oil Corporation Limited (IOC), New Delhi in the overall framework of a 'Study of Development of Green Belt and Afforestation of Agra Region'. This programme has also found place in the Ten Point Initiative of the Ministry of Petroleum and Natural Gas (1995)– 'Green is Clean'.

The origin of the project is the result of a discussion of the Princial Investigator had with Shri B.B. Chakrovarty, GM (S&EP) of IOC in 1994. When this idea was put up to him after the National Conference on Environmental Pollution and Preservation of Historical Monuments on Oct. 31 and Nov. 1, 1994, organised by IOC, he not only encouraged but offered valuable suggestions and recommended it for approval to the IOC. Other members of the IOC lent their ungrudging cooperation during the survey.

The present project which was necessitated for mitigating the pollutants in Agra as it had already reached a range higher than the prescribed limit and also to control the prevailing wind laden with sand particles coming from adjacent Rajasthan deserts was divided into three parts. Thus, Part A deals with the meteorology, hydrology and soil of the region; Part B deals with analytical studies of the region with a survey of the green belt– and in Part C, an estimated cost spread over five years for the implementation of the scheme, has been worked out. The report embodies recommendations besides a bibliography and appendices. The draft report has already been submitted to the IOC. Further work is an progress.

The exercise of providing a greenbelt in Agra region started mainly because of the conservation problems of the Taj Mahal. However, an appendix has been added which formed the basis of the guidelines issued on the maintenance and conservation of this monument as far back as 1942. Other appendices relate to list of plant species suggested by the studies of different organisations, Mughal chronicles and individual authors.

The survery of the area revealed that the present status of ambient air quality in the region is man-made and there is no coordination at any operational level, i.e. of Central Government with State Government and State Government with Local administration. After the establishement of Mathura Refinery, the State Government went on permitting the establishment of a number of industries on the Mathura-Agra road. In the present Master Plan of Agra (1971-2001) also one of the industrial zones has been proposed along the Agra-Mathura road.

Afforestation

Another factor worth highlighting is the mindless action of the State Government. The first forest policy emphasised 33% of the geographical area of the country under forest cover, although Landsat imagery records only 19.52% of the total geographical area which is ecologically not adequate forest canopy. In Agra Reserve Forest area along the river Yamuna, starting from Keetham to Sikandara on the one hand and from Shahadra to Chhalesar on the other, which is already on an inevitable course of degradation, a new concrete jungle has been allowed to come up. All steps have been taken to destroy the reserve forest cover with the active connivance of local administration. A clear-cut National policy on this issue is the need of the time. We may go on planting new saplings because funds are made available but what about the maintenance of natural vegetation cover of these forests which at places are dense pockets of standing shrubs/grasses of more than three metre high. The new plantation will no doubt help in greening the region but a determined step must also be taken to save and regenerate these Reserve Forests even with additional plantation as these forests fall between Mathura and Agra on one hand and Agra and Firozabad on the other. The development of open spaces lying in this axis, Mehtab bagh, Dhandhupura, Kuberpura and Burhia ka Tal, will further help in mitigating air pollution.

Observations

There are impressive schemes for afforestation, including the National Westeland Development Board and the World Bank aided socio-forestry schemes, in different States of India. What has really been achieved by these schemes, in Agra region, however, needs a close study.

Planting trees on the roadsides of Agra-Fatehpur Sikri be given priority as this will help controlling the dustfall which has a general tendency towards increase from April to June. The regeneration of the artificial lake created by Akbar by constructing Tehra Mori to store the rain water does not require much funds to make it functional except that the cost of the acquisition of land. The Ministry of Tourism, Govt. of India, may be favourably persuaded to finance this since this project will turn out to be a very viable tourist spot.

However, we are constrained to observe that the environs of Agra monuments is far from satisfactory. Whom one can blame, is difficult to say. The Archaeological Survey of India has no actual control on the area outside the monuments though legal instruments are there. Most of the places are under encroachments but there is no body to remove them. How long one has to continue with is situation ? Agra Development Authority increased entrance fees to monuments but without any integrated action plan. IOC believes that 'the green is clean'. Let us hope local administration will maintain it.

Recommendations

The following are the main recommendations based on the survey of 20 km radius around Taj Mahal and Fatehpur Sikri.

1. Creation of biosphere reserves for degraded Reserve Forest cover from Keetham to Sikandara; and from Shahadra to Chhalesar it will control polluants coming with wind from north-west and easern direction. As the area is under the Deptt. of Forest. Govt of U.P., they could be requested to submit the proposal to the Government of U.P. to regenerate the degraded forest. Moreover, no new constructions and ecroachment of land be allowed in Reserve Forest area as is going on at present. A notification in this regard should be issued by the competent authority. For offenders strict penalties be imposed.

2. The Industrial Zone as recommended in the Master Plan along the Agra-Mathura road should be completely stopped for any industrial activity.

3. The available open-spaces, specially between the east of Taj and Kuberpura, adjacent to Chhalesar Reserve Forest, Burhia ka Tal near Etmadpur and Sewal jat on Gwalior road have been proposed for dense planting. The open space on the left hand side of Yamuna facing the back of Taj Mahal has also been proposed for development.

4. The artificial lake created by Akbar in the back of Fatehpur Sikri has long back silted but the rain water still accumulates there and is used by villagers for irrigation purposes. If this waterbody could be developed, it would further restrict the chances of air pollution in this area. Part of area is under private possession and part under the U.P. Government .

5. The development of Road avenues in the city and around be entrusted to Deptt. of Forest, U.P. Govt. under Social Forestry Scheme because the present plantation in the city has also been undertaken by them. However, neem plantation be also included with other plants because it releases oxygen into atomosphare day and night and remains green practically throughout the year. The scheme should include different species so as as to make the whole as a compact system. The Agra-Bharatpur, Agra-Gwalior and Fatehpur Sikri-Bayana roads should be undertaken for immediate plantation of trees in three rows with tall trees in between the vacant

space with neem as one of the species. The neem tree will help in controlling the advancement of desert. Recently neem plantation was done in three rows in an area of 300 km to stop the advancing desert of Sahara, Africa.

6. As soon as the land for the proposed Ring-road of 45 km is acquired and demarcated, the process of plantation should be started. Besides reducing the volume of heavy traffic in the city, this road with a careful plantation scheme of species will also act as an effective screen against the natural sandy wind coming from Rajasthan.

7. A Land Use Authority is needed to regulate the land-use by even individuals for balancing the eco-system in Agra region even beyond the proposed Ring Road. This authority should eco-judiciously decide the introduction of various components or industries and others so that eco-friendly balance is not disturbed and a desired development may result in the long run.

8. The mass mobilization of rural population through public awareness programmes about the wasteland resource– use should be made by the State Govt. An incentive may also be given to them for growing trees around their homesteads, fields and common lands. Proper publicity may be given by the State Department of Information and Public Relation through video films. After receiving the proposals, a Steering Committee consisting of members from Ministry of Environment and Forests, Deptt. of Tourism, Govt. of India, Commissioner, Agra Division, Chief Conservator of Forest, U.P. and from industrialists may be made for pooling funds so that these proposals could be implemented. The Central ministries may be requested to take lead in the matter.

9. In the absence of proper maintenance, greening of Agra region may not pay dividend in the long run. Therefore, a Memorandum of Understanding may be formulated between the funding agency and UP Government for the maintenance of the greenbelt after the implementation of the scheme. As the Road Avenues come under Social Forestry and tall and other trees have multiple productive uses, including commercial, their maintenance after five years should be the responsibility of the Forest Department/other State Agencies as they are already maintaining the Road Avenues of the state.

K. N. Diskhit
Principal Investigator

Report of the XXX Annual Conference of Indian Archaeological Society held at New Delhi from Sunday, the 24th November Through Tuesday, the 26th November, 1996

The 1996 annual session of three Societies, namely Indian Archaeological Society, Indian Society for Prehistoric and Quaternary Studies and Indian History & Culture Society, in collaboration with the Deptt. of Archaeology, Govt. of National Capital Territory, Delhi, held jointly, was inaugurated at 10.30 a.m. on the 24th instant by Shri Sahib Singh Verma, Hon'ble Chief Minister of Delhi, in the premises of the Indian Archaeological Society, at B-17, Qutab Institutional Area, New Delhi-110016. Dr. Y.D. Sharma, a veteran archaeologist, was honoured by Prof. A.K. Narain, General President, by conferring on him the "Dr. V.S. Wakankar Award for Excellence in Field Archaeology" carrying a citation, a shawl and cash of Rs. 21,000/-.

Dr. S.P. Gupta, the Chairman, Indian Archaeological Society, who has completed 65 years of fruitful life, was, on the other hand, honoured by the Chief Minister, on behalf of the ISPQS, with his own *angavastram* and a *shriphal.*

Dr. Harshvardhan, the Education Minister of Delhi, the Chief Guest of the function, spoke about the collaboration of the State Government of Delhi with the Indian Archaeological Society in the field of Heritage Management. Shri Ajay Shankar, Director General, Archaeological Survey of India, who was the Guest of Honour, spoke on the occasion about the future planning of archaeology in India.

After the inaugural function, Shri Krishna Deva delivered the Presidential Address of the Indian Archaeological Society. Prof. R.K. Verma, delivered the Presidential Address of the Indian Society for Prehistoric and Quaternary Studies, and Prof. K.S. Lal, that of the Indian History & Culture Society.

The closing Function was held on 26th Nov. 1996. The Valedictory Address was given by Prof. Jagdish Mukhi, the Minister for Finance, Govt. of Delhi The function ended with a vote of thanks to delegates who had made it convenient to attend this Conference.

The list of the scholars who presented their papers in the academic sessions on Sunday 24th November, on Monday 25th November in the forenoon and afternoon sessions, and on Tuesday 26th November in the forenoon and afternoon sessions, is enclosed. As the number of papers was fairly large, parallel sessions were organised on Monday 25th November, 1996 and also on Tuesday November 26. The list of the scholars who presented their papers in all the three soueties are given below :

Sunday, 24 November : Forenoon Session

Inaugural : Chief Minister and Education Minister, Govt. of Delhi.

Sunday, 24 November : Afternoon Session

Professor H.D. Sankalia Memorial Lecture : Prof. A.K. Narain.

From the Yellow River to Oxus : The Tokharians and their Odyssey.

PRESENTATION OF PAPERS FOR "PROFESSOR H.D. SANKALIA YOUNG ARCHAEOLOGIST AWARD" BY THE FOLLOWING SCHOLARS

Lajwanti Shahani	Ethnoarchaeology of Harappan Sea-trade : A Preliminary Study
Anup Mishra	Chalcolithic Ceramics of Balathal : District Udaipur, Rajasthan
Alok Tripathi	Indentifying Dwaraka.

PRESENTATION OF PAPERS OF DIFFERENT DAYS AND IN DIFFERENT SESSIONS

D.P. Agrawal	Language, Technology and Human Evolution
Ravi Koriseter	Geological Context of Acheulian Sites in the Malaprabha Valley, Karnataka
Giriraj Kumar	Daraki-Chattan: A Palaeolithic Site in Rajasthan

Monday, 25 November : Forenoon Session

R.K. Ganjoo	Late Quaternary Fluvial History of Central Narmada valley
P. Rajendran	Studies on Palaeo-environment and Prehistoric Cultures of Kerala
Vijay Singh	Metrical Analysis of Lithic Tools from Jhinlhiri Rock Shelters, Jabalpur, Madhya Pradesh
Anupama Kshirsagar and Sheila Mishra	Relative Chronology of Mesolithic Culture–complexes in Gujarat, and Rajasthan
P.K. Thomas	Archaeozoological Evidence for Mesolithic Subsistence
P.P. Joglekar	Strategies at Damdama
Shanti Pappu	Site–formation Processes in the Kortallayar Basin, Tamil Nadu
Sudharshan Seneviratne	Situating Archaeological Site along Plate Boundaries of Sri Lanka: Implications for Archaeological Studies and Prospects for Future Mineral Resource Use
M.M. Hoque	Ancient Human Settlement Pattern of Bangladesh
Martha, E. Prickeit-Fernando	Ancient Sri Lankan Irrigation System and Archaeology: Recent Research
Sushama G. Deo and others	Geographic Information Systems for Archaeology: An Introduction

Monday, 25 November : Afternoon Session

Vijneshu Mohan	Re-examination of 'Oriental Despotism' in a Regional Harappan Context
V.H. Sonawane	Excavation at Bagsara– 1996: A Preliminary Report
P.P. Joglekar	Faunal remains from Padri
K.K. Bhan and Kishore Raghubans	Patterns of Craft Specialisation and Organisation of Production at Nagwada: A Mature Harappan Site in North Gujarat
P. Ajithprasad	Black Slipped Jars. Graffiti and Overseas Harappan Context
S.B. Ota	Excavations at Pipri and Utwad: Chalcolithic Sites in Nimar Area, Madhya Pradesh
Abhijit Majumdar	Harappan Burial Pottery from Pipli: A New Dimension in the Cultural Assemblage of North Gujarat
K. Krishnan and I.C. Frestone	Studies on the "Glazed" Reserved Slip Ware of the Harappan Period
V.N. Misra, , V.S. Shinde,	Excavations at Balathal: District Udaipur, Rajastan 1995-96:
R.K. Mohanty,	The Main Results
Lalit Pandey and	Chalcolithic Pottery and Antiquities
Jeevan Kharakwal	Architectural Remains of Iron Age
Anura Manatunga	The Terracotta Hoards Culture of Sri Lanka: An Interpretative Study.

Tuesday, 26 November : Forenoon Session

Sila Tripathi	Onshore and Offshore Explorations of Vijaydurg, Maharashtra Coast of India
Kuduposi Pulla Rao and V. Ramabrahman	Recent Archaeological Explorations in Chittoor District, Andhra Pradesh
Ramesh K. Pancholi	*Pragaitihasik Chintan ke Sakshya–Sailachitra*
Murari Lal Sharma	New Rock Art Sites in Western Rajasthan Region

A. Sundara	On the Geometrical Designs in the Rock Art of Karnataka
Sadisiba Pradhan	The Painted Rock Shelter of Lekhamoda in Orissa: An Excavation Report
R.K. Mohanty	Significance of Bead Industry at Mahurjhari, Vidarbha, Maharashtra
P.S. Joshi	Early Iron Age Tradition in Khandesh
P. Ajithprasad	Excavation at Ambakut and Mesolithic Settlements in the Sukhi Valley, Gujarat

Tuesday, 26 November : Afternoon Session

P. Rajendran and C.S.P. Iyer	Characterisation of Copper and Gold Ornaments of Arippa Megalithic Cultures in Kollam District, Kerala
K. Rajan	Archaeology of South Arcot Region
Chanchala Srivastava,	Diffusionary Trends in the Indian Timbers in Space and Time
Vibha Tripathi	Mortar and Oil Crushers through Ages
R.M.M. Chandraratne,	Faunal Remains from Salagha Watta Excavation in 1987-88, Anuradhapura, Sri Lanka: A Parallel Ethonographic Observation at Vishnupur
Malti Nagar	Pottery Manufacture and its Ritual function in Mewar
Subrata Chakrabarti	Anthropological Observations on the Birhors as an aid to Interpretative Archaeology in the Eastern Plateau of India
Ambika Patel	Blacksmithay in Baroda: An Ethnographic Approach
B.R. Subramanyam	A Stone Figure from Kambalapalli: The Oldest Cult Image?
Jagat Narayan	*Vilashgarh ka Gyarahvi Sati ka Bhauman-Kshtriyon ka Silalekha*

Parallel Sessions

Monday, 25 November 1996: Forenoon Session

Knak Tripathi	*Antardvand Parivesh Evam Parampara Darshati Matri Devi Murtiyan*
B.M. Kanduri, K.P. Nautiyal, Vinod Nautiyal, R.C. Bhatt and P. Saklani	Some New Megalithic burials from Sanana, Kumaun
S.B. Ota	Bangles from Khaparkhera: Metrical Analysis
R.D. Chaudhury	Excavations at Sriswya Rohan Assam
D.P. Dubey	A newly discovered stone inscription of 9th century from Dhata
A. Sundara	On the traditional names of the south Indian megaliths
Bhuvan Vikram	Trade and the Sindhu-Saraswati
Dr. Sudha Malaiya	*Tandava Tatha Lasya*
S.B. Ota and Prabhash Sahu	A note on Palas leaf impression on the buial pots from Chalcolithic Utawad
R.A. Sharma	Excavated pottery from Murar river valley
K.S. Saraswat	Harbal detergent and shampoo from pre-Harappan Banawali, Haryana
Rajendra Singh	The so-called Dalits and Sikh history
Vijaya Keshav Sinha	*Prachin Bharat Me Dalithoan ki Rooprekha*
R.N. Mehta	Migration of Yadavas from Mathura to Dwaraka: Chronological consideration of the myth in the Harivamsa

Monday 25 November, 1996: Afternoon Session

N.R. Patgiri	The Military System in Assam during Ahom administration
Bhagwan Singh	Aristocracy in the Indo-Aryan Society

B.R. mani	Urban growth in the trans-Ghaghra plains and identification of some city-sites in Siddharth Nagar
Baldeo Sahay	Trade Dominates Society
D. Bengra	Archaeological activity in Lakshdvip Islands
K.C. Deka and S. Das	Tradition of Human Sacrifice in Assam
P.C. Kashyap	Rigvedic-past still present in Himalayas
Amerendra Nath	Roman antiquities from Adam
K.B. Kaushik	*Budh Kalin Varidhi Smridhi*
Vibha Tirpathi	Advent of Iron in India: A Reappraisal
Archana Dubey–Asthana	Early Harappan Trade Contacts in Kutch Region

Tueday, 26 November, 1996:Forenoon session

Janardan Singh	Trade and Commerce in Protohistoric India
Shivaji Singh	The authors of Gandhara Grave Culture
B.R. Grover	Pattern of trade between north-western India and its impact on Social structure (1600-1900 A.D.)
S.K. Bhatt	Rudra: A Rigvedic god of *nishka*, the Rigvedic money
Janardhan Singh	Position of women in Vedic society
Raghubir Thakur	Some observations on Dating the Bedsa chaitya and stupa
K.S. Saraswat and	Botanical Evidence of the fire-
A.K.S. Pokheria	Sacrifice during the Kushana period at Sanghol

In the Business Meeting which was chaired by Prof. B.P. Sinha, the following were elected to the Executive Committee of the Indian Archaeological Society:

1. Dr. P.C. Prasad, Secretary (Prehistory)
2. Dr. Amrendra Nath, Secretary (Protohistory)
3. Dr. T.P. Verma, Secretary (Historical Archaeology)
4. Dr. R.C. Agarwal, Secreaary (Heritage Conservation)

Dr. K.M. Srivastava, Former Director, Archaeological Survey of India was elected President of the Society for the next conference at Srinagar (Garhwal).

On this occasion, the Archaeological Survey of India had arranged a photographic exhibition on Dholavira Excavation and also on conservation of monuments. The exhibition brought to light many hitherto unknown facet of Harappan Culture. The important conservation works undertaken by Archaeological Survey of India were also presented by the before and after conservation photographs of monuments.

The Department of Archaeology, Delhi State also organised a photographic exhibition on the excavations conducted by the state Deptt. of Archaeology. Prof. Kulkarni, Delhi College of Arts, took this opportunity of giving practical demonstration for the delegates to understand the stages of modelling of animal or other clay figurines.

The conference passed the following three resolutions:

One, the Archaeological Survey of India as well as various State governments and Universities explore and excavate dozens of sites many of which can make headlines in any world-class archaeological journals and magazines for mass circulation to create public awareness but in India we do not have any periodical published on glossy paper and meant for general public. It is suggested that the Indian Archaeological Society should undertake this job and the Archaeological Survey of India is requested to finacially support the Society to initiate one such magazine.

Two, The Government of India should send a delegation of DNA Scientists and Archaeologists to China to study the much publicised mummies of human beings found in northern Chinese Turkestan since it has been claimed that these people may have been closely connected with some of the stock of Indian people.

Three, Non-Governmental Organisations like Indian, Archaeological Society should be associated in the environmental development of monuments as well as historical structures by writing of status reports or expert advice on the complicated issues concerning conservation, field archaeology, etc.

B-17, Qutub Institutional Area
New Delhi-110016

K.N. Dikshit
General Secretary
Indian Archaeological Society

INDIAN ARCHAEOLOGICAL SOCIETY
BALANCE SHEET AS ON 31.03.1997

LIABILITIES	AMOUNT		ASSETS	AMOUNT
CAPITAL FUND			FIXED ASSETS	
			As per Books	21,85.329.52
Opening Balance	14,98,547.08			
Add. Life Membership	29,425.00			
Less: Excess of Expenditure	15,27,972.08			
over income	53,758.19	14,74,213.89		
Corpus Fund		15,00,000.00		
Building Fund		7,23,951.00		
Payables			Fixed Deposits	15,00,000.00
Loan from I.S.P.Q.S.		20,000.00		
Aquarelle		33,178.60	S.B.I. 45062	67,997.29
VAP Enterprises		23,291.57		
Audit Fee		8,000.00	S.B.I. 45082	2,777.19
			Cash in Hand	26,531.06
TOTAL		37,82,635.06	TOTAL	37,82,635.06

Sd/
GENERAL SECRETARY

Sd/
TREASURE

Sd/
For Rajan Sharma & Co.,
Chartered Accountant

Place: New Delhi
Dated: 12.09.97

INDIAN ARCHAEOLOGICAL SOCIETY

INCOME AND EXPENDITURE ACCOUNT FOR THE PERIOD ENDED 31.3.1997

EXPENDITURE	AMOUNT	INCOME	AMOUNT
To Honorarium	36,400.00	By Grant from I.S.P.Q.S. for Conference	25,000.00
To Ground Rent paid to D.D.A.	11,500.00	By Grant from Indian	
To House Tax	13,500.00	History and Culture Society	25,000.00
To Puratattva	60,347.17	By Membership Fees	2,300.00
To Award	21,000.00	By Donations	35,750.00
To Travelling Expenses	590.00	By Sale of Publication	66,401.00
To Telephone Expenses	7,454.50	By Delegation fees	30,479.00
To Conveyance Charges	27,968.50	By Bank Interest	98,306.72
To Printing & Stationery	8,577.75	By Excess of Expenditure	
To Conference Expenses	62,729.00	over Income	53,758.19
To Office Expenses	1,126.25		
To Repair & Maintenance	52,872.84		
To Staff Welfare	4,012.50		
To Postage	5,682.00		
To Accounting Charges	7,000.00		
To Audit Fees	2,000.00		
To Bank Charges	410.00		
To Miscellaneous Expenses	2,800.50		
To Depreciation	11,023.90		
TOTAL	3,36,994.91	TOTAL	3,36,994.91

Sd/
GENERAL SECRETARY

Sd/
TREASURER

Sd/
For Rajan Sharma & Co.
Chartered Accountant

Place: New Delhi
Dated : 12.09.97

INDIAN ARCHAEOLOGICAL SOCIETY
BOARD OF MANAGEMENT

Headquarters:

B-17, Qutab Institutional Area, South I.I.T., New Delhi-110016
Chairman 3388067 (R), General Secretary 6948971 (R)
(O) 6960654, 6523728 Fax : 011–6960654

OFFICE BEARERS OF THE INDIAN ARCHAEOLOGICAL SOCIETY

Patrons:

Prof. B.B. Lal
F-7, Hauz Khas Enclave
New Delhi

Prof. B.P. Sinha
68, Pataliputra Colony
Patna

Chairman:

Dr S.P. Gupta
148, Vigyan Vihar
Delhi-110029

General Secretary:

Shri K.N. Dikshit
B-322, Sarita Vihar,
New Delhi 110044.

Hon. Treeasurer:

Shri K.S. Ramchandran
C3/305 A SFS Flats
Janakpuri,
New Delhi 110058.

Secretaries:

Dr. P.C. Prasad
Former Director of Archaeology
Govt. of Bihar,
Patna

Dr. T.P. Verma
Reader, Deptt of A.I.H.C. & Archeology
B.H.U.
Varanasi

Dr. R.C. Agrawal
Director, ASI,
New Delhi.

Dr. Amarendra Nath
Director, ASI
New Delhi.

Members of the Executive Committee:
Prof. P. Singh,
Banaras Hindu University,
Varanasi.

Dr. V.D. Mishra,
Allahabad University,
Allahabad.

Dr. V.H. Sonawane,
M.S. University Baroda,
Vadodara.

Dr. D.N. Tripathi
Gorakhpur University
Gorakhpur

Prof. U.P. Arora
Rohalkhand University,
Bareilly.

Dr. W.H. Siddiqui,
Raza Library,
Rampur.

Asst. Secretary/Treasurer

Shri Jitendra Nath
National Museum
New Delhi

Editor Monographs/Newsletter

Shri K.S. Ramachandran
New Delhi.

Headquarters:

INDIAN ARCHAEOLOGICAL SOCIETY
B-17, Institutional Area, Mehrauli, New Delhi-110 016
Office: 6523728 Tele-Fax: 011-6960654
Tel: S.P. Gupta 3388067
K.N. Diskhit- 6948971
K.S. Ramachandran- 5598746

Mani : Siswania : Section Showing cultural levels.

Mani : Buddhi Khas : Yakshi
(circa 1st century BC).

1. Shashi : Eastern India : Mara's Attack (circa 8th century)

2. Bachchan : Betang : Avalokitesvara (circa 8 & 9th century AD)

3. Bachchan : Yala Province Avalokitesvara (circa 10th century AD)

1. Rashmi : Affected Rock Paintings.

2. Rashmi : Affected Rock Paintings.

3. Jitendra : Nalanda, Vajrasattva (circa 10th century).

4.Jitendra : Kashmir, Vajrasattva (Brass) with Consort (circa 11th century)

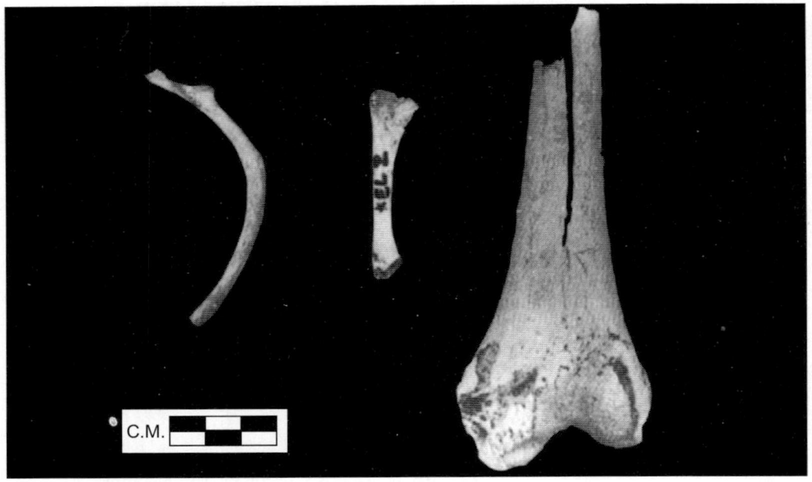

1. Joglekar; Kelshi; Human bones.
Left ù Rib; Middle ù mecatarsal;
Right ù Femur.

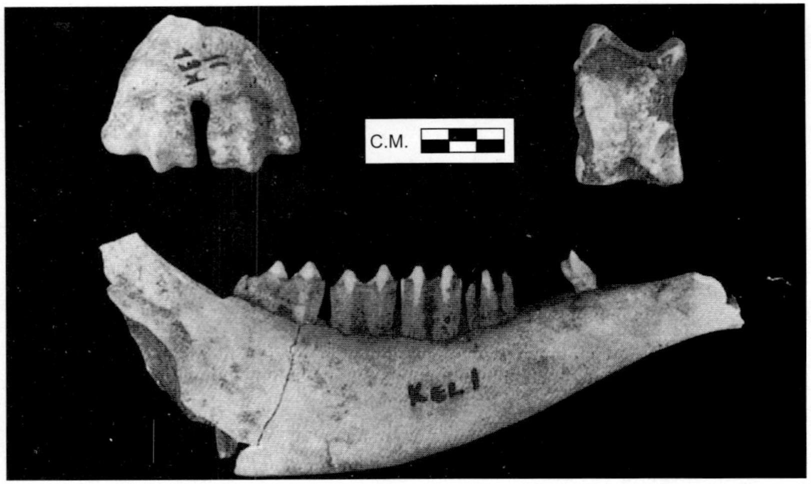

2. Joglekar: Kelshi; Animal bones.
Top left ù Metacarpal of buffalo;
Top right ù Astrogalus of cattle;
Bottom ù Mandible of cattle.

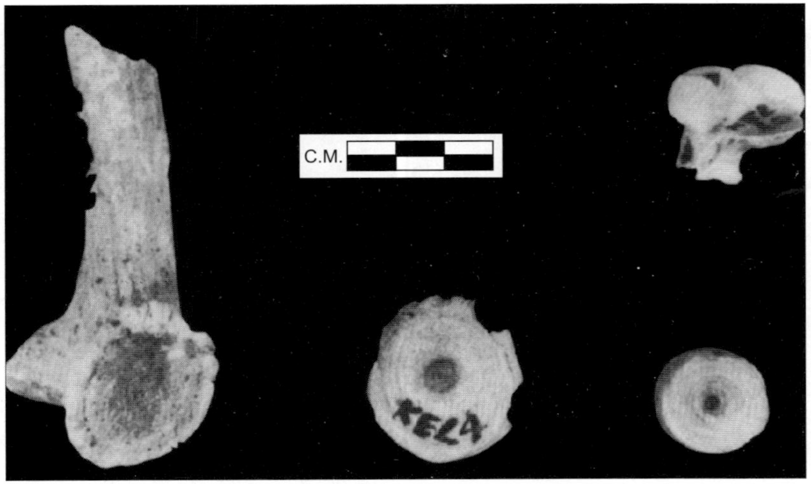

3. Joglekar: Kelshi; Animal bones and Antler.
Left ù Shed antler of Chital;
Middle & bottom Right ù First vertebrae;
Top right ù Femur of large marine turtle.

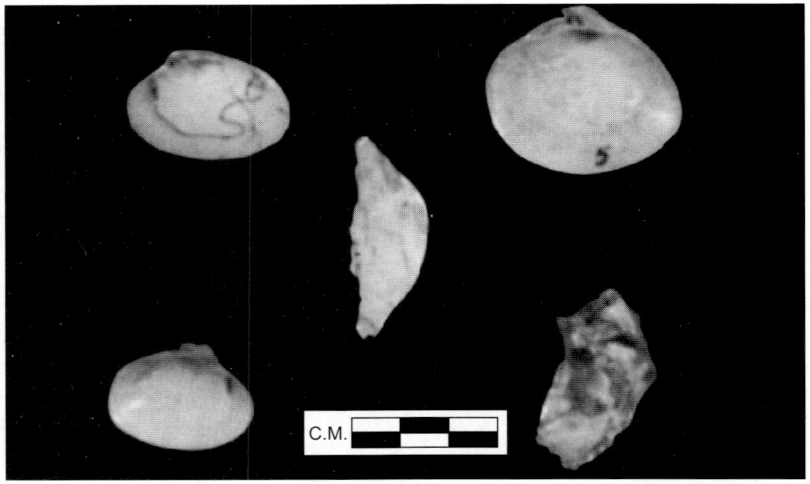

4. Joglekar: Kelshi; Molluscan shells.
Top left ù *Paphia sp.*, Top right ù *Meretrix Mererixt;*
Centre ù *Placuna Placenta;* Bottom left ù *Paphia Gallus;*
Bottom right : *Crassostrea Cucculata.*